Sex and Borders

Leslie Ann Jeffrey

Sex and Borders
Gender, National Identity, and
Prostitution Policy in Thailand

UBCPress · Vancouver · Toronto

Printed in Canada on acid-free paper ∞

National Library of Canada Cataloguing in Publication Data

Jeffrey, Leslie Ann, 1967-
   Sex and borders

   Includes bibliographical references and index.
   ISBN 0-7748-0872-1 (bound); ISBN 0-7748-0873-X (pbk.)

   1. Prostitution – Thailand – History. 2. Thailand – Social
conditions. I. Title.
HQ242.55.A5J43 2002   363.4′4′09593   C2001-911722-1

Canadä

UBC Press gratefully acknowledges the financial support for our publishing program of the Government of Canada through the Book Publishing Industry Development Program (BPIDP), and of the Canada Council for the Arts, and the British Columbia Arts Council.

This book has been published with the help of a grant from the Humanities and Social Sciences Federation of Canada, using funds provided by the Social Sciences and Humanities Research Council of Canada.

Printed and bound in Canada by Friesens
Set in Stone by Brenda and Neil West, BN Typographics West
Copy editor: Joanne Richardson
Proofreader: Craig Wilson

UBC Press
The University of British Columbia
2029 West Mall
Vancouver, BC V6T 1Z2
Ph:(604) 822-5959 / Fax: (604) 822-6083
E-mail: info@ubcpress.ca
www.ubcpress.ca

Contents

Acronyms

APSW	Association for the Promotion of the Status of Women
CEDAW	Convention for the Elimination of Discrimination against Women
CPCR	Centre for the Protection of Children's Rights
CPT	Communist Party of Thailand
CPWW	Committee for the Promotion of the Welfare of Women
DEP	Daughters Education Program
ECAFE	Economic and Social Council for Asia and the Far East
ECPAT	End Child Prostitution in Asian Tourism
EMPOWER	Education Means Protection of Women Engaged in Recreation
FAO	Food and Agriculture Organization
FFW	Foundation for Women
FOW	Friends of Women
GAATW	Global Alliance against Traffic in Women
ICAO	International Civil Aviation Organization
ILO	International Labour Organization
ISOC	Internal Security Operation Command
NCWA	National Commission on Women's Affairs
NCWT	National Council of Women of Thailand
NESDB	National Economic and Social Development Board
UNESCO	United Nations Educational Scientific and Cultural Organization
UNICEF	United Nations Children's Fund
UNTAB	United Nations Technical Assistance Board
WCC	Women's Cultural Club
WHO	World Health Organization
WIC	Women's Information Centre
WLA	Women Lawyers Association
YWCA	Young Women's Christian Association

Acknowledgments

First and foremost I would like to thank the many people who took the time to provide information and guidance while I conducted fieldwork in Thailand: Dr. Supang Chantavanich, Dr. Kritaya Archavanitkul, Dr. Suteera Thomson, Christine Beddoe, Wanee B. Thitiprasert, Jenny Visessiri, Dr. Chalermsook Boonthai, Jasmine Caye, Mary Packard Winkler, Suchit Tripitak, Khunying Chandhanee Santaputra, Therese Caouette, Sanitsuda Ekachai, Dr. Saisuree Chutikul, Sriwatana Chulajata, Thanphuying Ditti-karn Bahkdi, Siriporn Skrobanek, Maechii Khunying Kanitta Wicharoen, Dr. Darunee Tantiwiramanond, Suphalak Booranin, Dr. Pasuk Pongpai-chit, Khunying Ambhorn Meesook, Chantawipa Apisook, Rangsima Limpisawas, Dr. Napat Sirisambhand, Dr. Prathumpoon, Dr. Amara Phongsaiphit, Ranee Hassarungsee, Beth Greeney. Special thanks to Sukanya Hantrakul for her many insights and for the delightful and enlightening conversations.

For funding and support I would like to thank the Government of the Netherlands, York University Faculty of Graduate Studies, the Canada-ASEAN Centre, the Joint-Centre for Asia Pacific Studies, the Institute for International and Strategic Studies at Chulalongkorn University, the Atlantic Human Rights Centre, and the University of New Brunswick (Saint John). Many thanks go to Sandra Whitworth, Penny van Esterik, Shannon Bell, and Laura MacDonald for guidance and encouragement. Finally, of course, thanks to friends and family who supported me during the writing of this work, particularly Greg Cook (for the long hours of editing), Michael Fay and Fay Martin (for their support and encouragement), Elizabeth Philipose, Feng Xu, Yumiko Iida, Mary Young, and Joanna Everitt. I thank the Cook family for providing a "writer's retreat" as I finished the manuscript. Thanks also to the anonymous reviewers of the manuscript who provided very helpful feedback and advice.

Introduction

> There is no such thing as The Prostitute; there are only competing
> versions of prostitution. The Prostitute is an invention of policy-
> makers, researchers, moral crusaders, and political activists ... The
> Prostitute functions as a "magic sign" whose meaning always
> exceeds its definition.
>
> – Wendy Chapkis

"The Prostitute" has made frequent appearances on the world stage over
the course of the last century and a half, but nowhere has she been a more
enduring image than in post-1960s Thailand. As the go-go bars and "hired
wives" for American servicemen during the Vietnam War transmogrified
into an international sex industry centred in Bangkok, the Thai prostitute
has become a powerful international symbol, signalling, inter alia, the economic and moral decline of the so-called Third World, the international
sexual and economic exploitation of Third World women, the fantasies of
international business and leisure, and the nightmare of neo-imperialism.
All of these have drawn on the symbolic force of The Prostitute, although
none can be said to represent a singular "reality" pertaining to actual
women involved in prostitution. It is the symbolic force of The Prostitute
that has drawn my attention to the discursive construction of prostitution
as part of the international politics of representation. In particular, it has
been the raised voices of women from non-Western[1] nations asking for
attention to be paid to the ways in which non-Western women are represented – not merely as an issue of image, but also as a fundamental issue of
power. Underlying the discomfort of Thais, both women and men, with
the international discussions of the "Thai prostitution problem" is a plea
for an understanding of how important Western discursive dominance is
in shaping politics in non-Western countries such as Thailand. Because of
the way gender and sexuality have been invoked in both imperialist and
nationalist constructions of cultural identities, prostitution is a particularly
sensitive area of discussion in this regard. In this study, therefore, I examine prostitution policy in Thailand as the product of debates over gender
and national identity within the context of Western hegemony.

Prostitution in Thailand has garnered a great deal of international attention over the past two decades, with the seeming explosion of sex-related
industries. The sex-tourism industry has most recently been eclipsed in the
international spotlight by the growing awareness of the numbers of women
(from Thailand as well as other poor countries) working in the prostitution

industries of Europe, North America, and Japan. Pundits point to the "Asian cultural tradition" of dutiful daughters to explain this phenomenon, rarely questioning either the developed world's own complicity in the political economy of the region or Western men's demand for cheap, exotic sexual pleasure. Thai prostitute women appear either as innocent victims of a cruel cultural tradition or as heartless gold-diggers – in a repetition of the West's cultural stereotypes of prostitute women. (Not incidentally, Thai men appear as sexually rapacious and/or politically and morally corrupt.) These representations of Thai women and Thai culture have raised numerous protests from both the Thai government and Thai citizens who recognize in these characterizations the familiar strains of cultural imperialism – the differentiation and hierarchization of cultures that enables political and economic dominance – portraying Thailand as "backward," "debauched," and "primitive" and as incapable of Western "civilization."

Similarly, there have been numerous studies of prostitution in Thailand in recent years. Most have emphasized the interests of the Thai state and capitalist class in maintaining prostitution, particularly tourism-oriented prostitution, as a profitable enterprise for men and for capital. Alternatively, prostitution has been viewed as the product of an unchanging and uniform Buddhist-based culture that relegates women to secondary status. In this argument, women lack merit – the basis of rebirth into a state of Enlightenment – and are a source of pollution, even as they are deemed responsible for the maintenance of the family. On the whole, these studies view the Thai state and culture, particularly Buddhism, as unchanging and monolithic entities, and they view the interests of capital as unchallenged. Such studies fail to capture the changes and challenges to prostitution policy, and gender relations generally, that have occurred over the years. The result has been a growing resentment in Thailand of the failure of foreign academics and media to portray "what we're doing about it."[2] This complaint echoes postcolonial critiques of the portrayals of the Third World as inert and unchanging (without an infusion of Western impetus) and as less developed and less capable than Western states. Chandra Mohanty's classic study "Under Western Eyes" has clearly outlined the ways in which Western studies of Third World women tend to essentialize them in a way that deprives them of agency in the eyes of the West and that reasserts Western superiority.[3]

This debate leads us to recognize the fundamental importance of representation as part of the international power struggle between what are tellingly referred to as the First World and the Third World. The representational, or discursive, power of the West is salient with regard to the daily politics of countries such as Thailand. How Thailand is represented on the world stage is an issue of everyday discussion that plays out in national politics, particularly around the issue of prostitution. Within this context, prostitution policy becomes a forum for debates over national identity and foreign image, over who Thais are and how the world perceives them. How the Prostitute is constructed in Thai politics, therefore, reflects these concerns as much as it does economic interest or cultural predispositions. The debates around prostitution policy are a forum for the construction of national identity in the face of Western cultural imperialism.

Sex and Borders, therefore, addresses the issue of prostitution in Thailand not as a study of the whys and hows of the prostitution industry that has made Thailand (in)famous as "the world's biggest brothel" but, rather, as a study of the political discussion of and response to prostitution as a window onto the link between gender and national identity. In other words, rather than looking at how economics, relations between given men and women, or Thai culture have contributed to the growth in prostitution over the years, this book examines how the prostitution problem is conceptualized and how that conceptualization is linked to constructions of gender (masculinity and femininity) and national identity in a globalized world. In this way it shows how, over the years, prostitution policy has been shaped by an attempt to construct and to maintain a national identity.

In particular, the debate over prostitution policy in Thailand is a debate over women's bodies, which are seen as markers of national boundaries that are to be controlled by the state. In today's Thailand, the debate over prostitution involves a struggle over modernity and tradition, over masculinity and femininity, over the role of the state and the identity of the nation. In this era of globalization, as in the era of imperialism, states have responded with both resistance and acquiescence to global pressures and influences. These global pressures have not been simply economic or military but also discursive. Prostitution policy, as the site of the creation of the gender and sexual identities that undergird national identity, is shaped by the need to respond to Western representational power. Today, for instance, prostitution policy is guided by the desire of the Thai middle class to shape Thailand into both a modern state (as represented by the masculinity of the men who govern it) and a traditional nation (as represented by Thai women). In other words, prostitution policy seeks to discipline women, to regulate women's bodies, and to see that they occupy the "correct" cultural roles (e.g., mothers to the nation). In the particular history of the formation of Thai national identity, prostitute women have come to be interpreted as unable to control their own futures. In the discourse of the Thai middle class, prostitute women are icons of the decline of tradition and the (negative) result of a rush to modernity without the proper guidance of their "betters." In this way prostitutes' own voices and demands have been drowned out in the modern Thai polity, and these women have become the objects of policy rather than the subjects of politics.

By viewing the Prostitute, as well as gender and culture, as constructed categories, we begin to open up the possibilities of agency – of resistance and challenge. In this way we also begin to understand how those possibilities are made invisible by particular discursive renderings of identities; that is, rather than assuming that prostitute women are silent, or victims, or greedy consumers, we must assume that there is nothing essential about them at all and that the identities and modifiers given to them are, in fact, historical constructions imposed through power. Second, in order to understand how the Prostitute is constructed we need to examine the universe of political discourse in Thailand that produces this phenomenon. I view this universe as an arena of sense making within which various discourses are taken up by political actors who contend for hegemonic appeal. Third, in Thailand this universe is fundamentally shaped by the struggle between international/Western representations and Thailand's self-construction of national identity. And, fourth, because of the links between constructions of national identity, gender identity, and sexual behaviour, constructions of the Prostitute (and, by extension, prostitution policy) are informed by these discourses over national and gender identity.

Thus, I examine prostitution policy as a discursive terrain, one in which gender and national identities are produced and regulated. I argue that prostitution policy in Thailand is fundamentally shaped by concerns over gender and national identity; that is, I look at culture as continually constructed through operations of power rather than as a given. In particular, I look at that aspect of culture known as national identity as being constructed against imperialist representations of other cultures. Similarly, I look at gender as a construction imposed upon the fluctuating realities of sexed bodies – a construction that is interdependent with that of national identity. Constructions of gender have been central mechanisms of constructing national and imperialist identities. The Prostitute is a particular form of gender construction – a category with no inherent meaning but with a great deal of discursive power in the modern world because it is the dividing line between good (i.e., acceptable) women and bad (i.e., unacceptable) women.

Prostitution in Thailand

While historians have identified various forms of what may be called prostitution even in the ancient kingdoms that pre-dated Siam/Thailand, it was only with the Vietnam War that the numbers of women involved became an issue of wide public concern. Ever since then, despite the long history of prostitution in Thailand, prostitution has been strongly associated with the forces of globalization and modernization, and, despite the fact that most clients of Thai prostitutes are Thai, there has been a tendency to focus on the international aspects of the trade (foreign tourists and international

trafficking). The usual story of "the prostitution problem in Thailand" –
told by academics, feminists, and journalists both inside and outside Thailand – points to the Vietnam War and the stationing of thousands of American troops in Thailand as the beginning of wide-scale prostitution in that
country. Women, mainly from the poorer province of Isan in the northeast
and from the northern province of Chiang Mai, began to migrate to the
areas outside American air bases in Thailand as well as to the urban centres
where soldiers were taken for rest and recreation (R&R) leave. These women
were to provide sexual services in the mushrooming bars, discos, and massage parlours built to cater to the military and, increasingly during the
1970s and 1980s, to tourists. With the declining terms of trade in the rural
areas brought on by export-led industrialization policies, which drained
resources away from the countryside and into the urban areas, women's
responsibility to provide for their families led more and more rural daughters to seek work in the new sex industry. Police reports estimated that the
number of "persons clearly engaged in prostitution related activity" stood
at 171,000 by 1964 (in the early stages of American deployment in Southeast Asia).[4] The closest approximation in the late 1950s, from much less
thorough reports, was that approximately 20,000 people (mainly female)
were involved.[5] The perception of rapidly rising prostitution numbers was
highlighted by the number of women who were involved in the newly classified activity of "special service"; that is, working in the bars and entertainment districts. Here police estimated that there were some 426,908
"special service girls" in Thailand in 1964.[6] Even as American military
forces pulled out of Vietnam in the early 1970s, prostitution continued to
grow in Thailand as tourism agencies picked up where the military left off.

The growth of the prostitution-tourism industry in Thailand has been
the focus of a great deal of critical inquiry. Thahn-dam Truong's 1990 study
of tourism and prostitution in Thailand clearly laid out the interaction of
local and global capital and patriarchy in structuring and maintaining this
profitable industry.[7] Indeed, over the course of the 1970s and 1980s the prostitution industry continued to expand even as feminists and human rights
activists in Thailand, Europe, and North America organized against sex tourism, demanding that governments and international organizations address
the continued sexual exploitation of Third World women by Western men.

Feminist analysts pointed to patriarchal structures in Thai society – the
role of the dutiful daughter in maintaining family income and religious
teachings that placed women below men in the social hierarchy – along
with regional poverty as the driving factors behind women's entry into the
trade. Even as Thailand experienced its boom in the 1980s and early 1990s
through the rapid growth of export industries, the impoverishment of its
countryside continued to deepen. While rural poverty was three times
greater than urban poverty in the 1970s, it was five times greater in the

1980s. This poverty was concentrated in the north and northeast (Isan) provinces and manifested itself particularly among women, the uneducated, and the aged.[8] Since the majority of women were employed in the rural agricultural sector they were the ones who were most hurt by the rapid decline of agriculture as a contributor to the gross domestic product (GDP) (it went from 25.4 percent in 1980 to 12.8 percent in 1990).[9] Soon more women than men migrated from the countryside to Bangkok, only to find poorly paid and exploitative work in the export factories or even more demeaning work in domestic service. Work in prostitution, however, could provide an income twenty-five times greater than the median level of other occupations in which migrant women found themselves.[10] While regional and gender-based poverty explained the supply side of prostitution, feminists also pointed to the structuring of the demand for prostitution as a product of the interplay of patriarchy and political economy. In particular, they noted that government encouragement of the prostitution and tourism industries, along with the racist and sexist attitudes of Western men and governments, fuelled the demand for tourism-prostitution services. Not only were explicit sex tours being organized by international tourism agencies, but government tourism promotion also drew upon the sexualized image of Thai women to boost tourism numbers.

Reports of slavery-like conditions in the brothels and bars of Thailand intensified the investigations of national and international human rights and women's organizations in the 1980s. The deaths of several women, who were unable to escape a fire in a brothel in southern Thailand in 1984, generated further concern about the abuse of women in prostitution. Continuing reports of inhumane conditions, the buying and selling of women, the practice of indebting women or tricking them into prostitution, and outright abuse confirmed a general picture of the "sex slavery" that appeared to be rife in Thailand.

The industry also took on new forms in the 1980s. From traditional brothels and commercially organized sex tours – plane-loads of men from Japan, the Middle East, Europe, and North America arriving in Thailand – the trade expanded to include a reverse "traffic in women," with thousands of young women from Thailand and other developing countries opting, or being forced into, travelling overseas to work in the prostitution industries of the more developed countries. Even if some women knew that they would be working in prostitution once they arrived overseas, few were aware of the kinds of conditions they would face – conditions that included being controlled by the traffickers, or venue owners, who would demand repayment for all costs incurred in travel and housing, often preventing flight by holding on to the women's passports and documents. Often working illegally in an underground trade in a foreign country, women working in prostitution overseas had little recourse against abuse.

Adding further worry was the AIDS threat. HIV-positive rates reached proportions of 41 percent to 54 percent among commercial sex workers in brothels in the northern provinces in the early 1990s, and they reached a median prevalence of 24 percent among brothel prostitutes nationwide.[11] In 1993, the government reported that approximately 450,000 Thais were infected with HIV.[12] The threat of AIDS turned attention to the prevalence of prostitution use among the local male population. Reports of 88 percent or 90 percent of Thai men having visited a prostitute at least once in their lifetime made national and international news.

Children's rights organizations became increasingly involved over the course of the 1980s as information on the industry's use of very young children as virtual sex slaves began to come forward. Reports of poverty-stricken rural families selling their children into sex slavery in Bangkok became standard fare in the late 1980s. The growing threat of AIDS also contributed to an increased demand for younger children in the trade as people believed that young children were less likely to be infected. In 1991 the Center for the Protection of Children's Rights in Thailand reported that some 800,000 of an estimated two million persons providing sexual services in Thailand were children under the age of eighteen. While many analysts agree that the more likely number of people working in the industry as commercial sex workers is well under one million, the 1991 report indicated that there was a growing perception that the industry had spread to critical proportions.

Of further concern, though less frequently discussed in the press, was the number of migrant and indigenous hill-tribe women involved in the trade. While no exact numbers are available, the impoverishment of hill-tribe villagers has led hill-tribe women, like their rural lowland counterparts, to migrate to the cities in search of work, including work in the prostitution industry. Alternatively, tourists and "trekkers" are found in growing numbers in the distant hill villages offering money in exchange for sexual relations, and brokers are travelling to the villages in search of AIDS-free women for the urban prostitution trade.[13] Not only were the peripheralized hill tribes being drawn into the trade, but, over the course of the 1990s, analysts also noted increasing numbers of foreign women – particularly Burmese (including Burmese hill-tribe) and Chinese women – working in the Thai sex industry. This again raised the spectre of forced trafficking and dire economic circumstances as the underlying causes of women's entry into the trade.

However, it was also increasingly clear that the nature of the problem was very differently understood by various groups. Under international and national pressure to do something about the prostitution problem the Thai government, to much fanfare, adopted new legislation in 1996, increasing the penalties for procurers and brothel owners as well as punishing clients of underage prostitutes and parents who sold their children into prostitution. While the new legislation was greeted with enthusiasm by international organizations that viewed prostitution itself as a human rights abuse to be prevented at all costs, a number of women's organizations quickly remarked on the failure to remove penalties for prostitute women themselves. It was the illegality of prostitution, many argued, that led to abuse – by police, clients, pimps, and procurers. As long as prostitutes were themselves penalized, women had no possibility for redress, having to remain out of the reach of the law. The drive to "correct" the prostitution problem may have contributed to the continued abuse of prostitute women, and the overall understanding of women as "victims" in the trade may have contributed to patronizing and disempowering policies.

Therefore, I seek to understand how these policies have come about by more closely interrogating the story of prostitution. In reality, we know very little about the prostitution industry itself in Thailand. A great deal of activity takes place in roadside brothels and in more unstructured arrangements that involve hair-dressers, golf caddies (in Thailand these are mostly women), and waitresses. The conditions of work vary widely, as do the people involved. How, then, do certain, often simplified, representations of a complex reality come to dominate the public consciousness or, perhaps more important, the consciousness of elites and policy makers? Where do these representations come from and what are their implications? These are the questions that this book seeks to address.

Prostitution, Representation, and Power

The theoretical underpinnings of this book are drawn from social constructionist and postcolonial schools of thought. The constructed nature of the categories "prostitution/prostitute" has been made clear in feminist debates as well as in the history of the terms themselves. Prostitution is a highly elastic category. For this reason, debates among social scientists about what actually constitutes prostitution continue. Even the vague definition of prostitution as "the exchange of sexual services for material gain" is easily challenged. Consider, for instance, that actresses in seventeenth-century England were considered whores and that, in 1988, when a dominatrix was charged with keeping a bawdy house, courts in Toronto were preoccupied with determining whether "spanking is sex."[14] Similarly, in studying Thailand, Eric Cohen questions whether women who act as girlfriends to tourists during their stay in return for gifts can be included under the rubric of prostitution; others problematize categorizing women who were hired wives during the Vietnam War as prostitutes.[15] In most countries the definitional niceties (or lack thereof) are left to the police, who use their "common sense" to determine who is or is not a prostitute. They also decide at what particular moment and in what particular place a woman becomes a prostitute. The very flexibility of the category prostitution should alert us to the tenuousness of the link between reality and representation. Indeed, the feminist attempt to challenge masculinist representations of prostitution (e.g., as being functional to male sexual needs) by presenting a "truth" founded upon women's experience of prostitution (e.g., as being exploitative) foundered when analysts could not uncover a common experience. Prostitutes' rights activists have argued that prostitution is "just another job," while others, including former prostitutes, have organized against prostitution, characterizing it as a "degrading and dehumanizing" experience. Perhaps even more important, as organizers and activists turned their sights from First World to Third World prostitution, the problems of applying simplified notions of prostitution (as either a freely chosen occupation or a form of slavery) became increasingly clear.

While the structural constraints surrounding prostitution as a choice appear most glaring in the developing world, one cannot leap to the assumption that prostitutes in the Third World are without sexual or social agency. As Kemala Kempadoo has recently argued, despite the understandable reluctance to explore agency in prostitution in the Third World, and given the general over-sexualization of non-Western women (and the resulting histories of rape and abuse),

> in an era when women can no longer be defined exclusively as victims, where Third World women speak for themselves in various forums, where increasingly analyses have shifted focus from simple hierarchies and dichotomies to the problematization of multiple spaces, seemingly contradictory social locations and plural sites of power, it would seem that experiences, identities and struggles of women in the global sex industry cannot be neglected.[16]

In *Sex and Borders* I assume that there is neither any singular or generalizable experience of prostitution nor any singular prostitute; rather I view "the prostitute" as a subject-position constructed in discourse and imposed upon a shifting reality. I consider it important to approach the issue from this angle in order to address prostitute women's own concerns about the discursive power of the "whore stigma" and to recognize that women in prostitution in Thailand, as elsewhere, are aware of their own multiple subjectivity, of their simultaneous powerlessness and agency.[17] In taking this approach I draw upon the work of poststructuralist feminist theorists who uncover the ways in which female bodies are interpolated as women – including, for example, as victims or whores – and how this process constrains and structures their lives. From this perspective, the construction of the category "prostitute" is one of the forces that shape the lives and experiences of women, and it does so by delineating the boundaries of proper and improper female behaviour and seeking to penalize and/or regulate those who fall into the latter category. As Wendy Chapkis' opening epigraph makes clear, the regulatory function of the category "prostitute" makes its actual content highly variable rather than a simple correspondence between an embodied activity and an abstract label. Again, this is not to say that there are no women selling sex, no actual women engaged in the commercial-sex business; rather, it is to argue against a necessary experience, or reality, arising from this activity and to focus our attention on how, to paraphrase Denise Riley, actual women working in the industry are positioned *as* prostitutes.[18] Throughout I argue that law and policy are determined by, and reproduce, how prostitutes are seen and understood; that is, how they are positioned. Thus, we need to ask how prostitute women in Thailand come to be positioned as victims, or consumers, or backward peasants, and we need to examine the implications of such positionings.

My concern here with representation and the discursive constructions of prostitution is not simply theoretical. Indeed, it is feminists from the Third World – both scholars and those organizing around issues such as prostitution – who have called attention to the power of representation. It is my contention, therefore, that the struggle over the power of representation is a real and fundamental part of actual, everyday international and national politics. The theoretical insights of the postcolonial school into the power of discourse in shaping relations between North and South, the colonizer and the colonized, are made manifest in the protestations over how Thailand and Thai women are portrayed in the international debate over prostitution. Feminists from Thailand have been very sensitive to the need both to recognize Thai women's weak position within the global economy and to avoid presenting Thai women in prostitution as mere victims of larger processes. Similarly, both state and non-state Thai representatives have been sensitive to international media representations of Thai culture as the underlying cause of the booming sex industry. These protests are not simply about image or hurt pride; rather, they are about representations of the other – representations that, as postcolonial theorists have pointed out, have enabled political and economic imperialism.

Chandra Mohanty's ground-breaking article, "Under Western Eyes: Feminist Scholarship and Colonial Discourses," has drawn attention to the issue of power and representation in feminist theorizing. Mohanty argues that "Western feminist scholarship cannot avoid the challenge of situating itself and examining its role in [an imperialist] global economic and political framework. To do any less would be to ignore the complex interconnections between first and third world economies and the profound effect of this on the lives of women in all countries."[19] Mohanty points to the global hegemony of Western scholarship and its role in the reproduction of Western political hegemony. Specifically, she follows the understanding of "contemporary imperialism" put forward by Anouas Abdel-Malek as a struggle for "control over the orientation, regulation and decision of the process of world development on the basis of the advanced sector's monopoly of scientific knowledge and idea creativity." In other words, Western discourse attempts to delimit the political possibilities for the globe, such as the correct "path towards development" or the content of "modernity." Western knowledges and ideas, therefore, have a political power that must be "defined and named."[20] Naming the power of knowledge, Mohanty stresses, is essential if feminists are to forge international links between women's struggles. Western representations of a singular and monolithic "Third World Woman" are viewed as imperialistic and imperializing by many women in the Third World.[21] Third World feminists, therefore, call for a feminism that makes the links between First World and Third World, takes the time to learn about the different configurations of gender and power (and experiences thereof) in different societies, and listens to the voices of those experiencing it.

Unfortunately, much of the scholarship and writing on prostitution in Thailand (as well as on Thai politics more generally) has adopted an imperializing gaze, which often depends upon reified notions of gender and culture rather than upon examining how power informs the way in which such notions are constructed. For example, much blame has been laid at the door of Buddhism – the official state religion – for the second-class status of Thai women (which is seen as having paved the way for their entry into prostitution). Generally, it has been argued that it is more difficult for women to climb up the ladder of merit (women cannot, for instance, be ordained as monks – an important source of merit) and much easier for them to slide down (e.g., because of the demerit that is associated with female sexual misbehaviour but not with male sexual behaviour).[22] While such characterizations have sometimes been adopted by Thai analysts themselves, particularly when feminist academics first began to deal with the issue of prostitution, such an oversimplified (and negative) view of Buddhism has rankled many Thais as well as more sensitive analysts. Thai analysts such as Chatsumarn Kabilsingh point out that many of the misogynistic practices incorporated into Thai Buddhism are the product of earlier Brahmin, rather than Buddhist, influences.[23] Other analysts point out that such an explanation confuses, for instance, ideological, or textual, Buddhism with actual lived experience (one of the markers of an imperialistic approach, according to Mohanty), which is historically and regionally diverse. Indeed, Buddhism in Thailand lives in a complicated relationship with animist practices, which grant women a variety of spiritual roles and social powers. According to Penny van Esterik, even Buddhist textual doctrine does not necessarily support a misogynistic worldview; rather, a variety of contradictory images of women appear in the stories of the

Buddha, which can be, and have been, drawn upon and utilized by various groups for various purposes.[24] Indeed, prostitute women themselves draw upon images of themselves as "dutiful daughters" and view their contributions to the family income as meritorious. Young middle-class women in today's Thailand attend religious retreats in a form of resistance to the oversexualized image of Thai women. As Nicola Tannenbaum has pointed out in her thoroughgoing critique of the use of Buddhism as an explanation for prostitution, analysts have failed to uncover the "multiple possible meanings of Buddhism" and have instead produced an essentialized image that has more to do with "seeing the 'other' as being more religious, natural, etc., than the Western analyst."[25] Seeing the other in this way underwrites the superiority and power of the Western analyst, who is considered more modern, sophisticated, and "civic-minded."

It is these concerns that underlie Third World feminists' challenge to Western feminist representations of the situation of prostitute women in developing countries. First, in the debate over prostitution, feminists from Third World countries have been at pains to emphasize the role of the American military and the global economy in the spread of prostitution. Radical feminists' focus on the operation of sexual power alone was quickly challenged by feminists, particularly Third World feminists, who felt that the operations of power were not simply based in gender or sexuality. The overwhelming focus on sexual domination erases not only modes of opposition and resistance, but also modes of other forms of power as well. Women from Thailand who are working on the issue of prostitution argued that understanding prostitution requires understanding the international operation of the capitalist economy and its relationship to prostitution. Women are not simply victims of an international patriarchy: they are also the product of a capitalist system that positions them as cheap sexual labour.[26] Kathleen Barry's presentation of the Thai sex industry as a product of male sex right is countered by Thanh-dam Truong's analysis of it as a product of the global capitalist institutions – hotels, airlines, tour operators – that provide the infrastructure, and demand, for it.[27]

Second, the portrayal of women as mere victims makes Thai feminists organizing around the issue of prostitution very uneasy. They recognize the essentialized construction of the Third World woman as "passive victim," lacking the modern agency of her First World sisters and, therefore, being in need of their aid and direction. (Indeed, there is a frightening echo of the very language used by sex tourists themselves in the representation of Asian women as "passive.") Siriporn Skrobanek, for one, in her analysis of the "international sex-exploitation of Thai women," has always been careful to point out the efforts of women in the international marriage and prostitution trades to resist modes of power and to act on their own behalf (although not under conditions of their own choosing).[28] Sukanya

Hantrakul draws attention to the "spirit of a fighter," which she says exists in many Thai prostitute women, and she argues that the problem lies with the institutions of penal reform that attempt to discipline women into engaging in "acceptable behaviour."[29]

What these debates make very clear is that the politics of representation, the concern with the essentialized construction of identities, is not merely a theoretical point of interest; rather, it is part of the everyday political struggle and the operation of power, and it has historical consequence. In other words, the politics of representation is a vitally important part of international (and, as we shall see, national) politics and power that has been virtually ignored by political scientists. These concerns can best be addressed through a social constructionist understanding of politics in Thailand – an understanding that takes neither Thai culture nor Thai women as given but, rather, that views them as constructed within historical time and space and through the operation of power. Further, the above debate has brought into stark relief the importance of viewing Thai politics within the framework of the international struggle over representation. In particular, I focus on the struggle over national identity in the face of Western imperialism/ neo-imperialism and its link to gender constructs in order to understand prostitution policy as a terrain of contested identity construction.

Gender and the Nation

The construction and maintenance of borders is a complicated business. "Borders" must be mapped not simply on a geographic terrain, but also in the minds and on the bodies of the inhabitants of that geography. Without this deeper inscription, a line on a map is meaningless. "Nations," therefore, rest on the construction of national identities. Because of women's reproductive role, the regulation of women's bodies is an integral part of inscribing national/ethnic identities. As both the literal and figurative reproducers of the race (through biological reproduction and cultural reproduction, respectively), women and the control of their sexuality are key to the national(ist) project. The image of the prostitute, for instance, works to regulate women's sexual activity by confining women's proper sexual role to reproduction. Women who "squander" their sexuality (e.g., by engaging in sexual relations outside the confines of marriage or by engaging in sexual relations with more than one man) cannot be mothers to the nation. Such women, "whores," are duly confined to the margins of society as both a punishment to them and a warning to others. The construction of national identity, therefore, is closely linked to the construction of gender identity and the regulation of sexual behaviour.

Prostitution is a particularly rich ground for the investigation of the links between gender identity and national identity because of the centrality of women's sexuality in establishing and maintaining them. The classification of prostitution involves identifying correct and incorrect sexual behaviour on the part of women, and distinguishing between good and bad women. Women's correct sexual behaviour – usually within the bonds of marriage and family – grounds the categories of gender (what men and women should be and do). It simultaneously undergirds the categories of class (which men and women properly understand and apply) and national identity (which women are the mothers to our nation? The ones who populate the motherland that the manly state seeks to protect). Women's stepping outside the boundaries of proper sexual behaviour destabilizes these categories. The invocation of prostitution (understood to be a shameful and unacceptable sexual behaviour) serves to discipline women's behaviour into accepted modes and, therefore, to stabilize these other categories. With this understanding, I look at gender as a social relation of power, as a process of imposing certain hierarchical identities of masculine or feminine that are then read as natural and unchanging. Gender, rather than being a pre-given identity emanating from sexed bodies, is something that is constructed through operations of power. The construction of gender carries particular power because its constructedness (and, therefore, the operation of power) is so easily hidden in the apparently natural division between male and female bodies.

National identity, like gender, is also a constructed category invoked to unite certain peoples against an outside "other" and to legitimize state authority over a particular territory. Feminist theorists have drawn attention to what most theories of nationalism have ignored – that the nation is fundamentally gendered. Women stand in a different relation to the nation than do men. Some theorists of nationalism and gender, like Kumari Jayawardena, argue that moves to establish a sovereign nation – as opposed to clans or kin groups – also open space for women's citizenship rights by dissolving old kin-based loyalties.[30] Others point out, however, that the control of women and women's sexuality remains central to ideas of national identity. Floya Anthias' and Nira Yuval-Davis' now classic study, *Woman-Nation-State*, outlines five ways in which women have tended to

participate in ethnic and national processes and in relation to state practices: as biological reproducers of members of ethnic collectivities; as reproducers of the boundaries of ethnic/national groups; as participating centrally in the ideological reproduction of the collectivity and as transmitters of its culture; as signifiers of ethnic/national differences – as a focus and symbol in ideological discourses used in the construction, reproduction and transformation of ethnic/national categories; as participants in national, economic, political and military struggles.[31]

It is women's symbolic role as mothers and biological and cultural reproducers that is most central to my discussion here, since it is this role that is
central to discourses of national identity. The material effect of these roles
is the control of women's sexuality, which is seen as central to maintaining
national identity. This centrality leads to an "intense preoccupation with
women's appropriate sexual conduct," which "often constitutes the crucial
distinction between the nation and its 'others.'"[32]

Women's sexuality, therefore, can mark the very borders of the nation-
state – its purity, the purity of the nation; its defilement, the defilement of
the nation. The prostitute, therefore, appears as a liminal figure in relation
to the mother, as she marks the borderlands of female sexuality. She is the
internal "other" that threatens the purity of the nation. The rise of the
prostitute, in this formulation, signals the loss of control over female sexuality and, therefore, is a harbinger of the disintegration of national culture
and identity. Most threatening of all, the prostitute – seen as one who uses
her own sexuality for profit – is a subversive figure. While all women's sexuality can be viewed as at risk of "foreign invasion," the prostitute appears
to seek out such invasion. She is a potential fifth column within the
nation, which is anchored by female purity. (Indeed, that the prostitute
figures regularly as a spy in various literatures and histories comes as no
surprise here.) Other accounts of prostitution as sexual labour, or as the operation of male sexual privilege, must always vie with this powerful symbolism of the prostitute. At most, these accounts may argue for a more
sympathetic understanding of the prostitute as a victim of larger forces (a
symbolic rape victim). Within the context of concern over defending and
maintaining national identity (as in this period of globalization), however, the
perpetrators will appear as foreign (foreign militaries, rapid modernization/
Westernization).

As symbols, both prostitute and non-prostitute women are denied
national agency. Anne McClintock has argued that women's symbolic relation to the nation denies them active citizenship: "excluded from direct
action as national citizens, women are subsumed symbolically into the
national body politics as its boundary and metaphoric limit: 'Singapore
girl, you're a great way to fly.' Women are typically construed as the symbolic bearer of the nation, but are denied any direct relation to national
agency."[33] Indeed, the centrality of the symbol of women has rarely translated into full citizenship, although some women have been able to
trade on their cultural role in order to gain social power. As with women
more generally, therefore, the agency of the prostitute is always problematic. Seen as an agent, she is an accomplice in the destruction of national
identity; seen as a victim, she is sympathetic but also powerless. These portrayals encourage patronizing and stifling reactions.

With the rise of Western colonialism this symbolic national discourse was internationalized. The regulation of racial/sexual boundaries was central to the colonial project. Women's bodies were again important boundary markers in this process. The colonial community was consolidated through the call to protect White womanhood (pure, virtuous, and "civilizing") from the colonial other, which was figured as a sexual threat. Colonized women came to be read either as sexually voracious (i.e., prostitutes) or as unwilling victims of oversexed local males, the latter portrayal requiring the intervention of the colonial power in order to "rescue" them. White prostitute women, meantime, were represented as victims of an international ring of White slave traders. It was this process that underlay early international intervention in the field of prostitution – through international conventions on the White slave trade at the turn of the twentieth century. In this way a particular discourse of gender was internationalized.

The designation of bad girls and good girls, of proper gender identity and sexual behaviour, therefore, has long been a part of international politics. It is a process that deserves closer investigation because it helps to shed light on modern-day issues such as the sex trade in Thailand. In the present-day debate over the sex trade in Thailand, the prostitute's constructed status is often forgotten. A full understanding of the current situation requires that we recognize that prostitution is a symbolic terrain deeply embedded within gender and national constructions at precisely the point where the two identities intersect. How such constructions have worked to shape understandings of the modern-day sex industry in Thailand is what this book shall explore.

About this Book

Sex and Borders covers the development of prostitution policy in Thailand from the late 1800s to the present day, viewing it as a product of struggles and debates over national identity and gender. While male prostitution, child prostitution, and migrant prostitution in Thailand and elsewhere have become larger issues over the past decade, this study focuses mainly on Thai women because they constitute the majority of those working in the prostitution industry in Thailand and because it is the assumptions and concerns about these women, much more than those about men, that have shaped policy. The discussion of migrant and child prostitution has been an important part of recent attempts to address prostitution, and there is, therefore, some mention of these phenomena here; however, I have only discussed them in terms of how they are interpreted within prostitution policy. Similarly, because of the influence of Western colonialism and the continuing hegemonic status of the West writ large, I have focused solely on Western representations of identities as the constraining and enabling force in international politics. This is not to say that the regional dynamic is not an important influence in shaping the gender and national politics of Thailand. Indeed, other fascinating investigations are possible, such as those that focus upon the influence of Japanese constructs of identity (particularly given Japanese involvement in the sex industries of Asia). However, I limit myself to considerations of Western representations of Thailand and the Thai sex industry and hope that further investigations will some day examine the Asian regional context.

I also offer very little discussion of the role of Buddhism in Thai society. Buddhism's framework for understanding the self and human nature certainly informs Thai society, much as Judeo-Christian beliefs help to form the web of understandings within Western society; however, as mentioned above, Buddhism's explanatory power has been greatly overextended and applied to cultural determinist readings of Thailand, Thai politics, and Thai gender systems. For that reason I have generally avoided discussion of Buddhism, perhaps too much so; but I hope that this avoidance serves to highlight the more complicated process of cultural production that is at the core of the Thai sex industry. Suffice it to say, for those unfamiliar with Thailand and Theravada Buddhism, that some 90 percent of Thais profess to being Buddhist (although not necessarily practising, or practising devoutly) and that Buddhism figures as a central pillar of national identity (often styled, in the twentieth century, as "Nation, Religion, and King"). Further, the Buddhist belief system revolves around the concept of continual human rebirth, based on one's store of merit (i.e., good deeds), until one achieves the ultimate state of Nirvana, or Enlightenment. One's store of merit depends upon correct thinking and behaviour, such as avoiding causing harm to other living creatures, being generous, and avoiding desire for material things (which will only cause suffering). The idea of merit certainly shapes understandings of status and power in Thailand (those with power and money are assumed to have achieved them due to their large stores of merit), and particular interpretations of what is or is not meritorious shape general understandings of what is good and bad, moral and immoral (including with regard to sexual behaviour). However, while Buddhism provides part of the background of Thai society, vast generalizations about Buddhist belief give us little insight into the specifics of historically located responses to prostitution.

The research for *Sex and Borders* is based on both primary and secondary sources. In 1996 I spent six months in Thailand conducting field research for this book. During my time there I conducted in-depth interviews with some twenty-five key activists, directors of women's organizations, academic researchers, journalists, and bureaucrats whom I had identified through preliminary research or to whom I was directed by sources within Thailand. These people were perceived to be key players in addressing prostitution in Thailand. Given the attention generated by prostitution issues in Thailand over the last thirty years, there were certainly many more people who could have offered different perspectives and insights; however, a number of these perspectives are already represented in the literature, and I hope that those to whom I was able to speak represent important, though less well known, points of view (i.e., those of female politicians and female bureaucrats). Although I had achieved a basic level of (Central) Thai before beginning my research, the interviews were conducted in English, a language in which all interviewees were very competent. The interviews lasted anywhere between half an hour and two hours and were open-ended; that is, interviewees could direct me to what they deemed important (which often yielded delightful and helpful insights that I would not have discovered on my own).

The most important limitation of this research is that, as a discussion on the discourses that shape prostitution policy, it necessarily focuses upon middle-class and elite voices – the voices that have had the most direct influence on government policy. My conversations with prostitute women were casual. This is because I believe that, while it is indeed prostitute women's voices that need to be heard, my contribution as a political scientist (i.e., as someone trained to analyze those voices closest to the centres of power) could only be to create a space for them. While some excellent work, by those more capable than I (e.g., Pasuk Phongpaichit, Sukanya Hantrakul, the activists at EMPOWER), has been done to uncover these voices, I hope that much more will be done in the future. Here, I propose only to open up the possibility that such voices could contradict many of the assumptions being made in popular discussions of prostitution.

Documentary research for this project was conducted at the offices of the main feminist organizations in Thailand, particularly the offices of Foundation for Women and the Friends of Women (both of which have very helpful and patient staff) as well as several excellent research libraries in Bangkok and Chiang Mai. These included the Siam Society, the Thailand Information Centre, the Women's Studies Centre at Chiang Mai University, the United Nations offices in Bangkok, and the various libraries of Chulalongkorn University. I also closely tracked opinion and events through the two English-language papers in Thailand, the *Nation* and the *Bangkok Post,* from July 1996 to July 1997. While the language of publication necessarily limited what insights I could gather, my purpose was not to uncover "Thai opinion" but to trace the representation of "Thai identity" to the West. Additionally, these two papers are recognized as the key media of educated, Westernized, middle-class, and elite opinion making; therefore, they provided me with insights into how these particular groups sought to represent and to construct themselves and others. While my Thai language skills were not sufficient to allow me access to the wealth of information available in the very active Thai-language press, and while this limits the scope of this research, I do hope that this discussion will open doors for future research.

Further to the issue of language, throughout *Sex and Borders* I have relied upon the Thai transcription system of the Thai Royal Institute, which is based on phonetic transcription without tonal marks (except where common usage or the source being quoted dictates otherwise). I use "Siam" when referring to pre-1939 Thailand and "Thailand" after that date (despite the more complicated history and politics surrounding the change in name). For Thai names I have tried to follow the transcription used by the persons themselves; for historical personages I have used traditional transcriptions. In line with Thai usage, throughout this book Thai people are referred to by their given names rather than by their surnames, and they are entered in the Bibliography according to their given names. Titles are used where required, particularly where they are needed to denote class status. The terms "M.R." (*maum ratchawong*) and "M.L." (*maum luang*) for minor royalty, along with *Thanphuying/Khunying* for grades of "ladyship," appear throughout (with the exception of Lady [*Khunying*] Laiad, who is most commonly referred to in the English language historical literature by the English term). I also use *Phra* for monks of the Buddhist order (the *Sangha*).

Sex and Borders examines prostitution policy in Thailand from the semi-colonial period in Siam to modern-day Thailand – as the country moved from a traditional monarchy to military authoritarianism to democracy. None of these transitions was, of course, complete or clear-cut. The place of the monarchy in Thailand remains (or, more appropriately, has been made) central in many ways, even though it is no longer absolute. In the post-1932 era, the monarch is technically a figurehead who is subject to the rule of law through the Constitution but who continues to have a great deal of moral and symbolic influence. The monarchy, as a source of legitimacy and influence, is central to my understanding of class divisions in Thailand today. Before 1932 the monarchy was the core of political power. I have used the term "absolute monarchy" loosely here to refer to the monarchical system between the early fifteenth century (the *Ayutthayan* empire) and 1932, under which ultimate decision-making authority rested with the king. It must be pointed out, however, that some, like John Girling, would argue that the "absolutist theory of an all-powerful god-king (*chao chivit* 'lord of life') contrasts with the reality of a balance of power among king, princes, and nobility."[34]

Indeed, an extensive feudal elite, denoted by a system of "dignity marks" – the *sakdina* system, literally "power of the land" – worked to administer the kingdom's affairs. The *sakdina* system ranked each and every member of the kingdom, from royalty through slaves. The higher the rating of a noble, the more land and (more important) more labour (serfs, or *phrai*) controlled by the noble.[35] The influence of this class system is still felt today, particularly in the continuing power and influence of the elite class. I use "elites" broadly to refer to those with links to the more traditional centres of power in the monarchy and upper echelons of government. For example, the *khunyings* (ladyships) are women who have been recognized by the monarchy for their service and dedication to the nation. Elites and elite women also generally come from wealthy families, but it is important to distinguish them from the nouveaux riches of the post-1970s period. Today, elite women also tend to be an age cohort that is somewhere over fifty (i.e., women who were in their thirties or older during the 1973-6 democracy period), although this is not necessarily the case. This distinguishes them from the generation of student activists in the 1970s who are now, approximately, in their forties. The term "new middle class" refers to the new class of post-secondary-educated, often urbanized, individuals who work in particular sectors of the economy (e.g., the managerial and professional sectors). For the rural class, which continues to rely, at least in part, on the land for survival, I have used the generic term "peasantry" to distinguish them from the urban working class and rural elites.

Chapter 1 discusses the historical background of prostitution policy in both absolutist Siam and post-monarchical Thailand. In particular, it examines the links between gender and international representation that were established in the semi-colonial era as British, American, and European powers gained a foothold in Siamese politics and economics and the Siamese monarchy struggled to maintain its independence. The chapter then follows the developments in prostitution policy that followed the overthrow of the monarchy in 1932 and the establishment of modernizing dictatorships under Field Marshals Phibun and Sarit, who sought to make Siam/Thailand part of the international society of modern nations, in part through the manipulation of gender identities and the disciplining of sexual behaviour. Chapter 2 covers the period surrounding the "democracy era" of 1973-6, which shook the foundations of Thai society and politics. Sometimes referred to as the revolutionary period, this confluence of peasant uprisings/communist insurgency and middle-class student activism changed the face of Thai politics forever, as a military dictatorship was overthrown but then re-established with brutal force a scant three years later. It was during this period that the deep and lasting connections between peasant women's sexual behaviour (particularly in prostitution) and national identity were established, as students pointed to American military involvement in Thailand as the source of degradation of Thai culture and Thai women. Chapter 3 addresses the role of elite women in the reconstruction of Thai identity – particularly the attachment of the peasantry to the imagined nation – in the aftermath of the crackdown on the democracy activists and the re-establishment of a soft authoritarianism (or "guided democracy") under General Prem Tinsulanond, who oversaw the beginnings of tremendous growth and development in the Thai economy. Chapter 4 covers the flip side of these developments, the political economy

of prostitution tourism under Prem and the critiques of these developments by middle-class women's non-governmental organizations. Chapters
5 and 6 also cover two aspects of the same period, the 1990s, in Thailand –
a period of rapid political change as the new middle class, born out of the
prosperity of the late 1980s, began to make its claim for political power.
Chapter 5 discusses the construction of the new modern man in Thailand,
viewing it as the newly modernized, urban middle class's attempt to
respond to the relationship between its "international image" and the
prostitution problem. Chapter 6 explores the development of the critique
of the prostitute as a "material girl," viewing it as a response to the need for
an increasingly modern middle class to anchor its national identity in the
peasantry and in women's bodies.

Sex and Borders

1
Gender, Prostitution, and the "Standards of Civilization"

The importance of gender and sexuality in marking the difference between national self and other, and the power of particular gender constructs in establishing global authority, were made very clear during the imperial era. Their strictures, as defined by the West, shaped international relations into the twentieth century. The establishment of Western authority rested heavily on colonial discourses that marked the differences between Siamese and Westerners in sexualized and gendered terms. Thus, during the imperial era, Siam was represented by Westerners as feminine, or improperly masculine, and, therefore, as naturally subordinate to the "manly" Western states. The importance of proper gender and sexual behaviour to the "standards of civilization" were made very clear in the Western critique of polygamy and extended into the later international campaign against prostitution. Measuring up to Western standards of gender and sexual behaviour, therefore, became a central plank in Siamese/Thai policy as the country fought to maintain sovereign status and international respect; however, this also generated elite male resistance to the imposition of Western sexual standards. Thus, while polygamy was outlawed in 1935 and prostitution was eventually outlawed in 1960, elite men continued to resist these changes.

The accounts of British and American missionaries and diplomats in nineteenth-century Siam make it clear that their imperial status rested upon manipulating categories of gender and sexuality in order to establish Western states (associated with masculinity and sexual restraint) as legitimate and lasting and to establish the Siamese state (associated with femininity and sexual excess) as illegitimate and collapsing. In other words, Westerners pointed to Siamese gender and sexual practices as evidence of the "barbarity" of the Siamese. These characterizations and associations are particularly evident in the obsessive discussions of polygamy that are found in the journals of visiting diplomats and missionaries. It is the discussions of polygamy, rather than the discussions of prostitution (which did not gain momentum until the turn of the nineteenth century), that set the stage for future struggles over prostitution legislation.

Gender and Prostitution in the Early Modern Siamese State

The polygamous marital system of Siam was an integral part of the national and international politics of the tributary kingdoms of Asia. According to Thongchai Winichakul, the spatial conception of the Siamese nation was utterly different from the Western notion of contiguous boundaries and was, instead, based on a "sacred topography" – the spiritual realm of a king's sovereignty.[1] Rather than borders of defended territory, sovereignties were overlapping spheres of influence (conceived in a spiritual rather than a territorial sense), and relations between spheres were managed through tributary relations of gift giving. In many ways then, the king himself embodied the nation as well as the state, and it was the bodies of women attached to the king that were the ones most closely regulated.

Women played an important role in the harem as consorts and wives of the king, producing both heirs to the throne and staff for the state. As well, elite women provided a bond between rulers and between rulers and nobles in a state and inter-state system based on tribute and alliances. Gifts of women as wives from nobles to the king, and vice versa, cemented ties of loyalty and service between rulers of different spheres of influence. The sexual behaviour of elite women, particularly those within the king's harem, was closely guarded as their bodies marked the boundaries of the state. Thus, control of women's bodies increased with their closeness to the centre of influence, the king himself. One of the earliest available historical sources – the account of a French nobleman, Simon de la Loubère, in Siam on a diplomatic mission in the late 1600s – tells us that elite women were severely punished for adultery and promiscuity. The king's wives were most strictly guarded, being housed in the inner palace, which was peopled entirely of women presided over by the queen or principle wife of the king and guarded by female guards. The penalty for promiscuity on the part of a member of the king's harem was to be sold to a brothel owner or, sometimes, to be killed.[2] Thus, for elite women sexual misbehaviour was punished by being forced into sexual service, although this was most likely understood in terms of concubinage (as discussed below) rather than as prostitution in the modern Western sense of the term.

There was much less control over the sexual behaviour of women outside this immediate sphere of elite power. Marriage and divorce were a matter of relative ease, and virginity was not a requirement before marriage. Women traders exchanged sexual favours as well as goods, often contracting "temporary marriages" with foreigners. While non-elite women appear to have been fairly self-determining in their sexual practices, it is important to remember that Siam was also a slave society. Slavery in Southeast Asia was not the absolute slave system of Europe and America; while there were "absolute slaves" in the European sense (usually war captives), there were also a large number of bonded debtors who sold themselves or were sold into slavery and could buy their way out again. In the class system of Siam, women and children were not entirely independent actors: they could be sold into debt bondage by their husbands or fathers. Unmarried female slaves often acted as concubines to their masters or their masters' guests.

Commercial prostitution, as opposed to the indigenous practice of concubinage, appeared in Southeast Asia in the late 1600s.[3] According to Barbara Andaya, European disregard for the strictures of fidelity and support of the temporary marriage system rapidly eroded local practices and beliefs, and, with them, women's status. Increasingly, liaisons were contracted between European men and marginalized women (e.g., slaves, ex-slaves, and foreigners) who were far from the protections of home.[4] Within this context, the sexual relations between foreign men and local women began to more closely resemble modern understandings of prostitution as a commercial transaction. The proceeds from brothel prostitution were taxed by the king, but prostitution was not otherwise regulated.[5] In the 1800s, prostitution appears often to have been practised in boats anchored in city harbours, the prostitutes consisting mostly of women who had been sold into debt bondage.

Imperial Desire: Sex, Gender, and International Power

Interestingly, it was the practice of polygamy rather than prostitution that captured the attention of the imperialists. While the issue of polygamy had been of some fascination to the European visitors of the sixteenth and seventeenth centuries, it was understood in terms of the practices of the absolutist state. La Loubère explained to the French court that polygamy was not a matter of debauchery but of "Pomp and Grandeur."[6] Such pomp and grandeur were understood at the court of Louis the Fourteenth – the Sun King. By the middle of the eighteenth century, however, profound changes in the conceptualization of proper political rule, and the gendered nature of that rule, had been brought about through the Enlightenment.[7] The new ideas that swept across Europe in the eighteenth century created an association between absolutism, sexual debauchery, and "the feminine." Restrained sexuality, "manliness" defined as the natural opposite of "femininity," and proper rule were the order of the day. With the development of Enlightenment science, the conceptualization of the feminine shifted. Susan Hekman argues that nature as feminine, in the form of "nurturing mother or wild, insatiable *Fortuna*," was replaced with nature as feminine in its "passivity" and its subjection to domination and control by the (male) scientist: "A new image of the female emerged in the modern world, a female to be controlled and dissected. This image legitimated not only the domination of nature but that of women as well."[8] For example, control of female sexuality – through the differentiation of private and public spheres, and women's confinement to the former – was a central part of

French revolutionary and Napoleonic legislation. European literature moved from the celebration of openly sexual heroines like Moll Flanders to the sexually repressed heroines of Victorian novels.[9] Gradually, the division of the sexes into two distinct and hierarchically organized categories came to be viewed as natural and unchanging.

Masculine political rule was constructed and justified in terms of masculine rationality and control – in opposition to feminine disorderliness and emotionality. Masculine character was most specifically marked by rationality, and governance was rewritten as requiring rational control. Excessiveness and lack of restraint – now characterized as feminine – in either sexual or political affairs were expunged from the new ideology of masculinity. The new state in the West, therefore, established itself as manly in a particular sense – heterosexual, rational, and restrained. And, as Connell argues, "with masculinity defined as a character structure marked by rationality, and Western civilization defined as the bearer of reason to a benighted world, a cultural link between the legitimation of patriarchy and the legitimation of empire was forged."[10] Indeed, gender underwrote the establishment of Empire. The "natural" rule of male over female was extended to the rule over racial others who were characterized as feminine or, alternatively, as hyper-masculine, lacking the self-restraint of civilized manliness. Gender and sexuality, therefore, became important grounds upon which imperialism was legitimized and contested. The imperial era in Siam clearly bore the marks of this gendered struggle.

The Imperial Era in Siam and the Struggle over Gender

The beginnings of the imperial, or semi-colonial, era in Siam were marked, through Sir John Bowring, by the signing of a treaty between Britain and Siam. The treaty established immunity from Siamese law for British subjects and guaranteed the latter's full rights to residence and purchase of property in Siam. Siam signed a similar deal with the United States in 1856 and with several European powers thereafter. Although the treaties did not establish formal colonial rule, their provisions clearly established that Europeans and Americans had distinctive and higher status than did the Siamese and that Western powers had the right to abrogate Siamese sovereignty. Both of these provisions were hallmarks of imperial authority.

The gendered nature of imperialism was made clear in the continuing discussion of polygamy. Polygamy loomed large in the eyes of Westerners who dealt with the elite in Siam in the mid-1800s. The harems of notables were a matter of much concern (and titillation) on the part of missionaries and diplomats alike. The British envoy Sir John Bowring held numerous discussions with King Mongkut (1851-68) – while negotiating the famous trade treaty – on the practice that Westerners found "exotic, self-indulgent, and uncivilized."[11] Dr. Dan Bradley, the most prominent American missionary in Bangkok, who had a close relationship with King Mongkut, admonished the king in the *Bangkok Calendar* (an expatriate paper published by Bradley), saying, "virtue can never have much sway in Siam, nor any true prosperity, until polygamy is made a crime by the Government."[12] The enormously popular (in the West) accounts of life in the Inner Palace penned by Anna Leonowens in the 1850s often characterized the despair and cruelty of the lives of women "locked away" in the harem. The tyrannical treatment of women that polygamy was presumed to involve indicated to Westerners a lack of the kind of (gentle)manly virtues associated with Western governance. Such representations of native practices were commonplace throughout the Empire, legitimizing the imperial mission by presenting, as Gayatri Spivak puts it, White men saving "brown women from brown men."[13]

Polygamy, to Western observers, evidenced the lack of sexual control among the Siamese (men) and, therefore, in the imperialist ideology, the Siamese lack of "moral character"; that is, the quality that underwrote the imperial right to rule. The sexual excess that was assumed to be represented by polygamy was thought to bring about physical exhaustion, the degeneration of moral and physical character, and, therefore, the inability to govern. In the late 1800s, a memorandum from a British official in Siam who was worried about the likelihood of a French takeover read: "The King, who is honest, after a period of dangerous physical weakness, has regained strength, but is quite incapable mentally, exhausted by women, anxiety and opiates."[14] According to imperialist thought, such dissolute behaviour rendered rational, scientific, and morally upright rule impossible and, instead, led to an excess of cruelty. Joseph Balestier, an American diplomat in Siam in the mid-1800s, brought together the themes of excessiveness and the inability to rule when he remarked in his report to the secretary of state: "The present King of Siam is a *sensualist having no less than a thousand women in his harem* and a devotee of Buddhism with a retinue of forty thousand priests and forty wats or temples ... Upon these he spends the entire income of the kingdom. But *though he reigns he does not govern the State,* the administration of which is in the hands of rapacious and arbitrary lords who, by a heartless and relentless course towards their vassals and serfs and the Chinese are fast bringing about the utter ruin of the country."[15] According to this understanding, only the self-controlled behaviour of Western men could produce governance. Siamese masculinity, on the other hand, led to despotism.

While the critique of polygamy appeared to have the treatment of women at heart, in fact it did not. Throughout the colonial world the focus of such critiques was not the status of women. Indeed, Europeans almost universally regarded Southeast Asian women as sexually "loose," and the accounts of travellers and traders are full of bawdy stories of Southeast Asian women's sexual behaviour.[16] Westerners were never concerned about the actual daily lives of women; rather, as Lata Mani has argued in the Indian case, what concerned them was the fact that "women [were] the site on which tradition was debated and reformulated. What was at stake was not women but tradition."[17] In other words, the critics of polygamy were concerned with asserting the barbarity of indigenous culture and the superiority of imperial civilization. Indeed, when polygamy was finally rendered illegal in 1936 through, under British legal advice, the rewriting of the marriage provisions in the Civil Code, men were given the right to divorce their wives for infidelity but wives were denied the same right.[18] The focus of these reforms, therefore, was clearly not on providing women with more fair and equitable treatment in marriage customs. Polygamy in Siam, as constructed and represented by Westerners, evidenced Siamese inability to rule due to their lack of proper masculine behaviour and sexual control. Ending the practice of polygamy, therefore, was one of the conditions of Siam's entry into the company of "civilized" nations.

By targeting gender and sexual practices such as polygamy as representative of the essential barbarity of Siamese culture, however, the imperial powers also made gender and sexuality a key terrain of the power struggle between colonized and colonizing countries. Male Siamese elites resisted changes to the polygamous system, even producing a written defence of the practice for the edification of foreigners, defending it as a reflection of Buddhist culture and its particular gender system.[19] Male monarchs made various nods in the direction of changing women's status; however, as groups of modernizing Siamese elites themselves came to question the absolute monarchy and the polygamous system in the late 1800s, monarchs began to defend the practice more vigorously. King Vajiravudh (1910-25), despite his strongly nationalist program, which included making Siamese women appear "respectable" and "civilized" in the eyes of the world, abandoned his initial promise to remain monogamous and began to argue against the adoption of monogamy.[20] He argued, for instance, that polygamy at least provided protections for minor wives, unlike the system under which the so-called "modern elite" easily discarded their mistresses.[21] The monarchs and pro-monarchy elites, not unjustifiably, read the attacks on polygamy as attacks on the entire monarchical system, and the practice took on a certain intractability and importance for the defence of national identity (as viewed by the pro-monarchy establishment). Nonetheless, the monarchs and elites were well aware that changes to gendered practices such as polygamy and, later, prostitution constituted a key element to entering the company of the so-called civilized nations.

Prostitution in the Imperial Era and the Internationalizing of Western Gender Codes

It is within the context of the struggle over polygamy and gendered practices that the changing policies on prostitution, both national and international, need to be viewed. Beginning in the early 1900s, living up to Western standards of dealing with prostitution and the traffic in women became an important part of the Siamese government's policy with regard to becoming a full member of the international community. While polygamy had been the subject of constant Western condemnation from the early 1800s onward, thus firmly establishing sexual behaviour and gender roles as grounds for differentiating superior and inferior cultures, prostitution was the subject of much less attention – until the turn of the century. In part, this reflected the colonial powers' own awkward position vis-à-vis prostitution, which was generally viewed as a "necessary evil." In mid-eighteenth-century Britain it had been regulated through the highly controversial Contagious Diseases Acts, and, in mid-eighteenth-century France, it was regulated through licensed brothels. While polygamy was easily viewed as a foreign and barbaric practice, prostitution struck too close to home for European elites until the new middle-class imperialism of the social purity movement came to restructure sexual and class relations in the home countries.

In Britain, the Contagious Diseases Acts had touched off a storm of controversy. Josephine Butler and the Ladies National Association had protested the treatment of working-class women and the assumption of male sexual prerogative under the acts, which were designed to ensure soldiers' sexual health by subjecting women, particularly those suspected of prostitution, to examinations for venereal diseases. The campaign gained the support of the religious moral reform movement and, in Britain, managed to bring about the rescinding of the acts by the 1880s. Regulated brothels, which the social reformers linked to the international traffic in women (the forcing or enticing of women into brothels) remained in place in Malaysia and India as a convenient way to service male British nationals while avoiding interracial marriage and concubinage. Nonetheless, the growing political salience of the first wave of feminism and the social purity movement of the late Victorian era in Europe and North America soon put the prostitution problem on the international agenda.

Despite the continued acceptance of regulated brothels by some national and imperial governments, the campaign against the White slave trade eventually resulted in international agreements to suppress the traffic in women. In the hands of early feminists such as Butler the campaign against regulated prostitution had emphasized the economic and sexual power of elite men; in the hands of the popular press the issue of prostitution was translated into the White slavery panic, which built on stories of innocent (White) women and girls being abducted into the trade by evil (often foreign) traffickers.[22] In response to the panic, a number of international treaties to ban the traffic in women and children were signed in the early 1900s, including the 1904 International Agreement for the Suppression of the White Slave Traffic, the 1910 International Convention for the Suppression of the White Slave Traffic, and the 1921 League of Nations International Convention for the Suppression of the Traffic in Women and Children (see Table 1). According to Deborah Stienstra, these conventions "consolidated many of the gendered assumptions of the time, both about the role of women and men in society as well as about the role of the state in sexual relations."[23] Women were seen as passive victims who required protection from the (paternal) state rather than as social and sexual agents. Accordingly, the conventions criminalized procurement even when it occurred with the woman's consent. The result was the regulation of the travel of women and the careful monitoring of women's migration for employment. Men, on the other hand, appeared either as procurers and pimps or as protectors, the clients being conspicuously absent in the agreements and the discussions around them.[24] The thrust of these provisions, therefore, was not to provide women with social and sexual independence but, rather, to reform them and place them within their proper gender roles as wives and mothers. At the same time, these provisions left men's sexual prerogatives intact.

These treaties were part of the growing web of an international society of civilized nations. The terms of this society were set by the imperial powers and were formalized in the wake of the First World War with the establishment of the League of Nations. In insisting on international adherence to

Table 1

International conventions on prostitution and trafficking, 1904-49

1904   International Agreement for the Suppression of the White Slave Traffic

1910   International Convention for the Suppression of the White Slave Traffic

1921   League of Nations International Convention for the Suppression of the Traffic in Women and Children

1937   Draft League of Nations Convention on Trafficking

1949   United Nations Convention for the Suppression of Traffic in Persons and of the Exploitation of the Prostitution of Others

this gender code, the Western powers were seeking to impose not a more equitable gender arrangement but, rather, a gender code that reflected Western understandings of civilized gender roles.

Prostitution Policy in Early Twentieth-Century Siam

Ironically, it was the adoption of Western social practices, particularly the elimination of slavery in the early 1900s, that contributed to a sharp increase in the numbers of women involved in prostitution in Siam. In its attempt to modernize Siam in the eyes of the West, the reign of King Chulalongkorn (1868-1910) was marked by substantial changes to government and social practice, including the adoption of Western-style bureaucratic and legal procedures. Most important, the eradication of slavery in 1905 substantially reconfigured Siamese society, and the government was now faced with the problem of how to transform its subjects into citizens of a new nation. However, the government was much more concerned about the incorporation of men into the new citizenry, which it achieved through mandatory military service and education (also part of the standards of civilization), than it was the incorporation of women. Despite the warnings of bureaucrats and the queen herself that women now released from slavery would have to be provided with an education so that they would be able to live productive lives, King Chulalongkorn declared that the national budget, already under strain from the restrictions of the Bowring Treaty, simply could not sustain female education. Without education and without the supports of the old feudal system, women were left to fend for themselves.[25] As Suwadee Patana argues, "in [the] early period women were able to earn some money for their families by simply selling themselves into slavery. The process of abolishing slavery in the late nineteenth century made such things more difficult."[26] Sukanya Hantrakul surmises that a large number of women – now no longer the slave-wives of individual men or slave-women who had provided sexual service to visiting guests of their master – drifted into prostitution as a means of maintaining themselves and their families in the post-slavery era.[27] While slave status may have been officially eradicated, the practice of debt slavery, albeit in other forms, remained alive and well among the general populace. In that tradition, women were sold, or sold themselves, into brothel service for an advance, the idea being that they could buy themselves out again. Much to the surprise of Western officials, even when they were "liberated" through marriage, these women often insisted that their debt to the madams be paid off.[28]

To ensure the collection of taxes on this activity and, most important, to control venereal disease in an era of now continuous military training, the Venereal Diseases Act was proclaimed by the Siamese government in 1909. The act closely regulated entry into brothel prostitution, limiting the anonymity and ease with which women could move in and out of prostitution.[29] It required that anyone wanting to operate a prostitution business or to work as a prostitute must secure a licence (which was to be renewed every three months) from the government.[30] For women to obtain and renew their licences they had to prove themselves free of venereal disease and freely willing to engage in prostitution. Operators, for their part, were to ensure that the area used was clean and out of public view and that no prostitute was either confined or under fifteen years of age. Nor was the operator to accuse prostitutes of theft for losing things that he/she gave to them – a common technique of indebting prostitutes at the time.[31] Although women were not assumed to be enslaved through prostitution, provisions were required to ensure that no one was forced into, or forced to stay in, the trade. Nonetheless, the overall thrust of the legislation was to protect the male citizen-soldier from possible contamination by prostitute women; the act provided only minimal protections for women, while subjecting them to medical examination and control.

During the same period, however, in its attempt to become part of the international society of civilized states, the Siamese government became party to the social conventions on trafficking (which had become such a key part of international society's gender standards). Siam signed the 1904 International Agreement for the Suppression of the White Slave Traffic, which focused on the protection of women and girls, and the 1910 International Convention for the Suppression of the White Slave Traffic, which made procurement a punishable offence (see Table 2).[32]

Siam's international good behaviour did yield results. At Versailles, Siam shed its unequal treaty with Germany. In 1920, the United States relinquished both its fiscal and extraterritorial rights. At the same time, new treaties with Japan and France were under way. The British, however, remained reluctant, especially in regards to relinquishing extraterritorial rights. Britain objected to the "improper" administration of the Siamese juridical system. Chulalongkorn's successor, Vajiravudh (1910-25), advocated doing everything possible to please the British; however, it was only through the appointment of Francis B. Sayre of Harvard Law School as go-between with Britain and other European states that new treaties were finally signed in 1926.[33] The new treaties, which still retained some conditions to protect European nationals from the "not-quite-yet-up-to-standard" Siamese judicial system, were to remain in force for ten years, awaiting the finalization of the codification of Siamese law.[34]

It was within this context of trying to convince the European powers of the soundness of the Siamese legal system and its adherence to the standards of civilization that Siam signed the 1921 League of Nations International Convention for the Suppression of the Traffic in Women and Children. Then, in 1928, under King Prajadiphok (1925-32), Siam instituted its

Table 2

Siamese/Thai prostitution policy, 1909-66

1904   Siam signs International Agreement for the Suppression of the White Slave Traffic.

1909   Siamese government passes national Venereal Disease Control Act.

1910   Siam signs International Convention for the Suppression of the White Slave Traffic.

1920   US relinquishes fiscal and territorial rights.[1]

1921   Siam signs the League of Nations International Convention for the Suppression of the Traffic in Women and Children.

1926   Britain signs new treaties with Siam (some conditions remain in effect for ten years, subject to improvements in Siamese judicial system).

1928   Siamese government passes national Anti-Trafficking Act.

1932   Overthrow of the Siamese monarchy.

1935   Polygamy outlawed.

1936   Establishment of Committee Considering the Abolition of Licensed Brothels

1938   Plan for the Prevention of Venereal Diseases (not enacted). *Siam becomes Thailand.*

1941   Japan occupies Thailand.

1942   Venereal Disease Prevention and Suppression Committee proposes new legislation combining regulation (in necessary cases) and abolition. Not enacted.

1950s No further licences issued to brothels. Beginnings of reformist measures and vocational training.

1956   Penal Code penalizes procuring for the purposes of prostitution.

1957   Prohibition of Prostitution Business Act. Draft legislation to criminalize prostitution and establish reformatories.

1958   Phibun overthrown by Sarit.

1960   Prostitution Prohibition Act.

1966   Entertainment Places Act

---

1 Historical markers, unrelated to prostitution policy, are in italics.

own anti-trafficking legislation. The Siamese anti-trafficking act reflected European influences, singling out migrant women as potential victims of traffickers. It empowered officials "to examine all women and girls coming into or departing from Siam"; and, should there be a "reasonable suspicion" that a woman had been brought into or was to be taken out of Siam for the purpose of prostitution, then she was to be detained for investigation and returned to her country of origin (assuming the case were to be proven).[35] That the conventions on trafficking had some effect in at least keeping White women from entering prostitution in other countries appears to be borne out by the disappearance from Bangkok of Russian, British, American, and French prostitutes by the late 1920s.[36] This was no doubt reassuring to the imperial powers, for at least "their" women were no longer so visible in the Siamese trade.

The main target of the Siamese legislation, however, was Chinese women. The 1928 anti-trafficking act came into effect at a time when both the number of prostitutes and the number of immigrant Chinese women appeared to be steadily increasing. Between 1919 and 1929 the female Chinese population increased by 140 percent (however, it still remained well below the male Chinese population). Registered Chinese brothels also greatly outnumbered registered Siamese brothels during this period.[37]

Chinese women were assumed to enter prostitution unwillingly, to have been trafficked either explicitly for the purpose of prostitution or as *mui tsui* (young girls used for domestic service). The discourse around prostitution in China itself was, according to Gail Herschatter, changing rapidly at this time. With regard to prostitution, a discourse of pleasure, associated with the courtesan culture of the early 1900s, was quickly being replaced by a discourse of victimization and national humiliation.[38] Over the course of the early 1900s, the growing international consensus on the prostitute as victim put increasing pressure on states such as Siam to criminalize prostitution activities and to rehabilitate women involved in prostitution.

Post-Absolutist Prostitution Law and the Fight for "Civilized" Status
In the post-absolutist era, Thailand came under increasing pressure from the League of Nations and then from the United Nations to abolish the system of licensed brothels.[39] Despite the fact that elites continued to defend the licensing system as the best way to control the spread of venereal disease, some government bodies, particularly the powerful Ministry of the Interior, increasingly showed a willingness to entertain the possibility of abolishing licensed brothels. The 1932 overthrow of the absolute monarchy marked the growing strength of a modernizing bureaucratic elite who sought to transform the monarchical state into a modern and efficient administrative state. While attempts at democracy soon gave way to military authoritarianism, modernizing elements within the bureaucracy

continued to push for Western-style social welfare measures, including reformist approaches to prostitution. The militarization of Thai society, however, and the continued elite male defence of the regulation of prostitution, meant that there was still resistance to the abolition of licensed brothels. In post-absolutist Thailand the "woman question" reflected a tension between the desire to present Thai women to the world as modern wives and mothers within an equitable gender system and a continued defence of male sexual prerogative. While polygamy was officially illegal, it continued to be practised with "minor wives" who were now "mistresses" and who had none of the legal protections that went with the polygamous system. The beauty queen became a new national icon. And, in deference to the concern to protect male sexual health and access, until the 1950s government policy on prostitution moved slowly with regard to abolishing regulated brothels and, instead, emphasized venereal disease control.

In 1936, in response to the League of Nations Bandung deliberations on the control of prostitution, Thailand established the Committee Considering the Abolition of Licensed Brothels. However, in line with the concern over disease control, the government did not support the League of Nations Draft Convention of 1937, which called for the "almost immediate eradication of licensed brothels"; instead, the government opted for a policy of "progressive and gradual ... abolition of the system of licensed houses and the adoption of suitable administrative medical and social measures to accompany the same."[40] A plan for the prevention of venereal diseases was drawn up in 1938 (although not enacted), which suggested that the maintenance of brothels and licensed prostitution was important in the fight against venereal disease during a period of economic downturn, when more women were turning to prostitution.[41]

Indeed, the effects of the Great Depression had been devastating in rural parts of the country, and a growing number of women turned to prostitution to support themselves and their families. Since 1928, while the number of registered brothels had declined, the number of women practising clandestine prostitution had been on the rise.[42] In 1939 the issue of the increasing number of unregistered brothels was raised in the National Assembly. One member reported that, while sixty-seven brothels were registered with the police, he had discovered 274 in Bangkok alone. He had also discovered four girls from Denchai under the age of thirteen, despite the prohibitions on underage girls in the 1909 Venereal Disease Control Act. In response to his suggestion that unlicensed brothels be subject to higher penalties, the acting minister of the interior replied that higher fines would likely be ineffective in reducing the trade in underage girls; instead, the ministry made a case for the gradual abolition of licensing. Various attempts were made to control the industry more closely. The government raised the prices of prostitution licenses, put stricter medical examinations into place, and conducted a series of raids on illegal brothels.[43] Elite male opinion, however, continued to maintain that the abolition of licensed brothels would not be helpful in controlling disease or maintaining decorum. A *Bangkok Chronicle* editorial warned that the abolition of licensed brothels in the Straits Settlements had led to "no appreciable decrease in the spread of disease and 'rickshaw parades,' 'street-corner soliciting,' and other unseemly manifestations."[44] Newspaper articles on the issue often defended a stricter, Japanese style of control as the best response to these problems.

The outbreak of the Second World War in 1939, and the occupation of Thailand by Japanese troops from 1941 to 1945, leant new weight to the argument that disease control must be foremost in considerations of prostitution policy. While it is now well known that the Japanese took sex slaves in occupied Asian territories during the war, there is as yet no available evidence concerning to what extent this occurred in Thailand. Most often, Korean women were brought to "comfort stations" in Thailand to service Japanese soldiers. Nonetheless, the increased mobilization of the male Thai population, the continuing poverty of the rural regions, and the presence of Japanese troops no doubt contributed to a rising concern over prostitution. In 1942, the public health department's newly formed Venereal Disease Prevention and Suppression Committee had proposed a crackdown on prostitution. Its suggested legislation struck a balance between regulation and abolition. It prohibited "sexual relations for money," pimping, and brothel-keeping (which would be punished by stiff fines or up to one year's imprisonment) while allowing for the operation of brothels "in necessary cases," under a local government official, and with the agreement of the health officer and the minister of public health.[45] This legislation, however, failed to be enacted, and, with the end of the war, there was renewed pressure for Thailand to conform to international standards on prostitution.

Phibun and the New (Inter)Nationalism

In 1938, a year before the end of the unequal treaties and the outbreak of the Second World War, the Thai government began a nationalist program to modernize the country under the authoritarian leadership of Field Marshal Phibun Songkhram (1938-44, 1948-57). Phibun sought to reconfigure Thai identity in the eyes of the world as well as in the eyes of Thais themselves. To mark the beginning of a new era he changed the name of the country from Siam to Thailand and set about educating Thais in the proper mode of civilized behaviour. When the British and American governments failed to provide support to Thailand during the Japanese invasion of Indochina, Phibun brokered a deal involving guarded cooperation between Thailand and Japan. This cooperation with Japan during the war, however, meant a renewed struggle to maintain Thailand's sovereignty after the war. Britain demanded that Thailand pay war reparations;[46] the United States, however, blocked the British move. The United States had never received a formal declaration of war from the Thai ambassador in the United States, who instead convinced the American government to fund an underground resistance movement. The American government argued, therefore, that Thailand should not be treated as a defeated enemy. American interest in maintaining Thailand's friendship was heightened by growing concerns over the rise of communism in Asia. With the support of the United States, Phibun returned to power in 1948, reorienting Thai foreign policy squarely in favour of the United States and backing American anticommunist measures in Southeast Asia.

Phibun was determined to establish Thailand as a modern and civilized nation in the eyes of the Western powers, both before and after the war. To this end he and his lieutenant, the propagandist Luang Wichit Wathakan, established a program of national social and cultural renewal that aimed at forcing Thais to meet Western standards of appropriate cultural behaviour, including dress, social conduct, hygiene, and language forms. Proper cultural behaviour was considered key in maintaining the sovereignty of the nation. As expressed by one member of government, improper behaviour could lead to "foreigners ridiculing Thailand as being uncivilized, possessing no high morality and therefore not qualified to the same sovereign status as other nations."[47] Phibun passed a series of Cultural Mandates in the early 1940s, stipulating proper dress and manners. Although the Cultural Mandates were at first based simply on public exhortations by the Prime Minister's Office, after 1942 more coercive measures, involving fines and arrest, were employed, particularly to ensure that proper dress was maintained in public places.[48] According to Kobkua Suwannatha-Piat: "[it] became an offence to act or behave in public in a manner that would humiliate or tarnish the image of Thailand."[49] Foreign observers, such as Sir Anthony Eden, themselves recognized the campaign as an attempt to measure up to Western standards and to maintain world stature: "[the origin of the campaign] is probably to be found in the Thai desire to Westernize and modernize everything Thai[,] which [is] rooted in the inferiority complex of an oriental people which has only recently succeeded in establishing its theoretical equality of status with the European Powers ... [and has been] accentuated in the last year or so in proportion to Thailand's growing prominence in world affairs."[50]

Dress reform, for example, was considered particularly important in maintaining this image. Men, rather than wearing the traditional *pamuang* (a cloth wound around the body and hitched up between the legs) or Chinese silk trousers, were to wear hats, shoes, socks, jackets, and trousers; and women, who sometimes wore only a sarong with a simple cloth wrapped around the upper part of the body, and who could even go topless at home, were admonished to don a hat, skirt, shoes, and a blouse that covered the shoulders.[51] Phibun blamed France's reluctance to return territory to Thailand to the Thai people's failure to dress properly and to maintain a good image. As Kobkua writes:

> Phibun was singularly annoyed with a movie on "Siam" showing Thai women hawkers on the roadside chewing and spitting betel-nut, men crowding around a game of fish-fighting, and people in general going about their daily chores wearing only Chinese shorts ... and no singlet. The Prime Minister felt that such a public image greatly harmed the Thai request for the return of their territory from France. "The French could very well say that if this is what we are, how dare we demand for the return of the territory. It'd be more appropriate that [the territory] remain under their rule. They at least can keep it clean and hygienic."[52]

According to Phibun, maintaining Thailand's sovereignty demanded close attention to the dress and deportment of its citizens because this was what constituted the image of the country relayed to the world audience.[53]

Along with appropriate customs, Phibun sought to enforce proper gender identities. The dress reforms served to heighten gender distinctions in dress. Phibun also took offence at the ambiguous gender of some women's names and insisted that men's and women's names be distinct. He also sought to regulate marital relations between the sexes. Bureaucrats were told to kiss their wives upon leaving for, and returning from, work (in presumed Western fashion).[54] Wives were encouraged to join their husbands on healthy walks and to "improve relations with [their] husband[s'] friends."[55] Throughout this post-imperialist era, maintaining proper gender relations and gender identity in the eyes of the West remained an important part of negotiating Thai sovereignty.

In its drive to become a respected member of the international community the Phibun government enthusiastically involved itself in the United Nations. In the mid-1950s, Thailand was a hive of UN activity. UN organizations working in Thailand by that time included the Economic and Social Council for Asia and the Far East (ECAFE), the Food and Agriculture Organization (FAO), the UN Children's Fund (UNICEF), the World Health Organization (WHO), the UN Educational Scientific and Cultural Organization (UNESCO), the International Labour Organization (ILO), the International Civil Aviation Organization (ICAO), and the UN Technical Assistance Board (UNTAB).[56] This period also marked a rise in interest in human rights issues around the globe. Concern about the treatment of women and the problem of prostitution became a central part of the agenda of UN social agencies, which actively sought adherence to the new 1949 Convention for the Suppression of Traffic in Persons and of the Exploitation of the Prostitution of Others.

The 1949 convention was based on the 1937 League of Nations Draft Convention, which had died with the League itself, and echoed its moral reform approach (see Table 1). In particular, the new convention, like the old, excluded the possibility of prostitution as a choice (limited or otherwise); rather, the prostitute was viewed as a victim of pimps or procurers. It was assumed that no "normal" woman would choose to enter prostitution and that women required (male) protection and social/psychological reform. While the language of the convention was liberalized to reflect the aims of the 1948 Universal Declaration on Human Rights, the rights that were protected under its aegis were the moral rights of the community. As Deborah Stienstra argues:

> The 1949 Convention uses human rights language and conveys that "prostitution and the accompanying evil of the traffic in persons for the purpose of prostitution are incompatible with the dignity and worth of the human person and endanger the welfare of the individual, the family and the community." With these words, the Convention suggested that the protection of individuals, families and the community outweighs the rights of individuals to engage in prostitution. The rights to be protected are those that are judged "moral" by the international community.[57]

The predominant understanding of prostitution in the postwar period also leaned heavily on psychoanalytical models of human behaviour. Prostitutes were presumed to be sexual deviants who had an inordinate propensity for promiscuity, which required psychological treatment. The prostitute was now an object not only of medical, but also of psychological, concern. She needed to be readjusted, to be inducted into "normal" sexual behaviour. Thus, the convention emphasized the punishment of those who led others into prostitution. At the same time, it discounted the consent of the woman involved, who was presumed not to be able to choose; instead, it advocated the "rehabilitation and social adjustment of the victims of prostitution."[58] In other words, the convention positioned prostitutes as objects of reform rather than as acting agents.

Of particular concern was the "normalization" of women's sexual behaviour, the channelling of it into an appropriately passive sexual role. While the 1959 follow-up to the convention, *Study on the Traffic in Persons and Prostitution*, did not support the imposition of rehabilitation measures on unwilling subjects (those who are "not in the least victims of circumstances"), it did assume that many would benefit from, and take advantage of, facilities for rehabilitation, including those who may not be prostitutes per se but who "engaged in notorious promiscuity." The study argued that "promiscuity often leads to prostitution – in fact, it is often argued that between promiscuity and prostitution there is a difference only of degree," and it recommended "early detection and treatment of promiscuous propensities and mental deficiencies."[59] The 1959 study preferred to adopt the liberal language of "re-education" (as promoted by the International Abolitionist Federation), noting that, "in recent years, the process of rehabilitation of persons engaged in prostitution has been characterized by an increasing trend towards re-education; that is, rehabilitation through education to discipline the mind and character and to develop and cultivate the personality both mentally and morally." Re-education was meant to emphasize voluntary participation and the respect of the "liberty and dignity" of the person concerned, but it also emphasized the need to reattach women to the family unit – "the development of new psychological and family roots in preparation for married life." Difficulties in re-education were understood to derive from "the fact that these women generally show weakness of character, lack of will-power, instability, impulsiveness, suggestibility, etc. They have generally no aptitude for work, not even for domestic work, and some of them are physically sick or mentally deficient."[60] In other words, the rehabilitationist approach clearly viewed women in prostitution as social deviants rather than as women trying to survive, and it aimed to "normalize" women who did not conform to the Western middle-class norm of female social and sexual behaviour – the virtuous wife and mother.

In its effort to bring about greater cooperation with the convention, which had few signatories in its early years, in the late 1950s the United Nations launched investigations into the traffic in persons and the exploitation of prostitution. National committees to investigate prostitution and to establish prevention and suppression measures had been established in India, Sri Lanka, Burma, the Philippines, Indonesia, and Japan in the late 1940s and early 1950s.[61] Thailand came under renewed pressure to reform its prostitution laws as, by the late 1950s, it was the only Asian member of the United Nations to have legalized brothels.

In the aftermath of the war, however, as a step towards full abolition, the Ministry of the Interior had disallowed the opening of any new brothels.[62] Further steps were already well under way by 1956 (see Table 2). A small number of government officials and elite women were at work on the issue of prostitution – people such as Dr. Khun Pierra Veijabul, a member of the Ministry of Public Health (Venereal Diseases Division) since 1937, who had trained in medicine in France and established the Foundation for the Welfare of Women in 1956.[63] Dr. Pierra was representative of the small coterie of elite, professional women who studied abroad in this early period and who were part of the Women's Cultural Club. She sat on the Committee

Considering the Abolition of Licensed Brothels in the late 1930s, and, at the same time, she established the Maternity and Child Welfare Foundation. As part of a modernizing state elite, officials like Dr. Pierra sought to promote international standards of social hygiene.

Dr. Pierra made the abolition of prostitution and rehabilitation of prostitutes a personal campaign. In 1956, during a relatively open period of Phibun's government, Dr. Pierra established the Foundation of the Welfare of Women, which listed its purposes as: educating prostitutes to "encourage them to return to a normal life"; providing housing, treatment, education, and training to prostitutes seeking rehabilitation; researching the causes and prevention of prostitution; and researching venereal disease prevention and treatment. The foundation also sought to widen public awareness and involvement by persuading people to "help prostitutes to return to a normal life." Reflecting the growing internationalism of the period, the foundation also proposed to maintain international links with like-minded organizations abroad. Its board consisted almost entirely of government officials, the largest proportion coming from the National Institute of Culture as well as some from the Ministry of Health, the police department, the Department of Public Welfare, and the Municipalities of Thonburi and Bangkok.

The above bodies – the National Institute of Culture, the Department of Public Welfare, and the police department – had begun providing some vocational training to former prostitutes before 1956. They had also cooperated in returning "some newly recruited or prospective prostitutes to their homes."[64] Twenty-two young women were returned to their homes by the Department of Public Welfare in the period between May and December 1956, and a system of warning young girls of the practices of procurers ("often older women with promises of work or schooling in Bangkok") was in place in some provincial railway stations by 1956.[65] A revised Penal Code also came into effect in 1956, which strictly punished procurement, trafficking, and deception or coercion for sexual purposes, including prostitution (see Table 2).[66]

Phibun was anxious to demonstrate Thailand's cooperative international image as part of the "free world." Such an image was important with regard to guaranteeing continued military aid from the United States in the face of growing fear over communist insurgencies in Asia. In 1955, Phibun, along with his wife Lady Laiad, had completed a series of state visits around the world to promote this image abroad. The American public's growing criticism of the use of foreign aid to prop up a repressive regime led Phibun to vow to "democratize" Thai politics. In the 1956-7 period, Phibun legalized political parties, allowed for public discussion of politics, and removed many police and army troops from Bangkok. Lady Laiad and

Phibun also asked that further steps be taken to suppress prostitution, and the government began consultations with the United Nations Regional Social Defence Officer on how to rewrite the prostitution laws.[67]

Despite Phibun's desire to abolish prostitution and so stay in line with Western demands, some elites and the general public continued to be reluctant to do so. Morris Fox, the social welfare advisor to the United Nations who produced a report on prostitution in Thailand for the Thai public welfare department in 1957, noted that Thai men tended to view prostitution as "an accepted part of life," while women viewed it as a "necessary evil." He stated that "only a few persons in official or unofficial circles are working toward its suppression."[68] As a 1958 public relations department publication blithely reported: "To sleep out at night or to stay away from home is neither unusual nor badly regarded for a boy. They generally have their first sexual experience at the age of sixteen or seventeen with a prostitute. There is no stigma attached to the frequenting of prostitutes by either married or unmarried men. Prostitution is legal."[69]

The report goes on to defend the male sexual prerogative by dismissing the concerns of elite women as self-indulgent, stating that only the women of the upper class, "in which the woman regards herself as the equal of her husband, is offended by his extramarital activity, [and] has the leisure to be upset by her emotional difficulties."[70] The same report, however, notes with some discomfort the rapid changes, expressed in terms of young women's social behaviour, under way in Thailand in the 1950s:

> Westernization has lately received much comment in Bangkok ... Young girls are feeling the liberative influence of American ideas especially regarding dating and dancing, and this is considered to be affecting morality. The number of virgin brides in Bangkok where Western influence is strong, for example, is estimated 15% lower than in the country, and the wildness of Bangkok society girls imitating Western fashions taught by Hollywood films is notorious.[71]

"Westernization" was read in very gendered terms, reflecting the importance of women's behaviour to national identity.

The 1950s and 1960s in Thailand – a period of increased American presence – were marked by this tension over the maintenance of male sexual prerogative and the desire to maintain female purity in the face of foreign influence. Certainly the changes of the 1950s were provoking some concern among the urban population. Millions in American military aid had been poured into the Thai economy since 1950. American military and government advisors had swarmed the city, and the Thai military had ballooned in size and expense. The outpouring of criticism during the relaxation of media control in 1956 and 1957 testified to this concern.[72] For example, the public relations report noted that the demand for material goods that would enable Thais to live like Westerners was, according to its authors, leading to stress, family disintegration, and corruption as well as to "large numbers of nearly destitute people living in the worst kinds of slums" in the city.[73] Fox noted increasing coverage of the issue of prostitution in the newspapers in the late 1950s – "some devoting considerable space to it" – as well as the existence of an "almost universal concern for the young innocent girls who are tricked or 'seduced' into prostitution" and the influence of prostitution on children in the immediate neighbourhood (where children earned money by running errands for the brothels). There was also some fear that the growing "wildness" of Bangkok girls would lead them into prostitution. The "taxi dance halls," where young women went to dance and socialize, were considered a site where girls and women were procured for prostitution.[74] These concerns were translated into a need for increased control over female sexual behaviour.

In 1957 new prostitution legislation was proposed, and it echoed these concerns, emphasizing the reform of women engaged in the sex trade (see Table 2). Indeed, the first sections of the proposed act, which wished to abolish prostitution, dealt with the establishment and responsibilities of reform institutes, which were to be under the authority of the Department of Public Welfare. The building of a rehabilitation institution for those who sought to leave prostitution voluntarily was already under way, and plans for another institution were in the works. The legislation proposed that the institutions provide medical treatment, vocational training, and "placement in a suitable job."[75] The proposed legislation stated that "whoever habitually consents to be hired for sexual relations for compensation shall be deemed to be a prostitute," clearly defining a "problematic personality" that required treatment. Indeed, the legislation anticipated difficulties with inmates of the reformatories and so provided stiff penalties for whoever "willingly avoids going, violates the order or runs away." The bill did allow that not all prostitutes entered the trade willingly, providing punishment of up to seven years in prison and/or up to 10,000 baht[76] for whoever "treats any girl with any deceptive methods or threatens, compels, or forces her in any way in order to attract her into the prostitution business."[77]

Although the legislation appeared to reflect a strong commitment to abolitionism, the public remained ambivalent towards, and elite males continued to resist, the criminalization of prostitution. Indeed, in its rationale for the legislation the government emphasized that the public did not yet take the problem seriously. Government direction, therefore, was felt to be needed. The government was careful, however, not to use too heavy a hand in imposing penalties. The penalties for procuring were lighter than those listed in the 1956 Penal Code.[78] Clearly, there were continued tensions over the imposition of Western codes of behaviour, including sexual behaviour – tensions that were exploited by the Sarit government, which overthrew Phibun in 1957.

Thailand under Sarit: The Criminalization of Prostitution

Before the proposed prostitution legislation could go much further, the Phibun government was overthrown in a military coup led by Field Marshal Sarit Thanarat (1957-63), a long-time rival of Phibun. Sarit built his legitimacy on the growing resentment towards Western interference in Thailand – interference that Phibun had supported. Sarit described the kind of democracy brought in after the war as an attempt to impose foreign institutions on Thailand, and he appealed instead to what he defined as "traditional Thai values": social orderliness and proper conduct. According to Sarit, what the Thai people really wanted was strong leadership and progress rather than democracy in the Western sense. Sarit used this reformulation of traditional Thai values to underwrite the legitimacy of his dictatorship. Despite his anti-Western rhetoric at home, however, Sarit maintained Thailand's policy of cooperation with the West, particularly with the United States (i.e., regarding opposition to communism), in order to receive American military aid. His brand of nationalism continued to appeal to Western notions of civilization. Sarit resolved the tension between a pro-Western foreign policy stance and his anti-Western domestic rhetoric through the manipulation of class, gender, and sexuality; he built up his legitimacy through an appeal to the traditional Thai practice of polygamy, while imposing moral discipline on lower-class men and women, particularly through new legislation criminalizing prostitution.

In representing himself as a legitimate leader, Sarit styled himself a *nakleng* – a "hooligan" – drawing upon the imagery of the gangs of young men who were used to protect the villages from elite/administrative intrusion in the 1890s and who, in the 1950s and after, were often recruited by the communist movement in the face of Thai/American military intrusion.[79] Sarit became (in)famous for surrounding himself with beautiful women. He was "widely admired for having the effrontery to acquire mistresses on such a grand scale" as part of his *nakleng* image.[80] Sarit was known to maintain a "house-cum-harem" (as it is referred to by Thak), where he spent time among his mistresses; he also had houses built for several other mistresses in Bangkok. The year after he died, Sarit's affairs were the topic of two books, which discussed his liaisons with eighty-one women. The women were known to include "beauty queens, movie stars, night club hostesses, university and secondary school students, young and not so young. His elaborate network of procurers was the envy of many."[81]

Charles Keyes argues that there was a political motive to Sarit's affairs, that he "often chose as one of his mistresses a member of a family or group he wished to control politically," thus furthering his legitimacy as a great man by emulating the harems of past rulers.[82] Indeed, Sarit also fostered marital links among the elite and would get members of the royal family to sponsor elite marriages, gradually integrating bureaucratic, royal, political, and business families and conferring them with legitimacy.[83] Among those so joined were the daughter and son, respectively, of Sarit's two lieu-tenants, Thanom Kittikachorn and Praphat Charusathian (1963-73), the son being widely understood to be the heir to political power. Sarit's *nakleng* image was indeed a rejection of the outlawing of polygamy during the early years of constitutional monarchy as well as of the Western stan-dards of proper marital behaviour espoused by Phibun, and it appealed to the common practices of elite men.

At the same time, while espousing these behaviours for himself, Sarit ini-tiated a campaign of "social orderliness" that targeted the street *nakleng* of the cities, which Sarit now designated by the more negative term *anthaphan*, and prostitutes. These new urban poor were in fact a product of increasing migration into the city. The migration reflected the changing reality of rural Thailand, where, since the early 1950s, roads built by the military and funded by the Americans were changing the economic and migration patterns of the countryside.[84] Peasants increasingly responded to the pull of Bangkok, now labour-poor in the aftermath of crackdowns on Chinese immigration.[85] Sarit painted the migration as a sign of social dis-integration and a failure of proper behaviour. (Those intellectuals who crit-icized the elite exploitation of the peasants and rural labour, such as the famous Thai Marxist critic Jit Phoumisak, were branded communists – a term that was already well established as a dirty word and as "un-Thai.")[86] Prostitutes, *anthaphan*, and pedicab drivers were symbolic of "improper-ness" and disintegration. The government sought to reintegrate into the rural areas the young men who had left the productive work of agriculture "in favour of the unproductive profession of pedicab driving."[87] The unproductiveness of such activity was underscored by the link Sarit drew between it and opium smoking and between opium smoking and commu-nism. Sarit maintained that the communists sought to undermine the free world through such things as addictive drugs. Accordingly, in 1959 he announced that opium use in Thailand would terminate on 1 July, after which

we will be able to fully state that we are a civilized nation and national prestige will be liberated from international criticism ... the sale and use of opium is illegal, and I maintain that it is a major crime and whoever resists will be severely punished. Alien offenders will be deported and Thais will be marked as traitors who refuse to make sacrifices for the nation.[88]

However, rather than punishing those who failed to conform to his ideal of a people "agrarian in outlook and condition, leaving the government to look after their material needs," and who were "contented to remain on the land and go about their daily tasks in an orderly and proper manner," Sarit used his role as "father of the nation" to reform his wayward children.[89] In this fatherly role he attacked the problem of pedicab drivers and prostitutes through rehabilitation. He banned pedicab drivers from the capital in 1959 and organized rural communities to reorient these people to agricultural life; he also provided them with loans to start up new lives in agriculture. Prostitutes, on the other hand, were to be rehabilitated into "domestic" roles. Rather than recognizing the role of peasant women in the economic sustenance of the family, Sarit's program sought to reform these women, turning them towards the proper middle-class female roles of wife and mother. The tool for their rehabilitation lay close at hand in the proposed guidelines for a new prostitution law.

The Prostitution Prohibition Act, 1960, defined prostitution as the "indiscriminate acceptance of sexual intercourse or acceptance of any other act or the performance of any act for the satisfaction of the sexual desire of another for hire whether the acceptor of the act and the performer of the act are of the same or different sexes" (see Table 2).[90] As Sukanya Hantrakul has pointed out, this definition of prostitution emphasized the promiscuity of the act – that is, women's sexual behaviour – rather than the monetary exchange. The 1960 law outlined much more precisely the acts that constituted the offence of prostitution, penalizing street solicitation as well as brothel prostitution.[91] It was sufficient for a person to "wander" or "loiter" about the streets or public places in a "manner or way which *appears* to be an appeal to communicate for prostitution purposes" for her or him to be charged – a reflection of Sarit's concern to "clear the streets" for public approval.[92] Those convicted of prostitution were expected to pay a fine of up to 2,000 baht or to serve a prison term of up to six months. The legislation clearly targeted prostitutes as the source of the problem. The 1957 proposal's provisions pertaining to deceiving and forcing a person into prostitution were dropped, and the punishments for owners, procurers, and pimps were lightened, being now much lighter than those in the Penal Code.[93] While the modernizing bureaucrats who wrote the 1957 legislation had some concern that women in prostitution may have been victimized, the new law reflected Sarit's desire to reform the behaviour of lower-class women.

Accordingly, as with the 1957 proposal, prostitutes were also subject to remand to a reformatory for up to a year for "[medical] treatment and/or vocational training."[94] The women were not expected to submit to this training willingly, so provisions were made to punish those who escaped or broke the "disciplinary rules and work regulations" set by the Department of Public Welfare. The disciplinary function of the centres – to turn problem women back into good women – underwrote their "vocational training." Sukanya Hantrakul quotes from a 1963 Department of Public Welfare document on the Pak Kred reformatory: "Vocational training ... is designed to afford recreation and to keep the trainees occupied with work to such an extent that there is not much time for idle thoughts and emotional disturbances which may lead to the difficulty in administration."[95] Indeed, prostitute women did resist the discipline of the reform homes: accounts of escapes (by swimming across a 200-metre-wide canal) have circulated since the establishment of the Pak Kred reform home in 1960.[96]

The disciplinary programs of the reform system were designed to domesticate women rather than to train them for new occupations. Sukanya Hantrakul's study of the reform institutions set up under this law showed that they "equip[ed] most reformees for nothing better than employment as domestic servants."[97] The final training period before discharge involved:

> 1) Training in regard to the proper arrangement of sleeping quarters and methods of child care by officials specialising in health and sanitation. 2) Training in regard to proper home care and cooking by officials specialising in home economics. 3) Training in regard to proper codes of conduct in relations to morals and mannerisms by qualified personnel.[98]

There was also "follow-up after discharge to ensure resumption of a normal and decent way of life."[99] Even in the 1980s the occupational training provided consisted of "weaving foot-rugs, sewing and weaving clothes, laundry work, book-binding, beauticians (manicures) and cooking."[100] The domestic emphasis of the provisions is clear, as is the concern to "tame" unruly women into engaging in proper sexual and cultural conduct.

The training in "morals and mannerisms" reflected Sarit's campaign for traditional Thai values, but the new law also satisfied the international community's desire to abolish prostitution and to reform female moral and sexual behaviour. Sarit, meanwhile, could maintain his legitimacy through more traditional modes of male sexual prerogative. In other words, the appeal of this reconfiguration of gender identity and sexual relations was not widespread. It is not surprising, therefore, that a mere six years after the 1960 law was put into place, Sarit's heirs to power, Thanom and Praphat (1963-73), proclaimed the Entertainment Places Act, which effectively reinstated a regulated form of prostitution (see Table 2).

Conclusion

Prostitution policy in pre-1960 Thailand was clearly shaped by international pressure to conform to Western standards of gender and sexual behaviour. According to these standards men should maintain monogamous marital relations and women's sexual behaviour should be carefully controlled, particularly through legislation that punishes prostitution. Such standards demanded that prostitution be considered a criminal activity, that prostitutes and operators (although, significantly, not clients) be subject to punishment, and that prostitute women be subject to behavioural reform programs. Changes in the gender order did produce resistance. Some male elites resisted both limitations on male sexual access and Western intervention in the indigenous gender order. Various governments walked a fine line between maintaining the country's status in the eyes of the international community (and the indigenous modernizing elite) and maintaining the support of resistant elite men. Within this context prostitution policy became a marker of whether one was or was not conforming to international Western gender standards.

Resistance also came, albeit more subtly, from the women who continued to enter into prostitution in order to survive – women who, in the early 1900s, refused to operate within the brothel system and who, in the later 1900s, refused to submit to the disciplinary programs of reform and rehabilitation. Their resistances and demands, however, were inaudible in the debate between elites and the international community over prostitution policy, and they remained inaudible in the following period as prostitution became a nationalist symbol of foreign intervention.

2
Peasants, Prostitutes, and the Body Politic: Prostitution as Cultural Decline and Political Resistance in the 1960s and 1970s

Prostitution is rarely read in terms of resistance. Even during the era of the student demonstrations and peasant uprisings of the 1960s and 1970s in Thailand, prostitution is rarely seen as part of the resistance of country (*ban*) to city (*muang*), rather, it is seen as part of Thailand's cultural and economic breakdown in the face of modernization and Westernization. However, the period in which the modern prostitution industry in Thailand was established was also a period of profound social upheaval, a period in which the mainly peasant-populated countryside registered its discontent with the government's security and development agenda (backed by American military interests in the region), and a newly active middle-class student body took the opportunity to demand the democratization of the military-authoritarian political system. During the 1960s through the 1970s, prostitution and prostitutes became symbolic of the systematic degradation of the countryside that occurred in tandem with (1) the drive for development and security and (2) the Westernization of Thailand through the arrival of American troops. Prostitutes were symbolic because they themselves were rarely, if ever, participants in the debates; rather, they were spoken for, or invoked by, various groups addressing causes of, and solutions to, economic and political problems. Prostitutes' voices, which could have reflected on the complex realities of their experiences, were silenced, and their lives were simplified: they were victims of larger social forces.

This dominant understanding of the prostitution problem developed over the 1980s and 1990s, and it needs to be viewed in terms of the political discourse over gender, culture, and national identity that had its birth in the student democracy movement of the 1960s. During this period the peasantry, and peasant women in particular, became emblematic of the struggle to define Thai national identity. The newly active middle-class student body argued for the overthrow of the military dictatorship and the institution of a social democracy. The student movement based its claim to legitimacy in its appeal to Thai nationalism in the face of a growing American military presence, as a United States-Thai alliance formed to fight against communist "insurgency" in Southeast Asia. The symbolic importance of women, and women's sexual behaviour, in maintaining national culture and identity made the growing sex trade around American airforce bases in the Northeast a central subject of social and political debate. At the same time, the Thai military and conservative bureaucrats worked to pacify the countryside and to inscribe a Thai identity, based on "Nation, Religion, and King," upon a rebellious peasantry. In the reconfigured politics of the postdemocracy era, the peasant, too, became a symbol and an anchor of Thai culture. Peasant women, therefore, were doubly marked with national identity; and those who entered the growing prostitution industry were the source of a great deal of social anxiety in the following years.

Since the exponential growth in prostitution in the 1960s, the prostitution problem has consistently been read as the result of cultural decline. Pasuk Phongpaichit and Chris Baker, for instance, argue that, in the 1960s, village culture was increasingly under attack, the authority of village elders and other "natural" leaders was eroded, and village cohesion de-emphasized. It was this decline in "the importance of ancestry and place" and "the decay of local communities" that "led to large-scale migration by rural girls (and later also boys) to work in prostitution for the US soldiers, for an increasingly prosperous urban market, later for the tourist trade, and finally as an export commodity."[1] Such a reading assumes rather than analyzes the link between women and culture. The problem with such a reading of the events of the 1960s is that it subordinates the readings of rural peasants and prostitute women and fails to see how, during this period, the link between peasant women and national culture was forged – a link that worked to the benefit of elite rather than peasant women and that worked against prostitute women, who were blamed for abandoning and undermining cultural traditions.

The increasing migration of women and girls into the sex industry did not go unnoticed in the rural areas, but there is reason to believe that it was differently interpreted by various groups in different parts of the country. As Pasuk and Baker themselves point out, young women traditionally made up a large portion of seasonal migrants.[2] Women also figured among rural travellers as traders, entertainers, and spirit mediums. Sexual taboos and gender differentiations also differed across regions. In the North, where animism remained strong in spite of the predominantly Buddhist character of the country, women acted as guardians of the spirit. Sexual relations before marriage were viewed as an offence to the familial spirits, which could be ameliorated through an offering of gifts from the couple to the woman's familial spirits in a *phit phi* (wronging of the spirits) ceremony. Some analysts now view this particular ceremony as one of the links between women's sexuality and monetary value that has made prostitution more acceptable in the North.[3] Others, such as anthropologist Eric Cohen, have pointed out that "there is often no crisp separation in Thai society between emotional and mercenary sexual relationships."[4] Even more important, across the country women were viewed as wage earners and were expected to contribute a major part of the family income in order to show their gratitude to their parents. Peasant women, according to several anthropological studies, were economic partners in the household – working outside the home in the fields and markets, inheriting property equally with their brothers, and participating as wives in major household decisions as well as controlling the family finances.[5]

Most important, prostitute women themselves, particularly those from the North (the largest regional group), consistently interpret themselves as family wage-earners. Many women working as prostitutes, particularly those from the North, remit a large portion of their wages back to their families in the rural areas.[6] Within the context of rural resistance, this can be seen as a Robin Hood act, where young women are determined to take advantage of the resources offered by urban modernity and to transmit them back to the villages. As Mary Beth Mills has noted in her study of women's migration to Bangkok, "migration decisions ... are made both out of duty and a sense of adventure."[7] Ambitious young women who sought to leave behind the drab rural life of poverty and back-breaking labour migrated to the cities to seek a better life. For many, work in the sex sector offered the possibility of both quick financial return and contact with the new, the modern, and the global. While the conditions of work in prostitution rarely fulfilled these hopes, this fact does not diminish the agency of the women themselves. There is also an in-your-face resistance to elite codes of female moral conduct and propriety in sex work. Lenore Manderson has re-evaluated the sex shows of Bangkok's notorious sex district, Patpong Road, as sites of female sexual reclamation and resistance.[8] And, as we shall see in Chapter 6 , there were attempts to organize prostitutes as political actors in their own right. Such attempts, however, consistently failed in the face of the dominant discourse, which held that prostitutes were either victims or misguided. An understanding of prostitutes as women struggling to make sense of their own lives, and the changing circumstances around them, did not fit within a script that depicted prostitution as the result of cultural decline.

What the present chapter seeks to illustrate is the process whereby national identity was inscribed onto peasants and prostitutes. This identity did not come forth "naturally" from a pre-existing cultural core; rather, it was part of a disciplinary discourse of national identity and culture that silenced other possibilities and histories. While this chapter can only hint at what these silenced possibilities may be – a fuller delineation being the task of historians and anthropologists – it shows how political elites constructed this national identity, which served to enforce the notion of a monolithic and backward peasantry in need of instruction from elites, thus erasing the resistance and agency of peasants and peasant women. This process established a dominant understanding of prostitution as being the result of cultural decline. Prostitute women were accordingly interpolated into policy and politics as problems in need of elite solutions and, in particular, of infusions of "correct" cultural identity. This process clearly established elites as the proper authorities (in the face of the challenge mounted by students and peasants) and gave elite women a power foothold as the ultimate arbiters of tradition and cultural identity. Most important, having established the peasantry and peasant women as symbols of national culture, this discourse silenced their political and social agency and their voices; however, it granted agency to the elite women who could guide peasant women into the modern era (see Chapter 3).

Politics in the 1960s and 1970s
The 1960s were a period of enormous economic growth and social change in Thailand. Since the early 1950s, the country had received considerable economic and technical aid from its ally the United States. During this period, the growing American involvement in Vietnam and the concern about the containment of communism in Asia led to heavy investment in national development as a way to maintain national security. Indeed, according to Thak Chaloemtiarana, the official raison d'être shifted from the need for national improvement to the need for security.[9] Officials wanted to ensure "attachment to government" in rural/outlying areas through the provision of services.[10] More important, they needed to ensure attachment to Thai national identity and sovereignty. Thai identity outside of central Thailand was still not nationalized. The Northern Thai, for instance, maintained the shared sovereignty idea of a vassal state. A 1967 study shows that that following was a widely held sentiment in the North:

> About sixty years ago we were conquered by the Central Thai. We offered them ... signs of respect and loyalty. They became our ... "officials" or "rulers" ... and we pay them taxes. When the Communists come, they may conquer the Central Thai. Then we will offer them [respect and loyalty and call them rulers]. We will pay them taxes and all will be as before. We are the common people; what happens to officials does not concern us ... Whatever side wins, we will ... call them our leaders.[11]

Clearly Northerners did not see themselves as spiritually attached to a Thai nation. Thus, the "imagined nation" did not reach far beyond the Central Plains and the urban centres of Thailand.

Sarit Thanarat's (1957-63) nationalization program of Nation, Religion, and King was brought to the countryside through an education push that included the building of thousands of primary schools in rural areas. School teachers, government officials, and Sangha monks appeared in the villages with increasing frequency. These efforts themselves generated resistance. The teachers, monks, and officials "represent[ed] new sources of knowledge which claimed to be superior to village-based knowledge."[12] The focus on road building and communication, the purpose of which was to service American military needs, led to increased hardships for peasants in the form of expropriated land and increased taxes. Migration into the city increased, along with the class divide between urban elite and rural poor.

The exploitation of the countryside led to outlying areas offering increased resistance to Bangkok's intrusions. It was this resistance that Sarit had sought to undermine by classifying peasants in the city as a threat to stability and by implementing development plans to pacify the countryside. The development/security push, however, was itself an instigator of unrest. Sarit's hand-picked successors – Thanom Kittichakorn and Praphat Charusathien (1963-73) – extended the security/development regime after Sarit's death in 1963. In response to these changes, the Communist Party of Thailand (CPT), since the 1920s a largely urban, Chinese-dominated party, formally changed strategy. At a 1961 party congress it moved from focusing upon an urban working-class-based revolution to focusing upon a rural-based revolution. It moved its headquarters to the northeast in order to build a rural party base and to make contacts with the communist parties in China, Laos, and Vietnam (which would help with training), finally launching an armed struggle in 1965.[13] The Thanom-Praphat regime responded to the rural communist presence with search-and-destroy missions in the northeast. In one 1966 incident, a search-and-destroy team "tortured suspects, raped women, and carried out summary executions of supposed communists."[14] This and many other incidents of aggression by police and soldiers led to guerrillas approaching self-defence units in villages and asking them to join the communist insurgency. The hardships brought by the anti-communist drive actually increased the appeal of the communists, who promised, for instance, to end police corruption.[15]

At the same time, the influx of aid from the United States and the industrial boom that flowed from military investment led to a burgeoning of the middle class and an increase in the gap between rich and poor. Sarit embraced the development rhetoric of the international economic community, sending the king abroad to advertise Thailand's endorsement of *patthana* (development). The First Development Plan, instituted in 1961, echoed the World Bank's and International Monetary Fund's push for economic growth through economic liberalization. Sarit had thrown off former

prime minister Phibun's (1938-44, 1948-57) limited economic nationalism to open the country to foreign investment, banning trade unions,
abolishing limits on landownership, enforcing low wages, and offering
"very favourable conditions for the repatriation of corporate profits."[16]
Between 1960 and 1970, the number of people classified as "administrative,
executive, and managerial" expanded almost ten times (from 26,000 to
nearly 250,000), and "professional and technical" personnel more than
doubled. As well, university education expanded rapidly. The number of
students in university grew fivefold, from 18,000 in 1961 to 100,000 in
1972.[17] The income of these educated, middle-class groups grew accordingly. By 1969 average urban incomes were two and one-half times rural
income levels.[18] Urban centres expanded rapidly. Bangkok grew from a
city of 2.6 million in 1960 to 4.6 million in 1970 and 5.9 million in 1975.
Half the increase in the urban workforce was the result of immigration
from the countryside.[19] Nonetheless, Pasuk and Baker argue that the flow
of labour from countryside to urban areas was not so great, given that the
"expanding agrarian frontier still absorbed nearly sixty per cent of the new
addition to the labour force between 1960 and 1980 ... In 1980, seventy-
one per cent of all labour was still working in agriculture."[20] Seasonal
migration was also a long-standing practice in rural areas, and the effect of
the growth spurt of the 1960s and 1970s was to intensify this process as
migrants joined the urban informal sector. Migrants were mostly young,
often in their teens, and nearly half were female, reflecting the important
role of women in sustaining the rural household economy.[21] The remittances of these young women from more profitable labour in the urban
areas kept many rural families from starvation. Many of these women
became part of the growing prostitution industry in the tourist and urban
centres.

In the 1970s the political effects of these changes were felt in full force.
Benedict Anderson characterizes the early 1970s in Thailand as an era during which the rising expectations of the growing petite bourgeoisie – a product of massive American investment – were thwarted by the withdrawal of
American troops, the inability of the bureaucracy to take on many of the
newly educated students, a sudden onset of inflation, and the exclusion of
this class from political power.[22] The students took up a socialist/national-
ist campaign that criticized both the continuing undemocratic rule of the
sakdina (feudal) elite and the interference of foreign powers, particularly
the United States and Japan. In 1972 the National Students Committee of
Thailand launched a boycott of Japanese goods, protesting the growing
predominance of Japanese firms and investment in Thailand. Its actions
amplified a campaign launched by thirty trade associations the year before
and the growth of economic nationalism among some businesspeople,

state managers, and intelligentsia.[23] The students' nationalist stance made it difficult for the government to criticize them outright, even as their condemnation of Japanese influence implied elite Thai connivance with outsiders to bilk the Thai economy.[24] And, for the time being, the students' nationalist campaign worked in favour of the capitalist elite, who were growing impatient with military rule and interference with business.

Thanom and Praphat's dictatorial power had been increasingly opposed by business groups and civil society. Thanom had finally called elections in 1969, the results of which were a stunning setback for the military and the bureaucracy. In the new legislature 46 percent were businesspeople, 20 percent were professionals, and only 21 percent were civil/military bureaucrats. The results appeared to indicate the growth of a democratic political culture. The Parliament proved to be very active in criticizing authoritarianism, corruption in government, and military arms spending. In frustration, in 1971 Thanom revoked the Constitution and dissolved an increasingly fractious Parliament. The king, sensitive to the winds of change, was openly unhappy with this move. He encouraged the newly active student movement to continue to oppose corruption in government.[25]

Even elements of the military were unhappy with a situation in which Thanom and Praphat appeared to have lost touch with the military itself. In 1971 the head of the army, General Krit Sivara, was asked by members of the military to carry out a coup against the Thanom regime. He refused, but the growing activism of the student movement was rapidly making such a move unnecessary. When several students were arrested in October 1973 for handing out leaflets demanding constitutional government, the student body rose up en masse and insisted on their release. Several days later there were approximately 400,000 people – from all walks of life – marching on the streets of Bangkok.[26] A riot ensued and the government asked General Krit and the army to step in and crush the "revolt." When Krit refused, the king asked Thanom and Praphat to resign and leave the country. A new era in Thai politics began with the appointment of a liberal-minded Supreme Court judge and favourite of the king, Sanya Thammasak, as prime minister.

This period of "open democracy" lasted a scant three years, however, as the right wing gathered its strength in the face of labour unrest and student demonstrations. This led to the bloodbath of 1976, when students, demonstrating against the return of Thanom, were attacked by right-wing forces. Many were killed and many more were forced to flee to the hills to seek the protection of the CPT. The right had made progress through the careful cultivation of a conservative national identity based on Nation, Religion, and King. After the overthrow of the military government in 1973, right-wing groups within the military were increasingly concerned with stemming the tide of "communist" influence that they saw among the students and the peasants. The fear of communist insurgency, continuing labour unrest, and Prime Minister Kukrit's (1975-6) pledge to discontinue American military support provoked the military to reassert its role.

The Internal Security Operation Command (ISOC)[27] became the coordinating body for the military's resurgence. ISOC supported the organization of two right-wing vigilante groups – the Red Gaurs and Nawaphon.[28] Leaders and members of the Peasants Federation of Thailand were systematically murdered, as, after that, were the leaders of the socialist parties. On 6 October 1976, right-wing activists, including those from Nawaphon, the Red Gaurs, and the Village Scouts, attacked a student demonstration outside Thammasat University. More than 1,000 students were killed. An army coup that evening ended Thailand's period of democracy and led to the installation of a right-wing, virulently anti-communist Supreme Court judge, Thanin Kraivixien, as prime minister. The government ordered the arrest and imprisonment of "elements dangerous to society."[29]

Radical right-wing organizations such as Nawaphon and the Red Gaurs[30] espoused an extreme nationalism. The head of Nawaphon stirred up crowds of onlookers with shouts of "Do you love your King? Do you love Thailand? Do you hate communism?"[31] Their discourse connected the monarchy, religion, and anti-communism, presenting this combination as the correct Thai identity. All those who appeared to oppose Nation, Religion, and King were branded communists, and this group soon included Prime Minister Kukrit. The protesting students were defined as not Thai but Vietnamese, this being understood to also mean being communist.[32] As Thongchai Winichakul remembers, police lieutenant-colonel Salang Bunnag and a radio host joked about the beating of students, suggesting that their inability to speak clearly after the beating indicated that they must be Vietnamese.[33] Thongchai also points out how the students were constantly referred to as "the rioters" or "the deceived" in recountings of the 6 October massacre.[34] Not only was the terminology designed to depict the students as foreign and as a threat to Thailand, but it was also designed to render them as inhuman. In 1976 one monk, Phra Kittivuttho (a prominent supporter of Nawaphon), stated, in clear opposition to Buddhist precepts, that killing communists was not a sin because they were not human.[35] This urban anti-communist propaganda had its village shadow in the form of rumours of "penis-shrinking potions" being spread as part of a Vietnamese communist conspiracy in the Northeast. This led to attacks on Vietnamese-owned businesses. Other rumours described vampires (who looked exactly like students) sucking the blood of village children to provide transfusions for wounded communist guerrillas.[36] This discourse of the right wing clearly carried strong ethno-national messages. Within this context, the student movement was forced to maintain its nationalism in an attempt to appeal for political legitimacy. In doing so, however, the movement often painted women as symbols of national purity or degradation. Prostitute women came to be seen as representative of the decline of the Thai nation.

The Vietnam War and the Growth of the Prostitution Industry

It was within the context of these wide social and political changes that prostitution became a national issue. In the 1960s the number of prostitutes began to expand rapidly, from approximately 20,000 women working in the trade in the late 1950s to 171,000 persons "clearly engaged in prostitution related activity" by 1964.[37] Almost all analyses of the prostitution situation in Thailand today point to the arrival of American servicemen in increasingly large numbers in the 1960s as the reason behind the enormous growth of the prostitution industry.

The link between prostitution and the military has long been established. Certainly the idea that soldiers required sexual servicing was deeply entrenched in the American military system. As Cynthia Enloe has pointed out:

> A military base isn't simply an institution for servicing bombers, fighters, aircraft carriers, or a launch-pad for aggressive forays into surrounding territories. A military base is also a package of presumptions about the male soldier's sexual needs, the local society's sexual needs, and about the local society's resources for satisfying those needs. Massage parlors are as integral to Subic Bay, the Mammoth US naval base in the Philippines, as its dry docks.[38]

In the minds of many military officials, prostitution is an important part of maintaining order. The provision of sexual services through prostitution is considered to be both an emotional outlet and a reward for war-weary soldiers; a strategy for preventing the rape of local (ally) women; a counter to potential homosexual acts among the troops; and, when properly controlled, a way to limit the spread of venereal disease, which is a major threat to the health of soldiers. The at least tacit encouragement of prostitution around military bases, particularly in foreign countries, is a common practice among militaries, and the American military bases in Thailand were no exception.

At least some of the interaction between Thai women and American servicemen, however, occurred under the rubric of "hired wife," with servicemen living with local women and receiving sexual, emotional, and housekeeping services in exchange for money, upkeep, and/or gifts. In the countryside, where marriages were still largely unregistered, the women involved did not necessarily view the arrangement as prostitution.[39] However, the servicemen usually did not take their Thai wives with them when they returned to the United States; some of these women then began to work in the growing tourism-based sex industry.[40] The stronger cultural restraint on remarriage in the Northeast, where the air bases were located, facilitated the transition from working as a hired wife to working in the sex industry.

The attitudes of the American military men, who, for the most part, viewed the women as prostitutes rather than as girlfriends or wives, also contributed to the decline in women's status. According to one former serviceman's account, American soldiers viewed Thais as amoral. He recounts that "there was a popular attitude among Americans that activities such as prostitution and cohabitation were perfectly acceptable [to the Thai]."[41] A more damning account of the attitudes of American GIs is given by Nigel Brailey, who argues that the Americans in Thailand during the Vietnam War had a "gook" mentality with regard to Vietnamese and Thai alike.[42] Certainly such attitudes, along with the failure of military men to maintain their family responsibilities once they left the country, meant that cultural expectations were shattered and that women were increasingly looked down upon by their communities.

Indeed, the presence of American servicemen was not entirely acceptable to local officials, who, at private meetings between US airforce representatives and local officials, expressed their displeasure at the corruption of young Thai women. At the same time, "it was common knowledge that certain local officials at every base had a financial interest in the bars, massage parlours, and other activities that catered to GIs."[43] Concerns about venereal disease led to towns near bases instituting a system of registration and VD control cards, despite the formal illegality of prostitution. Nonetheless, local concern about the effects of the presence of American servicemen led to the establishment of the Civic Action Program, which promoted public relations between the bases and the local population through the provision of medical services to local townspeople, rebuilding programs, and the distribution of consumer goods.[44]

The Thai government's encouragement of the prostitution industry, however, became clearer over the years, as it built up the tourist industry on the basis of the infrastructure developed for the American military. The bars, nightclubs, and massage parlours built to entertain visiting American military personnel became part of a vast network of tourism-targeted infrastructural development. This process was facilitated by legal changes that created the legal category of "special service girls" as distinct from "prostitutes." In 1966 the government introduced the Entertainment Places Act, which was ostensibly designed to "control the operations of certain kinds of entertainment places which affect the public order and morals."[45] The law merely codified the police practice of ignoring military-oriented prostitution by establishing the legal category of special service girls, which referred to women who provided entertainment in bars, nightclubs, and massage parlours. At one level, the law appeared to respond to concerns over prostitution by allowing officials to inspect such establishments and to shut them down if sexual services were being offered. The law also appeared to provide heavier punishments for pimps and owners than did the laws codified in the Prostitution Prohibition Act, 1960.[46] In reality, however, the act further protected owners and operators by allowing them to hire women under the rubric of "entertainers" while profiting from prostitution as long as it occurred off-site. A system of bar fees was developed so that customers could hire out a woman by paying a set amount to the bar and then taking her to a nearby hotel for sexual services.

Women in the trade, however, remained at risk for punishment as the 1966 act provided for the arrest of those rendering sexual services. These people would, as under the Prostitution Prohibition Act, 1960, be remanded to rehabilitation centres by the Department of Public Welfare after completing their sentences.[47] Indeed, this is the only section of the 1966 act that has been regularly used. The lighter penalties for pimping and running a place of prostitution, which come under the 1960 act, are used in the few cases where offenders are prosecuted.[48] Clearly the government was paving the way for the use of women as entertainment attractions; nonetheless, it placed the blame for crossing the line from special services to prostitution solely on women's shoulders. While, according to the government, women were responsible for their entry into prostitution, they were not to be allowed to act independently within that trade. The 1966 act, while giving some status to prostitutes, did so only on condition that they work within a place of entertainment; thus the government continued to cede control to owners and managers and to penalize independent prostitutes.

The tourism industry only stood to profit from such a policy. The 1966 act was followed a year later by a deal with the United States to allow American forces in Vietnam to come to Thailand on R&R leave, effectively expanding the special services industry. The foreign-oriented sex industry now grew beyond the location of the air bases and spread to other centres, such as the southern coastal town of Pattaya, which was selected as an R&R site.[49] The contribution to the economy was immediate, as spending rose from US$5 million in 1967 to an estimated US$20 million in 1970. The financial interests in the entertainment and, increasingly, tourist industries were enormous. A 1974 survey showed that over 20,000 entertainment places had been established nationwide (including bars, nightclubs, and brothels).[50]

Increasingly, these places were being used not only by servicemen but by visiting tourists, the numbers rising from 80,000 foreign tourists to Thailand in 1960 to nearly three million by 1986. The Thai government had

undertaken a tourism promotion policy in the 1960s, following the recommendations of a report, commissioned by the US Department of Trade
and Commerce and widely touted by various international organizations,
that advocated a tourism promotion strategy for economic development in
the Asia-Pacific region.[51] Thanh-dam Truong argues that the sudden, intensive investment in tourism infrastructure (particularly hotels) in the late
1960s and early 1970s created a significant oversupply of accommodation
and entertainment facilities. Once the military demand for these services
began to drop off, the need to fill these spaces led to an intensification of
tourism as part of the export-led growth strategy that was taking hold in
the 1970s – a strategy that, according to Truong, "widened the R&R market
to a more international market."[52] Prostitution services – sold, for instance,
through joint venture links between hotels, travel agencies, and airlines to
sex-tour groups – became a lucrative way to fill the empty hotel rooms left
by American servicemen. Truong argues, therefore, that "the relationship
between tourism and prostitution can no longer be seen only as an issue of
employment alternatives available to women, but also as an issue related to
the internal structure of the tourist industry and to vested interests of a
financial nature."[53] Thus the structural basis of prostitution became well
entrenched during the 1970s.

The 1966 act clearly showed that the government was not adverse to, in
fact it even promoted, the use of women as entertainment attractions –
even as tourism officials argued that prostitution was merely an unfortu-
nate side-effect of poverty.[54] Women's images were used as promotional
vehicles for tourism, as in the advertisements for the national airline:
"Some say it's our beautiful wide-bodied DC-10s that cause so many heads
to turn at airports throughout the world. We think our beautiful slim-bodied
hostesses have a lot to do with it."[55] Beauty, desirability, and service were
symbolized through the feminine body. Thus, the state could promote Thai
services internationally without damaging the masculinity of the Thai state
and elites, which was attached to "possessing" women as a sign of virility
and power. Indeed, within the context of growing dependency on American military aid, the Thai military/state's feeling of being emasculated
by the more virile Americans may have been redressed through the overt
sexual use and proffering of women in an attempt to prove Thai military
masculinity.[56]

While the military and tourism industries may account for some of the
demand for prostitution, they do not account for the supply. Further, the
focus on these foreign causes of prostitution has obscured the role of
domestic demand. Even today, tourism accounts for a very small proportion of the prostitution industry. According to a number of analysts, the
majority of clients of prostitutes are Thai.[57] As Sukanya Hantrakul points
out: "The GI ways of recreation were overwhelmingly adopted by the Thai

males with their already permissive code of conduct."[58] Nonetheless, Thai men as clients of prostitutes rarely make an appearance in the analytical material or in the media. Nor is the behaviour of the Thai military examined, except in terms of the military elites' attitudes towards women. The Thai military's forays into the rural areas to suppress communism no doubt involved the use of local prostitution services and may have expanded them.[59] Indeed, while the continuity between acting as a hired wife and becoming a prostitute may hold for women in Isan, the Northeast province (where the bases were located), it leaves unexplained the entry of women from the Northern region – women who predominate in the sex industry. Here the more important explanatory factors seem to be the northern society's emphasis on (1) a daughter's duty to support the family and (2) the national ideology of femininity that prizes the fair-skinned women of the north as being particularly beautiful and "soft." As Pasuk Phongpaichit has argued: "If it was the Viet Nam war which drew in the North-east girls, it was the institution of the beauty contest which provided the channel for the girls from the North."[60] The beauty contest was supported by military-bureaucratic elites who, like Prime Minister Sarit, married former beauty queens or took them as minor wives.

These aspects of the sex trade, however, were often ignored amid the overwhelming focus on the effects of Western influence in expanding the trade. In the political climate of the 1970s, if one was not to be accused of being communist, then one's appeal to nationalism was paramount in launching a critique of the military-dominated government. Such nationalism, however, presented prostitute women as symbolic of the decline of "real" Thai culture – now understood to mean rural, peasant culture. While women students' organizations tried to bring attention to the elite gender culture that treated women as sexual objects, they continued to view prostitute women as "fallen." In other words, the divide between good women and bad women remained unchallenged, and prostitute women appeared as being in need of assistance in order to return to what was constructed as the good peasant tradition.

Rural Resistance
Analysts consistently describe the 1960s as a period when Western culture intruded into the previously untouched Thai culture of the rural areas.[61] As Pasuk and Baker point out, however, these communities were never isolated; rather, there was constant travel and communication between villages through visiting families, traders, travelling entertainers, and wandering monks. As they argue, "these 'wandering networks' acted as transmission lines for knowledge, information, and ideas."[62] Rural cultures, therefore, were hardly fixed and unchanging; they were, in fact, in a constant state of reformulation.

Within the context of growing urban and American interference in rural life and increasing repression of rural people, rural residents expressed their unhappiness; however, rather than this being the reaction of a "pure," "traditional" culture to a foreign influence, rural resistance mechanisms made use of the international flow of ideas and culture to express grievances. The expansion of radio and roads throughout the countryside in the 1960s enabled rural entertainers to broadcast their music more widely. The *phleng luk thung* (country songs) "reflected the appearance of new media which knitted together a single rural audience, and the emergence of new and common concerns arising out of the rural population's common confrontation with the city."[63] The songs drew on the earthy humour of the villages while expressing cynicism about urban interference. Their style, however, also reflected the urban and international influences of Latino stagecraft and nightclub music. Backup dancers (usually female) in flashy costumes became a requisite part of live performances. This musical culture appears to mark some space for an acknowledgment of sexuality in public discourse in the rural areas and a willingness to draw upon other cultures for inspiration.[64]

Later, however, as this musical form became part of an organized movement, in tandem with student activists demonstrating against foreign interference and government fascism, a more restrictive representation of female sexuality became increasingly dominant. By the mid-1970s female migrants had become a major theme of the *luk thung* songs, being cast as representatives of the hardships wrought by cultural dislocation. Songs were written about life inside a brothel, being the hired wife of an American soldier, or working as a masseuse in Germany. One study of *luk thung* titles in the late 1980s showed "as many as one fifth dealing with prostitution, including sympathetic treatments by male singers," who often linked prostitution to the need to earn money for the family.[65] Thus, for the rural cultural elite, prostitution became symbolic of rural cultural/economic decline and exploitation. The space for female sexual self-determination disappeared.

Resistance to urban intrusion also took the shape of what those in power termed the "communist insurgency."[66] The local disgust with the behaviour of the Americans, who "brawled with Thai over girls and money," became part of the communist arsenal of arguments to support their contention that the Thai government was acting as a puppet of the United States.[67] Dissident organizations decried the presence of the "US imperialists" who, according to the Thailand Independence Movement, "have propagandized their reactionary thoughts and rotten culture into our society."[68] In its inaugural statement in 1965, the Thailand Patriotic Front announced that "the U.S. imperialists suck our people's blood and each year take away tremendous amounts of wealth from our natural resources; at the same time they spread the rotten and poisonous American culture among our youths."[69] The Thailand Patriotic Youth Organization vowed to "oppose the derogatory culture and degenerating way of life of U.S. imperialism that are poisoning the minds of the Thai youth [and to] fight for the promotion of the excellent culture, tradition, and morality of the Thai nation."[70] The dissidents also responded to the concern over sexual relations between Thais and Americans by claiming that the American servicemen "barbarously rape Thai women" as well as injure and torture Thai people.[71] The emphasis on rape was designed to highlight the victimization and innocence of the Thai people in the face of American aggression (which was supported by the "corrupt," "fascist," and "dictatorial" Thanom-Praphat government).

That rape did indeed occur is very likely, given the attitude of the American forces personnel towards Thai women. To add insult to injury, even though the Americans had not formally negotiated a status of forces agreement to exempt American personnel from Thai law, Thai authorities usually handed offenders back over to base authorities without laying charges.[72] Conscious of the anger this must have engendered among the populace near the bases, in its statement the Patriotic Front linked these events to imperial disrespect of Thai sovereignty: "Worse still, they trample underfoot Thai law."[73] The threat of imperialism and loss of sovereignty in the American military's treatment of Thai women was made clear.

The Communist Party, for its part, made a pledge to adhere strictly to "ten disciplinary principles" adopted from Mao's Three Main Rules of Discipline and Eight Points for Attention, which included the order: "do not take liberties with women."[74] The Communist Party of Thailand made the following promise: "Women shall enjoy equal rights as men in the political, economic, cultural, educational and vocational fields; [and the party will] bring the role of women into full play in the revolutionary movement and production; promote fully welfare work among women and children, [and] ensure education and work for the youth."[75] Women, women's bodies, and women's sexuality were clearly becoming a battleground for issues of national identity, culture, and self-determination, and there was no room for the kind of ambiguities over women's sexuality suggested by other discourses.

Students, Elites, and the Threat of Cultural Decline
Resistance to the current regime was building throughout the 1960s not only in the countryside, but also among urban elites. The growth of a well educated and economically ascendant middle class spawned impatience with the dictatorial style of Sarit's successors, Thanom and Praphat. As the

number of university students had climbed, so had middle-class intellectual activity and unhappiness with continuing autocratic rule. Dissent was also apparent within conservative intellectual circles. In 1963, the renowned Buddhist intellectual Sulak Sivaraksa began the journal *Social Science Review,* in the pages of which critiques of Thai politics and society began to appear. Sulak also focused on the American influence on Thai society and culture.[76] He bemoaned the "mindless imitation" of Western practices without "careful evaluation." Cognizant of the workings of imperialism, he warned his fellow citizens in 1970 that such behaviour "invites paternalistic attitudes from our Western partners."[77]

A conservative nationalism such as that expressed by Sulak was becoming apparent among the wider circle of urbanites, including those from small-town, lower-middle-class backgrounds who had gone to the city to receive a higher education in the late 1960s. Suchit Wongthes, who later became a prominent supporter of the student movement, expressed a similar cultural nationalism. His early writings focused on the decline of Thai culture in the face of Americanization. These writings also illustrate the degree to which cultural decline was linked to women's inappropriate behaviour. In Suchit's stories women symbolize the corruption of Thai culture. In his short story "Second Nature," the local boy who has made good returns to his village to visit his sweetheart and finds that both she and his village have completely changed. As Anderson explains, "A countryman at heart (or at least so he thinks), he dreams of 'showing up' the corrupted (Americanized, by implication) women of Bangkok by marrying the simple village girl he had left behind back home."[78]

It is the women who appear as the personification of the corruption of culture both in Bangkok and in the villages. The local girlfriend appears pitifully ignorant in her attempts to mimic urban culture without the sophistication of urban women, wearing the stretch pants that now signify "looseness" in the sophisticated urban centre of Bangkok and engaging in the entertainment spectacles from which "nice girls" should abstain.[79] Suchit writes:

> He wanted to tell to her [sic] that stretch-pants were repulsive; but he held back, reflecting that he still had a few days left to explain to her that Bangkok boys with education and good taste regarded all girls who wore stretch-pants as low-grade whores; for any girl who clothed her body with such provocative tightness must be basically hard and far too forward. The young men were all agreed that a real Siamese beauty would never be brazen enough to display her bag of sexual tricks like that before the public.[80]

In this passage Suchit links Western consumer goods, particularly clothing, to an impure sexuality and to a lack of Thainess (no "real Siamese beauty" would wear those clothes). It also puts the male narrator in the position of authority, along with his friends, as the arbiter of what constitutes both real Siamese beauty and proper behaviour.

This conservative attitude towards the role of women in culture did not change with the increasing radicalization of the Thai student movement. Through the anti-war movement, Thai students studying in the United States in the late 1960s learned how their country was being used as a base for US military operations and were able to relay that information back home, where few were fully aware of the extent of American involvement. The number of US troops had increased from 3,000 at the end of 1964 to 9,000 in 1965, jumped to 35,000 in 1966, and reached a high of 48,000 in 1969.[81] Benedict Anderson notes that the students' critique of the changes taking place were a curious mix of disappointment with the Thai government for its failure to secure adequate American support to maintain Thai security in the face of communist encroachment and anger at the effects of the American military presence on Thai culture. He argues that such a mixture was "expressed in the combination of such sentiments as 'why have you let us down in Indochina?' and 'Look how you've corrupted our girls!'"[82] The nationalism of the student movement, however, was a key strategy in garnering legitimacy in the face of a conservative, military government that had the backing of the palace and the Buddhist religious order known as the Sangha. The students felt that they spoke for the "true Thais" – the peasants who were looked down upon by urbanites who had "come to regard Westerners as superior human beings."[83]

Indeed, the moral effect of the American presence became a central theme of this nationalism. There was a kind of nationalist machismo among male activists with regard to the issue of prostitution as they condemned the use of "our" women by foreigners.[84] In 1972, the students marched on the American embassy and denounced the US presence as the primary cause of "the rotten Thai society in which we are now living, one with 'hired wives,' prostitutes and half-breed children of all colours." Clearly, they constructed the threat to the nation in terms of the threat to the purity (both moral and racial) of women's bodies.[85] The students documented the growth of prostitution and the entertainment industry as proof of the demoralizing effect of the American military presence. A 1972 report published in the main vehicle for student critique, the *Social Science Review,* showed that by 1972 the town of Takli, the site of an American air base since 1961, had more bars and nightclubs (forty-six) than temples (forty-four). The report added that, in the wake of a 1972 all-out bombing campaign and its concomitant wave of American military men, "the number of prostitutes checking in for VD inspections rose from ninety-one in January 1972 to 2,954 six months later in June."[86] The decline of traditional culture was signalled through the rise of the prostitute.

The nationalist stance of the students gave them a ground from which to attack elites for their participation in the moral degradation of Thai culture. Even such highly respected figures as Buddhist monks were exposed to attack from the students, who saw themselves not as trying to undermine Thai culture but, rather, as trying to restore and purify it. Well known nationalists, such as Suchit Wongthes and Khanchai Bunpan, openly criticized the moral conduct of monks who endorsed "immoral establishments such as bars, night clubs, and massage parlours." At the same time they denounced elite, classical Thai literature as "erotic and morally corrupt with no social value."[87]

Over the course of the 1970s the students' critiques increasingly drew upon the work of native Thai Marxists such as Jit Poumisak and Gularp Saipraisdit, which had been banned by the military government. Yuangrat Wedel has argued that the Thai brand of Marxism was distinct from Maoism and international socialism in its emphasis on Buddhism and Thai national/cultural identity.[88] This nationalism remains clear in the analysis of women's status and the use of women's bodies. Jit, for instance, clearly saw women entering prostitution as a function of economic need both in the feudal (*sakdina*) and capitalist eras, but he also invoked the influence of European intrusion, echoing the concerns of the contemporary era:

> The nature of prostitution in the *sakdina* age and the capitalist age was identical i.e. many women who could no longer endure conditions of hunger and suffering had to sell their bodies. In periods when Europeans came to trade in the *krung*, their free-spending habits induced an even larger number of women who could not break free of such conditions to take up this occupation. At the end of the Audhya period it was notorious that increasing numbers of unfortunate women were being forced to grit their teeth, shut their eyes, and sell themselves to foreigners.[89]

The illegitimacy of the feudal elite was illustrated through its own treatment of women and its sexual "perversion." The feudal elite "did nothing to correct the situation, because it saw women's 'basic nature' as being lustful. All the *sakdina* did was wait around to collect the tax." Indeed, Jit characterized the *sakdina* class as licentious and sexually perverted, "using women as objects in which to release their desire. A woman's condition was thus that of a female animal waiting to receive the Land-Lord's lust."[90] Jit studied classical literature to find examples of how a woman was viewed as "good only when she ha[d] an interesting body, good only for sexual release."[91] Jit's invocation of sexual depravity demonstrates the symbolic importance of women's bodies in provoking a nationalist response, a need to save Thai women from the perverted ruling class and from the foreigners to whom they are sold. Women themselves appear as objects passed from hand to hand rather than as agents.

The student movement of the late 1960s and early 1970s could openly espouse such criticisms on the grounds of defending Thai culture against encroaching American imperialism. Nonetheless, the external focus and nationalism of much of the students' critique also allowed the government to appropriate their rhetoric. Thanom himself told the American military that their behaviour was prompting Thai hostility to "foreign culture based on materialism." And he was able to turn attention away from his own government, and its complicity in the changes being wrought in Thai society, by focusing on "foreign culture":

> Foreign culture based on materialism has flowed swiftly into Thailand, being brought into the country directly by tourists or indirectly by mass media ... These changes are rapid and have in a short time shockingly damaged the good morale and culture of certain groups of people ... pretty girls turn to the business of being mistresses, bar hostesses, masseuses, or prostitutes, [while their brothers] rob and extort honest persons.[92]

It is important to note, however, that Thanom made this pronouncement at approximately the same time as the government was forced to admit that Thai air bases in the northeast were being used to bomb North Vietnam. This had been suspected by some members of the public but was not generally well known. Kirk argues that "Thanom may have wanted to counterbalance the adverse propaganda effect of this admission by appearing to agree with sceptics and critics who had already expressed doubts privately about U.S. activities."[93] Clearly, however, the nationalist rhetoric did not challenge the conservative elite's views about the role of women.

The Thai student movement made prostitution an issue of social and symbolic importance during the 1970s. The prostitute powerfully evoked women's link to national culture and identity, and her abuse was synonymous with the abuse of the nation. Rachel Harrison has uncovered the symbolic importance of the prostitute in modern Thai literature as a woman unable to be a mother, a phenomenon that is demonstrated by complications in pregnancy and childbirth.[94] While Harrison links this view of prostitute women to Buddhist beliefs about the dangers of uncontrolled female sexuality and traditional gender structures that define good women in terms of their duty to the family, it is no small coincidence that a number of these stories appeared in the 1960s and 1970s, when concerns about the reproduction of the nation were very high. The symbolic importance of these stories lies in their evocation of a nation unable to reproduce its citizens, of women who are not "good mothers" (i.e., women who reproduce the nation) but, instead, prostitutes (i.e., women who cannot be mothers and who, therefore, embody national decline).

As symbols, prostitute women were granted little agency; their voices were interpreted through social and political commentators. Harrison's analysis of male writers' treatments of prostitution during this period finds that they were ambivalent in their dealings with the prostitution issue. She notes that, even as they detail sensational information about prostitution (which indicates some first-hand experience), they pose the prostitute as an object of pity and a symbol of social/cultural decline. The commentary in one short story illustrates this objectification of women in prostitution:

> Every time I meet a woman in this situation there are the same old ques-
> tions and the same old thoughts: here was yet another Thai prostitute, a
> woman leading a lifeless life, existing only in order to satisfy the sexual
> desires of men, without the least understanding of the deadly blows soci-
> ety dealt her. She merely led this terrible, putrid life until the day when she
> would become little more than a lump of rotting flesh.[95]

Prostitute women are seen as pitiable both as victims of society and as being people "without the least understanding." It is not surprising that these authors should view the prostitute as in need of rescuing and as a per-fect symbol of the state's failure to govern properly. As one author con-cludes his story on prostitution: "All I want to know is what the country intends to do about all this." Another poses his narrator as an observer who wishes to "save her rather than sleep with her."[96] The Thai student movement spoke *on behalf* of the prostitute, using her degradation as a weapon against a corrupt government and Western/capitalist intrusion. Prostitute women's own interpretations of their lives (e.g., as workers try-ing to support their families) were rendered mute. Their ability to intervene in political affairs and to put forward their own interests or desires, such as better working conditions, was extinguished.

University Women's Groups
Female students were very much involved in the Thai student movement, and they tried to inject the question of women's lower social status into the movement's debates. A small group of women students at Thammasat Uni-versity formed the organization *Klum Ying* (Women's Group) in 1973 and began publishing the periodical *Lep* (*Fingernails*), a publication that featured the writing of both male and female students and that contained articles on women's liberation in the West, birth control, abortion, and sexual free-dom.[97] The early women students' organizations of the 1970s took issue with the portrayal and use of women as sex objects and their patronizing treatment as "flowers" (i.e., decorative objects) – a metaphor frequently

used in describing women. They linked prostitution to the rise of capitalism and to the male demand for women as sex objects and as symbols of male prestige.

The most well known woman activist was Jiranan Pitpreecha. In 1975 a small group of women at Chulalongkorn University published Jiranan's *The Fourth World,* a Marxist feminist reading of women's oppression. According to Jiranan, the blend of capitalism and Thai values led to women being reduced to the status of "commercial goods or objects to denote prestige" (as may be seen in the fact that elite men often collected numerous wives). Jiranan read prostitution as an outgrowth of the "decorative" status of women. She argued that women were forced to become "minor wives, mistresses and even prostitutes to cater to the male need for prestige." She characterized the beauty contest as a "capitalist device aimed at improving the stock of living merchandise."[98] For Jiranan and her colleagues, women were devalued through capitalism as well as through the sexual culture of polygamy and concubinage, which promoted a view of women as sexual objects.

Rachel Harrison's research on the prostitute in Thai literature of the 1970s notes the development of a sympathetic attitude towards prostitutes – an attitude that blames the development of capitalism for prostitution. However, she also notes a continuing divide between good and bad women. Harrison argues that, while male and female writers tended not to differ greatly in their writing on the topic of prostitution, "Thai women's fictional writing on prostitution has, on the whole, only served to confirm traditional gender-based beliefs through its compliance with the given hierarchies of male/female roles in Thai society. That it does so with apparent sympathy for the prostitute does not detract from its underlying standpoint that, despite herself or otherwise, the prostitute has transgressed from the realm of the 'good' woman to that of the 'bad.'"[99]

Therefore, the growing recognition that prostitution may result from economic circumstances led only so far as sympathy for the prostitute for having failed to remain a good woman. It did not challenge the good girl/bad girl divide. Some put further distance between themselves and prostitute women by continuing to argue that there may be some psychological abnormalities that lead women into becoming prostitutes.[100] Just as the nationalism of the student movement gave it legitimacy within the wider society, so being good girls legitimated members of the women's groups – because promiscuous sexual behaviour on the part of women continued to be condemned.

Conclusion

As we shall see in the following chapters, today the prostitution problem is very much viewed as the product of cultural decline in the face of growing

Westernization and globalization. Such a reading of prostitution, however, assumes that cultural identity is indeed embedded within peasant women, and it poses their sexual degradation as symbolic of cultural and national decline. This assumption erases the struggle over national identity, the resistance of the peasantry to centralized control, and the state's forcible imposition of that identity in the form of the military's intensive training programs. The 1960s and 1970s, as we have seen, was a period of intense struggle over national identity, particularly between the rural and urban areas. Peasant women, in particular, were emblazoned on the national imaginary as symbols of national culture.

This reading is itself the product of the politics of the 1960s and 1970s, within which prostitution first came to be recognized as a "problem" in the full political and social sense. In the 1960s the arrival of the American forces, along with peasant unrest and dislocation, led to a sudden increase in the number of women working as prostitutes and hired wives, particularly in the Northeast of Thailand. And, in the 1970s, these numbers expanded still further with the growth in the tourism industry. While women working in the sex industry may have seen themselves as family wage earners, or as women willing to take risks in order to take advantage of the modern and the foreign, to the growing middle-class student movement they represented the degradation of Thai culture through Americanization. For the students, rural women's bodies marked the borders of the Thai nation. Their sexual use by foreigners indicated an invasion by a foreign other, and the production of mixed-race children signalled a dilution of the ethno-racial essence of the nation. Prostitute women soon became icons of cultural decline. In the following years, this understanding of prostitute women – as symbols rather than as agents – underwrote elite programs to discipline and guide peasant women.

3
Elite Women, the Reconstruction of National Identity, and the Prostitution Problem

While the prostitute became a symbol of cultural decline in the discourse of the student movement, this symbolism only gained its power when it became part of the hegemonic political project of the post-1976 period. This new power structure combined both progressive and conservative elite forces in a national program of economic growth and political stability, which crystallized under the guiding hand of General Prem Tinsulanond (1980-8). A key ideological plank of this program was the construction of a hegemonic Thai identity that worked to stitch the national psyche back together in the wake of the upheavals of the mid-1970s. This new identity drew upon the symbolic force of the peasantry as the "backbone of the Thai nation," erasing years of peasant struggle by carefully crafting an idealized image of the happy and contented Thai peasant who upheld the customs and traditions of Thai culture in the face of rapid modernization. This new discourse around the peasantry emphasized stability and continuity with an idealized past, making it easy to forget the violent struggles of recent years. This national reconstruction project opened opportunities for elite women to participate in the construction of the "good peasant woman." They would guide peasant women who had strayed from their proper roles – most particularly, prostitute women – by relinking them to their (newly reconstituted) traditions and customs. By participating in this project elite women legitimized their own role in national affairs, particularly their fight for gender equity in marriage laws, as good Thai women protecting and promoting Thai culture. Thus, in the development programs that marked that period, the prostitute figured prominently as an object of reform and re-enculturation at the hands of the elite.

Crackdown and Reconstruction: Reconfiguring Thai Identity
By the early 1980s the communist threat had been contained by the security forces in Thailand, and an eight-year period of semi-democracy under General Prem and his alliance of royalists, military, and provincial politicians

began.[1] Although the fear of communist encroachment remained strong during this period, even the military had come to view outright repression as the wrong approach. The Kriangsak Chomanand government successfully squeezed out the Communist Party of Thailand (CPT) by renewing formal links between Thailand and China, the CPT's major backer. According to one of the foremost scholars on the Thai radical movement, the students themselves had come to see the CPT and its pro-Beijing, Maoist stance as counter to their own democratic ideals and were slowly slipping back into the towns and cities and out of the jungle.[2] Prime Minister Prem and his entourage sought to stabilize Thai society in the wake of the events of the 1970s.

This period of "Premocracy" has been characterized by John Girling as a classic example of Gramsci's *transformismo*, or passive revolution: "the growth of an ever-more extensive ruling class, through absorption of elements from other social groups within the established framework."[3] Peasant revolution was replaced by guided democracy and development. Progressive elites and technocrats found a foothold within the government, advising on development programs and managing economic growth. While the military retained its influence through the Senate and its threats of force, its appeal was declining as business and the middle class grew in importance. Nonetheless, the military continued to provide the "stable" atmosphere within which business could prosper, infiltrating unions and weakening the working class, pacifying the countryside, and policing the security of Nation, Religion, and King.

Most important, the post-1976 regime sought to stabilize a new Thai identity grounded in the rural areas. The active construction of a peasant-based national identity had been a key part of the security forces' agenda beginning in the 1970s. The peasant unrest of the 1970s had made it clear to some organizations within the military and security apparatus that national identity needed to be inculcated within, rather than forced upon, the rural peasantry. In the early 1970s, even before the student uprising of 1973, the Internal Security and Operations Command headed by Saiyud Kerdphun turned to "a 'political' strategy of killing communism against the patently unsuccessful military strategy of trying to kill communists."[4] The Border Patrol Police formed the Village Scout Movement in the far northeast as a way of instilling loyalty among the villagers and vigilance against communist insurgency. The Village Scouts organization was a major state attempt to engage in what Katherine Bowie has called "cultural management": "an effort to both mould the consciousness of the more compliant citizens and to intimidate the more intractable elements into inaction, thereby changing the balance of forces in favour of the state."[5] The movement attempted to win over the hearts and minds of the peasant populace through an intense indoctrination program of "love of King, country and religion." Its nine-point code included a commitment to pre-serve Thai customs and rituals, and the use of Thai products. The move-ment was quickly absorbed by the central state apparatus as part of the national security and identity-building project. After 1973 the Ministry of the Interior became involved in nationalizing the movement beyond the northeast by giving recruitment quotas to local officials.[6]

A prime function of the Village Scouts movement was to attach the peas-antry to the monarchy. While the monarchy had been largely sublimated under the Phibun regime, Sarit had drawn upon it as an indigenous base for legitimacy. In the Thanom-Praphat era, the king and queen began to make regular appearances around the countryside, supporting royal pro-jects in agriculture (the king) and handicrafts (the queen). These activities took on increased significance in the post-1976 era as conservative ele-ments in the military and bureaucracy began to advocate an enlarged role for the monarchy in the national culture. The public relations department and the military-owned television stations increased coverage of the royal family. On military television the royal report became a daily segment of the news. In this coverage, the monarchs were clearly presented as "friends of the peasant."[7]

The Village Scouts stand as a prime example of the programs being undertaken by elements in the military and bureaucracy to reassert control during this period. Among the chief architects of the counter-insurgency measures were people who were to make their mark on Thai politics for the next twenty years: Prem Tinsulanond, who became prime minister in 1980 and oversaw the "guided democracy" of those years; Saiyud Kerphun, who, after the demise of ISOC, became head of Poll Watch, the election "watch-dog" organization; and General Chavalit Yongchaiyudh, who was elected prime minister in 1996 in what he termed a "graceful rise" to the top after many years as head of the New Aspiration Party and member of several coalition governments. Prem's idea of counter-insurgency was to use Maoist guerrilla methods against the insurgents, using not only military might but offers of development assistance and amnesty for complete sur-render. Along with the Village Scouts (which had a membership of three million by 1980), the counter-insurgency forces organized the National Defence Volunteers and the Military Reservists for National Security. These paramilitary groups and officials "made it clear that failure to join the organizations might indicate disloyalty or communist tendencies."[8] A number of women's groups designed to promote national security, anti-communism, and Thai identity were also formed between 1976 and 1985. These were often associations of officials' wives (e.g., The Housewives to Protect Thailand, Army Housewives, Air-force Housewives, and Housewives of the Ministry of the Interior).[9] The paramilitary organizations also offered propaganda through lectures and entertainment programs that

"often emphasize[d] the evils of communism, the heroism of Thai ances-
tors, Thai national identity, and the democratic process[,] which include[d]
how to properly elect parliamentarians."[10]

A 1977 coup put General Kriangsak Chomanand into power and saw a
return to somewhat more open government. The "Thai-ification" programs
of the counter-insurgency were so successful that the government felt comfortable enough to welcome back its delinquent student population. Those
who had been ejected as un-Thai were now to be reabsorbed into the population, their radical ideals dashed by the harsh conditions of the jungle. In
1979, the government allowed some student, labour, and farmer groups to
organize on a very limited basis. And, in 1980, Prem and Chavalit designed
Order 66/2325, which offered amnesty to the students who had taken
refuge in the hills after the 1976 crackdown.[11]

Building on its success, the government formed the National Cultural
Commission and the National Identity Board to promote a new hegemonic
identity by defining and promoting *khwampen thai* (Thainess). The commission's mandate clearly recognized the political importance of having "*a*
culture," stating that culture, "a distinctive characteristic of nationhood,"
was essential in maintaining the stability and integrity of the nation.[12]
National security was firmly attached to the maintenance of a particular
national identity – especially in the rural areas. The national culture championed by the new organizations relied on the three-tiered vision of the
nation as promoted by King Vajiravudh – king, bureaucrat, and peasant.
The peasant, who, only recently, had been considered a potential communist insurgent, now became a symbol of all that was to be considered essential to Thai identity: Buddhism, respect for the monarchy, and contented
agricultural lifestyles. As the elites reconfigured and reconstructed Thai
national identity for a modern era, the symbolism of the peasant and peasant culture provided a timeless link to a primordial past, thus giving this
new identity legitimacy. Even democracy, that most modern of political
forms, could be given a rootedness in the past by linking it to traditional
peasant culture. In the early 1980s, for example, the National Identity
Board declared: "Despite increasing industrialization, some 40 million ...
Thais still live in villages where democracy is practised in its purest form."[13]
Even as this interpretation of national identity linked modern forms to a
traditional past, it also contained peasant culture within that newly
invented past, protecting or restricting it from the temptations of modern
living. In 1984, the National Identity Board boasted:

> The village is a peaceful place, its slow pace reflecting the serene, unas-
> suming nature of the villagers themselves ... most farmers are content to
> earn enough to support their families ... *wealth is not something most villagers*

actually crave ... The natural affection Thai villagers feel for their land *minimizes population migrations*. Moreover, villagers have little ambition to change their lifestyles.[14]

This reinterpretation of village culture and the peasantry reflected not only the peasant identity enforced by the counter-insurgency movements, but it also echoed the romanticism of the student movement's ideas about village culture. And it stood in stark contrast to the actual events of the 1960s and 1970s. The power of this interpretation was that it provided a foundational myth that linked the past, present, and future of the Thai nation in a smooth and uncontested transition and, thereby, legitimized the power of the elites who guided the process. This new representation of Thainess held into the 1990s. As Craig Reynolds argues, "the current official formulations of what is quintessentially Thai never fail to include the peasant and the village."[15]

The peasant as the conceptual anchor for Thai identity had particular ramifications for peasant women because of the already established link between women and tradition. Peasant women who engaged in prostitution were viewed as having failed to live up to the behavioural norms of peasant culture, as defined by the government. They had stepped outside the boundaries of acceptable behaviour and were in dire need of reintegration. A suitable guide for this process of re-enculturation was found in that class of women that had the "skills and wisdom" to preserve national culture even as it partook of the benefits of modernity. The role of elite women as preservers of tradition, evinced in their desire to re-enculturate peasant women, provided an opening through which they could make political demands for greater gender equality.

Elite Women, the Protection of National Culture, and the Struggle for Gender Equality

The approach of elite Thai women to gender issues hinged on the need to gain admittance to, and acceptance within, the halls of power. It quickly became clear that only by capitalizing on their role as protectors of national culture, as symbols and guides for other women, could elite women gain some influence over the political agenda and hope to gain some semblance of legal equality between the sexes (the lack of which was most particularly galling for elite and middle-class women). This pragmatic approach to achieving gender equality is, of course, a common tactic, particularly in the South, where women have often been confronted with conservative and defensive governments, and it has proven an effective method of achieving some gender goals even if at the cost of others. It is, as Hamideh Sedghi has argued, a double-edged sword, involving promoting both national interests (not just as a tactic but because women, too, resent the imposition of Western/international power) and gender-specific interests, thus running the risk of having the latter subordinated to the former. However, this may be the only available means of advancing gender equality at all.[16] For the purposes of this discussion it is important to understand that the defence of national culture adopted by many elite women was an effective method of gaining some political influence in the face of continued male resistance to gender equality; however, it also limited how the issue of prostitution, in particular, could be approached.

Elite women's concern with establishing gender equality can only be understood within the historical context of the long struggle for legal equality during the course of the 1900s. While Thai gender relations had often been presented within the early anthropological literature as equitable, this generalization was most difficult to uphold when applied to elites. Elite women were the most affected by unfair marriage and divorce provisions, legal restrictions on women in business, and career restrictions on women in government. While peasant practices and distance from or resistance to governmental/legal intervention gave peasant women some leeway, elite and, increasingly, middle-class women found themselves hemmed in by inequitable laws and practices. The most frustrating of these was the continued sanctioning of male sexual freedom and the restriction of women's ability to seek divorce. Elite women had campaigned for more equitable gender laws since the end of the absolute monarchy. In 1932 elite women activists had campaigned for legislation that would end polygamy and advance equality between the sexes. The new anti-polygamy law of 1935, however, failed to protect women's independence and instead increased a husband's control over his wife's business affairs. As well, while polygamy was no longer officially legal, the practice remained in place, and elite men continued to acquire mistresses as a symbol of their status and wealth. Other provisions in family law still effectively sanctioned polygamy – for example, men were still able to register all their children, whether or not they were the offspring of a formal marriage.[17] This made it more difficult for married wives to protect their children's legal rights against other claimants. Finally, women had little redress against their husbands taking minor wives because a husband's adultery was not considered grounds for divorce whereas a wife's was.[18] As Gail Omvedt has argued, the 1935 legal changes

> merely institutionalized a bourgeois form of patriarchy which made it
> more difficult for women to get a divorce, and required that the husband's
> consent be given for any contract entered into on the part of the wife.
> (Outlawing polygamy legally while it continued socially meant only that
> second wives no longer had any protection; ironically, women who often

controlled significant property could no longer act independently of their husbands: in this way, "modernization" – carried through largely by Sino-Thai legal experts acting on western advice – meant worsening the position of Thai women.)[19]

For elite women, the struggle to remove these discriminatory provisions was a central political campaign for most of the twentieth century.

Political influence for women, however, remained extremely limited. While women had been given equal voting rights in the new Constitution and the right to run in elections for the legislature in 1932, no woman was elected until 1949, and, even today, the numbers of women in the legislature remain extremely small.[20] With the growing anti-socialist feeling of the 1930s, women's groups that focused upon issues of women labourers had also been pushed out of the political field. One women's newspaper, *Ying Thai,* which opposed the government's invitation to women to run as candidates in elections on the grounds that "the honour given to a few women did not guarantee equal treatment to the other seven million women," had been shut down in the early 1930s on suspicion of communist leanings.[21] The space for women's organizing, therefore, was very narrow, forcing women to work within the government's state-led nationalist approach.

During the state-building years under Phibun, elite women had taken advantage of the opportunities provided by their role as "mothers of the nation." Phibun had emphasized the role of women as symbols of Thai civilization. Accordingly, women took on a new importance as guardians of culture and mothers of the nation. Phibun made the following announcement: "Women are mothers of every Thai as women are mothers of all things. They are the mothers who give birth to children and they are the mould of the nation ... Mothers are the mould of the character of men since childhood ... If we have no good mould, we can never build the Thai nation."[22] In 1942 Phibun had institutionalized the link between women and national culture in the National Cultural Council, which was divided into five departments: Spiritual Culture, Traditions, Arts, Literature, and Women.[23] The women's department was actually proposed, and then chaired, by Phibun's wife, Lady Laiad.[24] The women's department became a vehicle for upper-class women to proselytize on behalf of the government's nationalist program. It took up the social hygiene campaign, training women in proper dress, housekeeping, and childcare. Lady Laiad also founded a private women's organization, the Women's Cultural Club (WCC), in order to gain the active participation of elite women outside the government. The WCC had similar goals to the women's department, including encouraging proper homemaking and making women "more compatible partners of their husbands."[25] A branch of the club was set up in each province under the guidance of the wife of the provincial governor, giving its provincial associations semi-official status.[26] Although the official work of training professional social workers became the prerogative of Thammasat University in 1954, the associations continued to teach "modern practices" to poor and rural women as part of their philanthropic efforts.[27] Emblematic of the elites of the WCC were women like Dr. Pierra Veijabul, who was so key in the design and acceptance of the 1960 anti-prostitution law discussed in Chapter 2. In 1956 the WCC evolved into the National Council of Women of Thailand (NCWT), modelled after the International Council of Women, which took up many of the objectives of the WCC, including, as Darunee Tantiwiramanond and Shashi Pandey put it, promoting "better roles of wives and mothers within a nationalistic framework."[28] Today the NCWT is one of the largest women's organizations in Thailand, with strong participation from elite women and close association with government.[29] The institutionalization of women's role in national identity building provided a new route to political influence. It was a route still limited by its dependence upon women's role as wife and mother, but it also provided avenues into the new profession of social welfare work and gave some elite women a quasi-official role in governance – a role they could not easily achieve through the election process or careers in the bureaucracy.

The changes wrought by the upheavals of the 1960s and 1970s provided new opportunities for elite women to campaign for women's rights. Several new professional women's associations were formed during this period. Many of the reforms sought by these organizations aimed at removing discriminatory laws that blocked women's equal access to careers and legal equality. The Women Lawyers Association (WLA) began to push for women's equal treatment in the workforce, targeting those laws that limited the professional level a woman could attain in the military and bureaucracy. It also worked to correct employment practices that led to women factory workers being paid 30 percent less than men. Most important, however, the WLA sought to change those laws that affected married women's status. The WLA considered the divorce law in particular to be a key pillar in the maintenance of elite male sexual prerogative and the double sexual standard.[30] While the WLA's proposals to change the law were rejected by the Thanom-Praphat government, the 1973-6 period provided renewed opportunity for the WLA's lobbying efforts.[31] The National Assembly appointed in the wake of October 1973 put sixteen women into the 299-member assembly.[32] Prime Minister Sanya, an expert on family law, was also known to be sympathetic to the women's lobby. In 1974, his government enshrined equal rights for men and women in the new Constitution. Sanya announced: "Under the present social, economic and political conditions, as far as the status of women is concerned, the age of privilege of men is passing and the era of equality is approaching."[33]

Even in the democratic era, however, equality provisions continued to meet with only partial success, particularly in marital matters. While the women's lobby forced changes to the divorce law in 1976, these changes only went so far as to allow a woman to sue for divorce if she could prove that her husband and another woman were indeed living together as husband and wife. This clause severely limited the applicability of the new provision since most men remained resident with their wives while establishing separate homes for their mistresses. The new law also continued to encode male sexual privilege, framing a man's primary responsibility to his wife as financial rather than as a matter of loyalty or sexual responsibility.

In the postdemocratic era women made only gradual gains in equality laws. While the new 1977 Constitution did not include a gender equality clause, the government-enacted legislative changes, begun in 1976, included an act granting the right for "a woman to perform a legal act without her husband's consent if it concerns her own properties."[34] Women were also included in the fourth national development plan, which contained equal status provisions and an affirmative action plan for women in government.[35] Changes in regulations allowed women to assume diplomatic posts to foreign countries as well as senior administrative posts in private business and international agencies.[36]

While elite women's professional roles expanded, women continued to be discriminated against – again in ways that denote their "border-marking" roles. The importance of women's bodies to the Thai nation was reflected in several practices and regulations. Krannich and Krannich noted that "legal changes in the status of women have not necessarily resulted in corresponding changes in government personnel practices."[37] The Department of Public Welfare, for instance, which housed a large number of female bureaucrats, kept women out of superintendent positions in its project for resettling the landless poor. Male supervisors were concerned that women "must be kept out of settlements because of the physically demanding and dangerous conditions. After all, many settlements are located in remote and politically sensitive areas."[38] Similarly, running for political office remained plagued with difficulty for elite women whose sexual conduct – especially while campaigning in the far reaches of the country – was the object of constant speculation and rumour.[39]

Thus, the position of elite women remained wedded to their role, as wives and mothers, in the maintenance of culture and tradition. Prime Minister Sanya, like most elites, saw women's role in the household as being chief among her duties and necessary for family contentment.[40] Prime Minister

Kukrit's attitude towards women was also paternalistic. Kukrit endorsed the traditional beliefs about women's role, writing an article in the largest national newspaper (which he owned) in 1972 approving the Ten Oaths of the Women's Safety Pin Club, which include accepting male superiority; being "gentle, sweet and beautiful"; and playing the role of loving, supportive, and unquestioning wife.[41] Women's symbolic role in national culture is illuminated in Kukrit's most famous work of fiction. The central character of Kukrit's epic novel *Four Reigns*, a historical fiction set in the first half of the twentieth century, clearly demonstrates the virtues of a good wife. Ploi's devotion to her husband is unflinching; she even offers to allow him mistresses in his old age in order to rejuvenate him.[42] Ploi remains devoted to king and religion as well as to husband and family, and she watches with fear, and little understanding, as the old world of the monarchy, religion, and stately tradition passes away under a new modernized and Westernized regime marked by war, political struggles, and business concerns. Ploi clearly embodied Thai culture and Thai womanhood as defined by the royalist elite. While derided by student activists in the 1970s as a "mouthpiece of the Thai royalist elite" rather than the Thai people, the novel remained extremely popular, being reprinted many times, serialized in newspapers, and, in 1973, being turned into a television movie and a stage drama.[43]

Within this context, which involved celebrating women's roles as wife and mother while punishing any attempt to step outside them, many elite women championed conservative social values. Many women elites supported Kukrit's and Sanya's views of proper Thai womanhood. In its social outreach programs, the largest women's organization, the NCWT, encouraged all Thai women to adopt "proper Thai values."[44] Elite women generally exhibited more conservative attitudes towards social issues than did their male counterparts, and they were at least as conservative on political issues. Elite attitudes towards sexual morality were clearly reflected in the 1979 statement of the Committee for Promoting Moral Values of Thai Ladies, which endorsed the moral advice of the Law of the Three Seals: "A good woman should not let more than one man gain access to her body."[45] Rangson Prasertsri's research on women in the Parliament of 1979-83 showed that the only significant difference between men and women in Parliament was that the latter were somewhat more conservative than the former on social issues.[46] Half of the women in a survey of women in government and business also pointed to "moral and crime problems," or "incorrect social values" due to "improper culture,"as the major social problem facing Thailand.[47] Further, elite women demonstrated a commitment to the maintenance of traditional order and stability. They strongly supported the efforts of the Village Scouts and accepted the notion that military intervention might be needed in order to preserve stability. As

Abhinya argued, however, "if women are apparently apolitical, it is because they lack a stake in politics, and if women are conservative, it is because patriarchy has obliged them to acquire a stake in the traditional order."[48] Indeed, given the failure of attempts to achieve legal equality for women, it was by drawing upon their traditional and conservative role in promoting national culture that elite women were able to carve out a space for themselves in the political sphere. Elite women would be the ones to inculcate correct behaviour in other women.

This careful approach to women's organizing was undertaken not only by conservative women, but also by progressive elites who had supported the demands of the student movement and who looked to the international movement for women's rights and development to engender changes in Thai society. The liberal legal equality approach espoused by the early conferences for the United Nations Decade for Women appealed to progressive elite Thai women, who, while not considering themselves feminist, recognized that they shared with other women an experience of paternalism. The action plans adopted by the conferences and, ultimately, the development of the Convention for the Elimination of Discrimination against Women (CEDAW) provided elite Thai women with standardized tools to evaluate, and to set out objectives concerning, women's status in employment, education, marriage and family life, law, and so on. These international standards also provided Thai women with the legitimacy to lobby government for programs directed at raising women's status. Indeed, as a direct result of this process, in 1981 the Thai government established the National Commission for Women's Affairs (NCWA), which promotes CEDAW's (and other women's development) goals within Thailand.

While progressive elite women sought to use these tools to bring down the legal barriers that still faced women in 1970s Thailand, they understood that the radical protest approach of Western feminists would not work in their country. As one member of the Thai delegation to the 1975 Mexico meeting for the Decade for Women remembered:

> It was there I met these women from Australia and the US and they were very frightening, Germaine Greer and Betty Friedan. They were absolutely frightening, too aggressive. You see, we learned something ... These ladies, they won't go anywhere. They can do it in their countries but it won't work in our countries. And that has been the philosophy here in dealing with men, we have to have a velvet glove. Oh they were shouting and banging.[49]

Instead, within the Thai context, careful negotiation was required. As this delegate pointed out:

If you want to know about Thailand – and I consider myself a professional – I mean that women's affairs can be very delicate, because Thai men can be very clever, they don't antagonize us they flatter us, which is more dangerous than being aggressive. Which is what I've told them. During that time they have laughed in my face: "Oh, we think we have given everything to our women folk and all this and all that, why should women want to be free of all this?" I said, "it is because we ourselves are not perfect, we have to improve ourselves and we want to help the men to free from prejudices and narrow-mindedness." They said, "oh don't talk to her, she gives it back to us."[50]

This approach was echoed in the introduction of the Thai report to the 1980 Mid-Decade Copenhagen meeting, which, while emphasizing the need for change in attitudes towards the roles of the sexes, pointed out that, "in the past, Thai women have been admired for their subtlety. Thai women of the present day can learn something from this tactic so that equality and participation can be achieved harmoniously and happily."[51] The necessity of this tactic became clearer over the 1980s as non-governmental women's groups considered too critical of male behaviour were often labelled as Westernized and, therefore, as being without political legitimacy. Given the events of the mid-1970s, those advocating women's rights tried to present themselves to the established order as non-threatening. One female government member, for example, understood the dominant political discourse and knew she would have to deal with the fundamental conservatism of the Thai government and its continued fight to contain communism at the turn of the decade. As she described it:

I remember [that] to start one of the series [there were] seven ministries working together – interior, agriculture, industry, etc. They didn't think about it but they had been working with women a lot. And even the ministry of justice. Not to mention the PM. They say they can't work together – they're so individualistic. I said well let's try, using women's issues, because then people thought it was not dangerous, non partisan, non political. So it worked to our advantage. We asked for money, [they said] "okay, okay." Whereas they were worried about communist encroachment, not realizing it was really women who had a lot of influence in the family, whether or not their men become communists depending a lot on the women. But we who were working on this, we kept it very quiet. That's our technique, and you can put it in your [book] for the others to learn, because we have done rather well, not antagonizing the men but including them. But some of them are very clever, they caught on. Thanat Khoman, who was the minister of foreign affairs, said in a meeting that "[she] is a very dangerous lady."[52]

Foreign Minister Thanat's comment reflected the precarious position of those trying to get women's issues on the development agenda. The potential subversiveness of gender issues is clearly underlined. Elite women had to carefully balance their roles as wives, mothers, and defenders of culture with their desire to change women's status. Appealing to traditional culture – acting in a way considered Thai as opposed to Western, and treating men with kid gloves – allowed elite women access to power.

Elite women were willing and able to take advantage of this role in order to gain political influence. The period of Premocracy offered a new opportunity for elite women who sought to redress gender relations and to influence policy, particularly through supporting the drive for "socially relevant" development on the part of both the government and the international community. While more progressive elite women sought increasingly radical changes in gender relations – by, for instance, openly criticizing male sexual behaviour – they grounded their legitimacy in appeals to the maintenance of tradition and culture. This need to work within the hegemonic framework shaped elite responses to the issue of prostitution throughout the postrevolutionary period.

The Prostitution Problem and the Elite

The growing prostitution problem was already on the agenda of socially conscious elites in the 1970s. The attitude of the conservative elite towards prostitution is illustrated in Kukrit's 1954 short story about a prostitute. Phanni is a poor, rural, fatherless girl who becomes a domestic servant. She falls in love with, and is seduced by, the son of the household, thus bringing down upon her the wrath of his mother, her employer. In escaping this intolerable situation Phanni is sold into a brothel where she is well treated. Gradually, she comes to enjoy the life of a prostitute and determines to make her fortune by it. Phanni's greed, rather than her sexual activity, is the central theme in the story. As her greed grows, her character becomes less and less appealing. Kukrit paints her as falsely playing an innocent in order to entice more money out of her customers. At the same time, her lack of worldly sophistication is played up in the way she mangles both the Thai and English languages in her attempts to appeal to foreigners. Phanni is coarse and unrefined as well as grasping and greedy. Her difference from sophisticated, "modern yet modest" elite Thai women could not be more apparent. She fails both to maintain traditional behaviour and to negotiate the demands of the modern world. In the end, Phanni lies dead on a beach, ogled by the youths who find her. Kukrit dismisses his protagonist as unworthy even of escape in death; her body lives on as a sullied object: "Even after she had breathed her last, Phanni's body still aroused lust, and was still public property."[53] Not only does the story play on the Buddhist condemnation of lust and greed as the source of unhappiness, but it also emphasizes the fact that Phanni reached beyond her station in life: a country girl who goes to the city to make her fortune is doomed to failure. Country girls, the moral of the story seems to say, should stay where they belong rather than challenge the given order of things. Prostitution, in this fictive world, served as a punishment for those who would try to gain what they did not deserve. It also served as a reminder of the legitimacy of elite rule, of elites' inherent ability to properly control wealth and power. Elite attitudes, therefore, revealed a certain level of condemnation of, and disgust with, prostitute women. In this view, prostitute women were themselves to blame for their predicament in life; they were deserving of neither pity nor aid. Indeed, the predominant belief was that prostitute women were in some way mentally defective, lacking the natural attributes of proper Thai womanhood.

Some elite women, however, began to challenge the way women in prostitution were treated. Having fought against the way women were treated in marriage and divorce, a number of elite women understood only too well the problem of male sexual and political power and women's weaker position. While many continued to view prostitution itself as inevitable – the product of male sexual needs combined with the availability of morally loose women – they objected to allowing women in prostitution to suffer needlessly. Incidents of forced prostitution that reinforced their understanding of male power rather than female corruption as the underlying cause of prostitution had begun to appear in the press. In 1971, for example, the newspaper *Thai Rath* published a letter from a woman working as a prostitute in the Suan Mali Hotel in Bangkok. It told of the atrocious working conditions of the 220 (mostly Northern) women working there.[54] Newly formed elite women's organizations, including the Association for the Promotion of the Status of Women (APSW) and the Committee for the Promotion of the Welfare of Women (CPWW), took up the issue of prostitution in the early 1970s and pressed for legalization measures.[55]

For elite women at the time, legalization measures appeared to be the most sensible way to protect women in prostitution from harm as well as to protect society from the dangers of venereal disease – a very real threat for elite women themselves as their husbands assumed the privilege of unrestricted sexual activity. As one of the women involved in pushing for legalization measures recalled:

> I started attacking the problem by considering the fact that we should have just resolved the houses of ill-fame, we should go and rearrange the situation. That's what we thought. That these houses should be one, registered; two, there should be perhaps a police force that should go in and see whether someone was forced to come in and so forth, and then we should

have a social worker, and doctors to go in and take care [of the women]. If
a woman wants to be a prostitute she has to be taken care of.[56]

A number of elite women also felt that it was unfair for prostitute women
to suffer blame and misfortune when so many profited from the trade. One
woman involved in the debate remembered that there was concern over
the profiteering of the brothel owners. Many felt the owners should be
taxed to provide funds to take care of prostitute women.[57] Others, however,
were critical of the implied acceptance of prostitution that went with legalizing the trade. Member of Parliament (MP) Khunying Jintana Yossoontorn
argued that it was the dislocations of modernization that were to blame for
prostitution rather than the women themselves. She refused to endorse the
bill for legalization on the grounds that it would damage the image of Thai
women by making prostitution acceptable. Prostitution, she felt, needed to
be addressed by improving women's standard of living.[58] Among these few
women a more sympathetic attitude towards prostitute women was developing, one that recognized the unfairness of blaming them. Nonetheless,
most still felt that the registration of prostitutes would be in their own best
interest. While a bill for legalizing prostitution did make it through Parliament in 1974, indicating wide acceptance among politicians, it was not
promulgated before the dissolution of the House in 1975.[59]

By this time, the strength of the student movement's critique of prostitution was becoming apparent. Prostitution was increasingly viewed by students and elites alike as symbolic of the degrading effects of foreign culture
on the peasantry. For elite women, the postrevolutionary reconstruction
offered both an expanded role and legitimacy within national affairs as
they attempted to counteract foreign influence and to reintegrate peasant
women into a Thai identity. In the second half of the 1970s and into the
1980s prostitution was addressed through development programs rather
than through legislation, reflecting the hegemonic reconstruction project
of the period. On the advice of such women's organizations as the CPWW,
the Community Development Department of the Ministry of the Interior
launched a number of women's development programs, including a non-
formal education project for rural women in order to deter them from
entering prostitution.[60] Such development projects were part of the newly
forming hegemonic structure of the postrevolutionary period, and they
were meant to bring the countryside into the national project. The non-
formal education program, for instance, was clearly constructed to accord
with the Ministry of the Interior's interests in reforming peasant identity as
well as to reflect elite women's concern to promote tradition.

Elite interpretations of prostitution increasingly reflected this concern over
the loss of tradition. Women in prostitution, according to this interpretation,

had failed to have character and moral strength, had failed to uphold traditional values in the face of foreign influence. According to elite women, this failure could be corrected through elite guidance. Peasant women who were tempted to enter the prostitution industry needed to (re)learn traditional skills and become *good* workers in industries such as traditional crafts (which were part of an effort to market Thailand externally) or domestic services such as sewing and hairdressing. This understanding was expressed in 1977 by a professor of history at Thammasat University, Srisurang Poonthupya, who argued that the increase in prostitution resulted from foreign influence. Srisurang's representation of the problem powerfully resonated with the government's links between national identity, women, and the peasantry. She argued that American influence had created the new phenomena of "partners" (hostesses/prostitutes) and "a-go-go" dancers "who seem quite shameless to ordinary Thai women. They dress themselves in minute bikinis and dance suggestively on stage to make the men feel the need for prostitutes afterwards." According to Srisurang, Japanese influence had meant "unskilled women who like *easy money* will go to work in the 'massage parlour.'" European influence had resulted in "blue movies" and the phenomenon of the "exported Thai wife." Clearly drawing the distinction between elite protection of culture and peasant susceptibility to foreign influence, she argued: "The bad [foreign] influence causes a section of Thai women, especially the poor and the ignorant, to sink down to the lowest level. The Thai Government and the more fortunate Thai women realize the seriousness of the situation and are looking for a solution to the problem."[61]

For elite women, the answer lay in teaching lower-class and peasant women the traditional skills they appeared to have abandoned in the search for "easy money." That this was the function of the queen's endorsement of local handicrafts, as well as of the programs offered by such elite women's groups as the NCWT, was illustrated in the same paper:

> Girls from upcountry, who are often enticed by the *fun and easy life of the city* to become prostitutes, will be encouraged to *learn the traditional skill of their region*. For example, they learn how to weave or how to make the lacquerware. The native products are being promoted by Queen Sirikit as well as the Government. The personal care of the Queen who often visits them in their home makes these girls proud of their work and their region. In this way, it is hoped that the bad foreign influence will eventually lose its grip on Thai women.[62]

The "fun and easy life of the city" and "bad foreign influence" were juxtaposed to the "traditional skill of their region" and the "native products" promoted by the queen. Rural and national identity – evoked in the powerful symbolism of the queen – were fused in opposition to, and were seen as superior to, the foreign and urban. Such discursive renderings of women clearly indicates their proper place in rural/national identity. Such representations powerfully resonated with the government's reconstructions of peasant/national identity.

The CPWW was one of the elite women's groups that offered education and development programs to rural women. The content of the classes offered by the CPWW, the purpose of which was to prevent peasant women from turning to prostitution in the city, clearly reflects the concerns of the elite and the state to pacify the countryside by inculcating what they considered to be traditional Thai values. The courses taught "general knowledge, proper conduct and ability towards honest livelihood," which involved both skills and religious training, with a basic course in "sewing, handiwork, cooking, nutrition, hygiene, social manners, moral precepts and citizenship."[63] The leadership course for both the nuns and girls who had completed the basic course – and who were designated as village leaders and who would go on to work as instructors – included not only skills training, but also "Thai history and culture, comparative religions, the Thai language, and the concept of 'Land of Dharma and Prosperity.'"[64] The concept of the "Land of Dharma and Prosperity" was drawn from a larger government sponsored program of the same name which sought to promote Buddhist values in the villages. Philip Hirsch explains the Land of Dharma and Prosperity Program as being

> based on ideological training sessions that emphasize unity, individual virtue through abstinence from "*abayamuk*," the Buddhist vices of drink, gambling, and adultery. Model *Phaendin Tham Phaendin Thong* villages to be emulated are often villages where these vices used to be rampant and associated with violence but conversion of the *nakleng* (strongman) village head or *kamnan* to *Phaendin Tham Phaendin Thong* results in a new era of peace and harmony.[65]

Hirsch argues that the program is part of a totalizing discourse of the ideal Thai village designed to render the countryside "administrable" and, therefore, politically controllable by imposing particular ideas about the village. This discourse is also found in military schemes such as the 66/2523 policy, "which from 1980 set about the task of 'pacifying' the Thai countryside by political as well as military means, largely through a variety of initiatives that came under the rubric of rural development."[66] In this discourse: "*The* Thai village emerges as a particular physical, social, and administrative ideal toward which such programs aspire. The ideal is a subtle blend of, among others, populist and traditionalist ideas, administrative convenience and control, urban and modern values, and democratic forms."[67]

The Land of Dharma and Prosperity Program then, serves to impose the centre's concept of rurality on the countryside. It is "an attempt to impose a rural identity that at once incorporates Thainess and positions the village within a larger entity."[68] So positioned, the village and, therefore, the villagers are more easily controlled by the urban elite. Thus the program was clearly designed to bring the countryside into Thai national identity. The CPWW's adoption of this program into their training of rural women and girls indicates that the CPWW was attempting to bring peasant women under the control of the Thai state by ensuring their identification with "Thainess" and the protection of Thai culture.

Assessments of the CPWW's education program throughout the years (it ran until 1989) often pointed to the importance of this aspect of the program. The governor of Buriram (in the highly sensitive and poverty-stricken Northeast) reported that, in assessing the program in his area: "Of particular importance is [the program participants'] understanding of the need to preserve the Thai tradition and culture, shown by their gracious manner and courtesy, which is highly impressive." And in Loey (in the north), an area "threatened by Communist insurgency": "They also learned about hygiene, family planning and citizenship, to the gratification of government officials and villagers alike."[69] The continued usefulness of the courses for capitalist enterprise in the 1990s is made clear by requests such as one from a glove-making factory in Songkhla, which wanted to provide training to their employees.[70]

Elite women were able to gain political and social power by remoulding the character of peasant and lower-class women to properly reflect what was now deemed Thai culture and national identity. As well, these women needed to be inculcated with the attitudes appropriate to good workers and by being provided with a work ethic that would lead to national development and prosperity. Through the Village Scouts and other social retraining programs, elite women instructed peasant women in proper cultural values, the lack of which was understood to lead to improper behaviour, especially prostitution. In this way, elite women were able to resolve the tension between increasing their own social and political power and avoiding social disruption since their increased role was based precisely on keeping other women in line with tradition. Elite women were clearly being positioned as the only ones who could inject the needed inspiration for (proper) change.

The defence of the role of elite women, however, occurred not only within a national, but also within an international, context. In accordance with international development ideology, peasant women had to be brought into the modern era. As Abhinya argues, Thai women elites "regard technological underdevelopment in Thailand as arising from the lack of technological know-how and training from poverty and from psychological and personality handicaps such as laziness, uneconomical habits, lack of initiative, selfishness, and lack of moral standards."[71] Further, Abhinya points out that

> Thai women elites, and perhaps Thai elite groups generally, tend to assume that Thailand lacks both capital and will to originate economic progress, and that it is necessary to inject the inspiration for change and the ability to change from the outside. This assumption implies a need for an attempt to manipulate and change the socio-cultural characteristics of the people to fit the claimed norms of Western industrial societies.[72]

Elites like Prime Minister Thanin blamed the people's laziness for their poverty: "Not a small number of Thais are lazy. No one will deny this fact. This is a major cause of poverty in our land. A large number of us work on a day-to-day basis. If they earn more, they stop working; but, more, they also turn to drinking and gambling. When they earn extra income, they think it is time to celebrat[e]."[73] Here too elite women were constructed as the only possible source of development and modernity. Professor Srisurang argued that "the majority of women, especially in the lower class or in the rural area are still submissive to their husbands. They still feel it is the right thing and are quite happy in their condition. Only the educated women demand more rights and more active roles."[74] Thus, peasant women's activism, their participation in rural resistance, and their taking it upon themselves to capture the benefits of modernization for their families by migrating to Bangkok for work was dismissed by elite women as further proof of their "backwardness."

The Committee for the Promotion of the Welfare of Women (CPWW) reflected the same approach to peasant women. From its three-year study of prostitution it had concluded that the lack of education beyond *Prathom* (Level 6) left village girls unequipped with either skills or a "sense of direction with which to face the future" – a lack that left them open to becoming victims of circumstance and that led them into "undesirable" situations, particularly upon migrating to the cities. The first assessment of the program, which was made in 1972, stated: "In a short period of 3 months beautiful but shy Dokkamtai girls were *transformed from completely passive and unresponsive* persons into *alert and attractive* individuals, with good deportment and self-confidence. They also learned how to keep their homes neat and clean, how to cook, how to sew for their family needs, and how to dress appropriately for different occasions."[75]

The measure of success and development clearly reflects state and elite concerns about instilling Thai values – an instillation that is instigated by elite Thai women who convert the "passive and unresponsive" village girls into "self-confident" women who, at the same time, have "good deportment" (i.e., hold true to "Thai values"). Thus, elite Thai women, and through them peasant women, have successfully negotiated the opposition between (Western) modernization/development and Thai tradition.[76]

Girls who resisted such instruction were thought to be lazy. For instance, when village girls resisted the CPWW's program for domestic service training, the CPWW reported that "village girls are not interested in the course, considering it degrading to serve in the homes." It went on to insist that "many of the girls do not wish to work. They are accustomed to poverty and inertia."[77] However, as Mary Beth Mills points out,

> [domestic service] carries little aura of modernity (excluding new domestic technology) which is one reason why village women seek urban employment in the first place. In addition, servants' wages are generally lower than those for all other types of urban employment available to migrant women, even when free room and board are counted. A 1980 survey of Northeastern women working in Bangkok found a mean monthly income for domestic servants, including payment in kind, of 800 baht or US$32 (Pawadee 1982: 103). This compares to 1200 baht (US$48) per month for factory production workers (ibid).[78]

Women who needed to support their families and who were seeking some of the promise of the modern era would understandably find domestic service "degrading."[79] That they resisted elite attempts to contain them within an elite-designed rural lifestyle demonstrates their refusal of the strengthening grip of the elite on the peasantry.

The development agenda was championed not only by social conservatives, but also by progressive elite women. Progressive elites were critical of the top-down, security-driven development approach of conservatives and hoped instead to use the development agenda for social change. It was, of course, the strength of the development push generally, and Premocracy particularly, that they could absorb and contain both conservative and progressive agendas. Progressive elite women were thus able to gain a foothold in the corridors of power due to the changing imperatives of the Prem government, which sought more socially conscious development that would simultaneously uphold traditional Thai culture as defined by the state. Progressive women joined forces with the National Economic and Social Development Board (NESDB), the advisory body on development issues responsible for the five-year National Development Plans. A group within the NESDB was sympathetic to the need for socially relevant development, advocating the "basic-needs" approach of the International Labour Organization (ILO). This same group was able to obtain greater emphasis on rural poverty in the Fifth Development Plan (1982-6) and had supported non-governmental organization (NGO) initiatives, setting up a joint committee to promote cooperation between NGOs and government in 1981.[80] The board formed the National Commission on Women's Affairs (NCWA). With funding from the United States, a task force was put together to write a twenty-year women's development plan to integrate into the government's five-year plan and to present at the mid-decade conference in Copenhagen.[81] A number of progressive women who would remain key in women's organizing and advocacy for the coming decades were drawn onto the team.[82] The committee's report moved far away from standard celebratory publications of famous women in Thai history, or elite women's contributions, and made some remarkable demands, such as for men's increased responsibility for birth control and housework. The results of the preliminary study and seminar in 1978 were included in the report of the NCWA to the 1980 Copenhagen meeting and then further developed into a twenty-year women's development plan.

Elite women clearly understood the need for modernization as perceived by the government, and they could make use of their position as conduits between tradition and modernity. Elite women would lead the way for other Thai women to become developed and modernized without jeopardizing Thai culture. Both the preliminary and the long-term reports clearly reflect a liberal approach towards women in development – the need to bring women into the development process (envisioned as intensified production and generation of national wealth), which is associated with better living standards (health, education, income) and reduced social conflict (including reduced urban migration). Echoing elite beliefs about the abilities of the common people, the committee argued that women's efficiency needed to be increased, that women needed to be taught initiative (presumably by the elites) and how to overcome their traditional roles in order to fully contribute to greater production and national development. At the same time, however, the reports emphasized the importance of the maintenance of traditional moral and cultural values by, in fact, using women and development (particularly education) as instruments to ensure that women expand their role in cultural promotion. The initial report remarked that "existing society tends to prefer material values and is more interested in art works that violate moral and ethic[al] codes" and that the media, arts community, and parents have not sufficiently cultivated "cultural, ethical and moral codes." The report, therefore, recommended that women "combine their efforts to fight against emerging allurements and values that are detrimental to moral and ethic[al] codes"; that the government define guidelines for the promotion of the nation's cultural heritage, including the conservation of traditional "arts, handicrafts and folkways"; and that "women's groups and the government should carry out campaigns for the application of the principles of Buddhism's precepts in daily life."[83] The report also emphasized the importance of this task of the preservation of national identity, especially among those who "live in remote areas who are under influence of other cultures" – a clear reference to the need for women's cultural vigilance in the face of communist incursion.[84] Elite women, therefore, walked a careful line between tradition and modernity, maintaining national identity while modernizing society.

Prostitution was featured as an example of women's need for development and guidance. The report presented prostitute women as misled: "Many rural women are being led or persuaded to become prostitutes. This causes a prevalence of venereal diseases." Prostitution, the preliminary report continued, needed to be resolved by addressing both socio-economic problems and attitudes, for instance, through education, which "should inculcate more appropriate social values, and should be designed to enhance more employment opportunities." The report also stated that prostitution should be addressed through legal measures to suppress "the crime of forcing women to enter prostitution and being ill-treated," to control venereal disease, and to promote the development of occupations that yield higher income. The government "should devise appropriate measures and seriously enforce these measures to control various entertainment services."[85] The long-term development plan, however, went further, demanding that not only should there be heavier punishment for owners and procurers, but also that "criminal liability for prostitutes [should] be abolished and replaced by occupational training and health care."[86] Elite women, plagued by unfair divorce laws and limited in their professional and personal lives by gender constraints, resented the unfairness of laws that punished women for sexual misconduct but failed to punish men. Rather than seeking to legalize prostitution, therefore, they sought to criminalize male behaviour and to redress female behaviour through development and education measures as well as legal ones.

The call for cultural vigilance also allowed for a radical critique of male behaviour. The initial report argued that "necessary measures should be developed to improve social surroundings such as controls on the use of women pictures in advertisement to depict sex appeals [sic], as well as other sex based entertainments, etc." It also openly questioned the promotion of tourism "that draws tourists with carnal pleasures as attractions."[87] The final report went so far as to demand that the government curb "the entertainment activities offered by officials who welcome visiting government officials or guests by providing sexual services of local girls." Further, it pointed out that "traditional attitudes" that allow sexual licence to men and attribute inferiority to women

> have had the effect of inhibiting women's enthusiasm to develop themselves. When faced with family problems or economic pressure, therefore, some women are led to sell themselves into prostitution. Factors contributing to

such a plight are: lack of discipline, declining morals, sensual temptations, and examples of excesses which are far more abundant than reminders of moral conduct and human dignity in our modern society, apart from this, the attitude that prostitution is an "evil necessity" has also contributed to the continuing expansion of this profession.[88]

Elite women were thus able to critique male sexual privilege as a barrier to development. At the same time traditional women, who were thrown unprepared into the modern world, were doomed to end up in undesirable situations, such as prostitution. Development (particularly education), as overseen by elites, was the conduit between the traditional and the best of the modern.

Conclusion

Over the course of the 1970s and early 1980s elite women took on new importance in their roles as protectors and promoters of traditional Thai culture. The hegemonic project of reconstructing Thai identity in the countryside opened new paths to social power for elite women. Prostitution, which in the democracy revolution had come to be seen as symbolic of the decline, or lack, of national culture among peasant women, was now to be addressed through having the elite inculcate proper Thai values into peasant women. Such a role for elite women was strongly legitimated by the postrevolutionary government's national project of identity reconstruction. By associating themselves with this project, elite women gained new prominence and power. This same project was present in the language of development that was taken up by progressive elites. By appealing to the reconstruction project, women elites gained enough legitimacy to be able to make public criticism of the male sexual prerogative – a prerogative that was institutionalized in the divorce law so resented by elite women – and to change predominant attitudes towards prostitute women (who were viewed as mentally defective) so that they took into account an understanding of the economic and social conditions surrounding prostitution. Within the development paradigm, however, prostitute women became objects of governmental reform. Interpreted as unable or unwilling to help themselves, as incapable of coping with the changes wrought by rapid modernization, they were interpolated into development programs and plans as people in need of elite guidance and intervention rather than as social agents who deserved a voice in determining their own future.

4

Women's Groups and the Prostitution Question: Prostitution Law under Premocracy

In the 1980s Thailand underwent rapid economic growth and social change. The Prem Tinsulanonda (1980-8) government carefully managed this expansion by allowing the expression of social interests but controlling their potentially disruptive influence. Labour was repressed, while labour organizations were infiltrated to prevent union unrest. Non-governmental organizations (NGOs) were allowed to form but were strictly monitored by the military and security apparatus. Premocracy, the period of "guided democracy" under Prem, worked to absorb and neutralize potentially radical elements, providing a stable atmosphere for rapid economic growth despite severe repression.

The prostitution-linked tourism industry was a central contributor to this rapid growth. While prostitute women made demands for better working conditions and pay, their campaigns failed to find much support among the weakened labour unions or the newly formed non-governmental community. For the middle-class women's groups that came together in the aftermath of the 1976 crackdown, because the government and the tourism industry used women's bodies to attract greater profit, it seemed more important to draw attention to the exploitation of women through prostitution than to focus on prostitute women's labour rights. Prostitute women were often painted as innocent victims of greater forces. In the popular imagination this quickly translated into their being the victims of evil foreigners. Such portrayals strengthened rather than challenged the elite image of prostitute women as rural girls who required re-enculturation. The focus on women's victimization also resulted in government responses that increased controls over prostitute and lower-class or rural women rather than empowering them.

Premocracy, Politics, and Growth

The period of government under Prem marked the consolidation of a national hegemony based on a particular understanding of national identity and interest. As we saw in Chapter 3, national identity was anchored by the imagery of the idealized peasant and contented rural lifestyles. That imagery helped the nation to forget the upheavals and peasant resistances of the past, and it also worked to suppress consciousness of the exploitation of the peasantry that undergirded the economic miracle of the Prem period. While the national identity was based on images of bucolic bliss, the national interest was defined as rapid economic growth and modernization. To achieve this national interest the Prem government balanced the forces of military and business under the rubric of guided democracy – democracy that served the national interest of stability, security, and growth. While NGOs were allowed to form, they were closely monitored to ensure that they did not damage this national interest. Indeed, the military itself usurped many of the potentially radical critiques of the left-wing and emerging social movements by claiming that its role was to protect the national interest against the foreign interests served by urban capital.[1]

While the claim of national interest was used to keep the military's hold over politics and the business community, it was also used to ensure that labour and social organizations did not disrupt the return to a "good investment climate." Prem, himself, sought to balance business and military forces in order to achieve such a climate. He supported the technocrats within the bureaucracy – such as the National Economic and Social Development Board (NESDB) – in order to carefully manage the country's return to prosperity. At the same time, he allowed the military to maintain close control over democratic groups in order to ensure continued stability. The strikes and demonstrations against foreign economic control in the 1970s had taken their toll on foreign investment. Investment confidence returned only with the October 1976 coup, and, even then, the excessiveness of the Thanin regime kept much foreign investment at bay for fear of internal unrest. The new hegemony under General Kriangsak, and then Prem, restored investor confidence through its careful blend of the rubrics of growth and social justice. The fourth development plan (1977-81) balanced the concerns of business and the military and "urged foreign investment, but economic growth was to be tempered with 'social justice,' and there was an emphasis on decentralisation, employment, and income distribution."[2] Nonetheless, according to Pasuk Pongpaichit, the policies were "designed not to channel too much social investment into the countryside, not doing anything which would raise the expectations or the bargaining power of the farmers, not allowing the rural interests to develop any real political torque."[3] The plan marked the ascendancy of an export-oriented industrialization strategy as advocated by the World Bank and the International Monetary Fund. The economy grew quickly, reaching levels of 7 percent to 8 percent growth per year almost steadily from the late 1970s, hitting double digits in the late 1980s, and continuing to grow until the fiscal crisis of 1997. The economic policy of the 1980s was summed up in Deputy Prime Minister Boonchu's open-door policy, known as "Thailand Incorporated," wherein "Thais would retain control of economic policy-making, but ... there would be fewer restrictions on the movements of capital, both domestic and foreign."[4]

This spectacular rate in growth was, in large part, achieved through cheap labour. Labour was repressed by the government in order to provide a profitable investment climate for business. The strikes of the mid-1970s were often forcibly put down. The attack on striking Dusit Thani hotel workers in 1975 by right-wing thugs, and the smashing of women textile workers' picket lines in 1974, presaged the violent crackdown on students in 1976.[5] Benedict Anderson argues that perhaps the most important factor in encouraging the 1976 crackdown was that the Thai press presented the strikes of the mid-1970s as "'anti-national' in the sense that they scared away the foreign investors on whom the 'national economy' so depended."[6] In the 1980s the military completely co-opted the labour movement. The Labour Council of Thailand was headed by two men closely linked with the Internal Security Operation Command (ISOC) and who used the organization to support military bids for power.[7] In 1980 the *Bangkok Post* could boast:

> While the minimum daily rate in Bangkok is proposed to be 54 baht (US $2.20) in the North and North-east ... Thai workers have been found by many companies to be willing, dextrous, remarkably quick learners and conscientious, dependable workers ... Another point about Thai labour is that it is not militant. There have been many strikes, of course, but in general most disputes are settled amicably ... [L]abour leaders understand the present situation in the country and have decided that unity is more important than large wage increases.[8]

Under the Prem government, the labour leadership had been co-opted into working for "unity" and the national interest over and above workers' rights.

The social cost of such co-optation was high. As Kevin Hewison has written, despite changes in the early 1980s leading to the development of a more regularized relationship between capital and labour:

> The state does not encourage unionism, and the majority of workers remain outside the union movement, exploited and oppressed. Those unions which do exist are routinely infiltrated by the military. Child and "slave" labour, unsafe and unhealthy conditions in sweatshops, and subsistence wages remain facts of life for many of the working class.[9]

The NESDB reported in 1985 that 350,000 children, from eleven to fifteen years of age (among whom the girls outnumbered the boys), were working in factories and households, 15 percent of them in Bangkok. They were working more than eight hours per day for very little pay.[10] In 1985, Thailand's well known human rights advocate, lawyer Thongbai Thongpao, reported to the Regional Council on Human Rights in Asia that the minimum wage was insufficient for daily expenses, given the rising prices brought on by inflationary pressures. To make matters worse, "over sixty percent of workers still were not paid according to the minimum wage."[11] Young women were particularly affected by the labour conditions. Export manufacture had become the biggest industry, staffed mainly by young female labour amidst notoriously poor working conditions.[12]

It was within this context that young women were also finding work in the burgeoning service and tourism industry. Work in the tourism-oriented prostitution trade could be one of the better paid options for young women even if the conditions of work were often inhumane. Some government officials explicitly stated that the "entertainment" industry was a key part of Thailand's economic recovery:

> Within the next ten years, we have a need of money. Therefore I ask all governors to consider the natural scenery in your provinces, together with some forms of entertainment that some of you might consider disgusting and shameful because they are forms of sexual entertainment that attract tourists. Such forms of entertainment should not be prohibited if only because you are morally fastidious. Yet explicit obscenities that may lead to damaging moral consequence should be avoided within a reasonable limit. We must do this because we have to consider the jobs that will be created for the people.[13]

With their bodies, women were to serve the national interest in economic growth. This, however, brought them no status as workers with rights; rather, it emphasized the sacrifice of any social concerns in the service of economic growth.

The Prostitution-Tourism Industry

The tourism industry became a cornerstone of Thailand's economy in the 1980s. Building on the R&R industry of the 1960s and 1970s and following recommendations from the World Bank that touted tourism as the cure-all for Third World development, the government supported increased investment in tourism infrastructure through the establishment of the Tourism Authority of Thailand. The new agency aggressively marketed tourism, declaring official tourism years in 1980 and 1987, respectively. The profits from tourism leapt from 200 million baht in 1960 to over 37 billion baht in 1986.[14] According to Chris Dixon, tourism became the "single most important export policy success of the 1980-88 period, especially the 1987 Visit Thailand Year. By 1988 tourism accounted for approximately fifteen percent of income from the export of goods and services."[15]

A key ingredient in the success of the tourism enterprise was the marketing of sex. Truong argues that smaller operators in the tourism industry turned to marketing sexual services as a result of the favourable position that Thai investment policy granted to large-scale enterprises in the hotel industry. Small-scale operators had to find new ways to compete – ways that included partnerships with tour operators. In doing so, "a dearth of regulations ... allowed tour operators to include more and more services of a personal nature, in particular sexual services, to give their packages particular appeal."[16] Thus, advertisements for tours to Thailand often featured the availability of Thai women. International tourism agencies peppered their literature with references to the "exotic" women of Thailand. Sex-tour operators and marriage agencies were explicit in describing the sexual fantasies available with "passive," "adoring," and "willing" "sex slaves" in Thailand who could be had for a full night at very low costs. Unlike the "overbearing" and "demanding" women of Europe and North America, Thai women were, according to these advertisements, happy to serve. White men could live like kings in this exotic kingdom.[17] Such enticements were also alluded to in business magazines and advertisements proffered by official Thai organizations. Thai International Airline, for one, was known to use women's sexual allure in its advertising. One advertisement crooned: "Smooth as silk is a beautifully prepared meal served by a delicious hostess."[18]

As the demand for sexual services in the tourism industry grew, so did the supply of women from the increasingly impoverished rural areas seeking work in the urban centres. The tourism-centred sex industry provided one of the few better paid opportunities for peasant women whose other choice would be work in the poisonous and exploitative factories. While a 1974 police survey placed the number of women working in prostitution at approximately 400,000, by 1980 that number had reached somewhere between 500,000 and 700,000. In 1978 officials estimated that at least 248 hotels in Bangkok "hosted prostitution as a means to increase gross income."[19] The estimated numbers of women involved in the prostitution industry continued to climb throughout the 1980s, reaching, by one estimate, more than two million in the early 1990s.[20] The actual numbers involved, however, continue to be hotly debated by researchers and the media. The highest numbers most likely reflect increased anxiety over the incidence of prostitution rather than the actual incidence itself.

Working conditions within the sex sector, as in most industries, were often well below acceptable. Women working in bars and brothels handed over approximately half of all their earnings to bar owners and managers. Some bars established systems of fines and fees that punished workers for not conforming to house discipline. Protection money might also have to be paid to police. Some women were indebted by bar owners and/or procurers and were forced to work to pay off "debts" for being housed, fed, and/or transported. Indebted peasant families, particularly from the North, could also pressure daughters to undertake work in the sex sector and/or to send money home, with the result that the women themselves kept very little of their hard-earned cash. Less independent women could end up living in the bar or brothel, staying in crowded rooms and having minimal freedom. Other women worked fairly independently but still faced the often dangerous working conditions typical of the sex trade. Work hours could be extremely long, and the pressure to receive many customers in one night could be very intense. Women in the crowded tourist bars had to compete for the attentions of customers, talking a customer into buying as many drinks as possible from the bar and working hard to talk him into taking her "out" for the night by paying a fee to the bar. Once outside the confines of the bar, however, women also had to work very hard to avoid being bilked out of payment by an unfeeling client and/or being physically abused. Sexually transmitted diseases remained a constant threat, of which women may or may not have been aware (this is particularly true of HIV/AIDS, which came to public consciousness in Thailand only in the 1990s).

Prostitute women were by no means passive victims in this process, but their attempts to organize were quickly put down by the anti-labour government and were discouraged by those around them. The repression of labour meant that prostitute women had no allies to draw upon in the battle for improved working conditions. Although women were predominant in the new export industries that were fuelling the Thai "economic miracle," their activism had been brutally crushed in the 1970s. Siriporn Skrobanek argues that "rape as well as other forms of sexual harassment were employed to suppress the struggle of female labourers."[21] In keeping with the tenets of the national interest, attempts made by female labourers to organize in the 1980s were also quickly suppressed.

Nonetheless, prostitute women continued to demand better working conditions. In 1981, 100 masseuses at the Amarin Hotel in Bangkok staged a protest to argue their right to refuse clients.[22] In the same year, a strike by prostitutes held at the reformatory for women was broken up by police.[23] In 1984, a group of prostitute women formed the Night Girls Right Guard to fight for prostitutes' rights, but they were pressured to dissolve the organization both by families (who were afraid of the stigma) and by owners and police.[24] Another attempt to organize prostitute women in 1987 met the same fate. While individual prostitute women continued to resist management authority in their own ways (e.g., by taking money under the table, coming to work late, using toilets reserved for customers, etc.), organized action remained extremely difficult.[25] Besides the lack of support for labour rights, prostitute women also faced an increasingly violent trade run by the very people expected to enforce and uphold the law. The police, military, and politicians were well known to be involved in running the trade. Bar owners were known to keep a careful eye on the activities of the women and to exact payment for infractions of bar rules and discipline in order to ensure maximum profit.

The appeal to address prostitution was taken up, instead, by non-prostitute, middle-class, and elite organizations that, in the 1980s at least, tended to focus on the victimization of women in prostitution and trafficking rather than on the rights of sex workers. Such organizations worked within the narrow confines of Premocracy. Within this context, as we saw in Chapter 3, elite women's ability to appeal to the maintenance of tradition while promoting development enabled them to achieve the strongest voice on prostitution policy. But middle-class, non-governmental women's organizations also tried to draw attention to prostitution as a social problem. For these middle-class groups the growth in the prostitution trade was an exemplar of the sexual and economic exploitation of Thai women within a globalized economy. Thus the prostitute was an important symbol of the exploitation of the Third World. In their portrayal of women as victims rather than as agents, however, the early feminist campaigns tended to reinforce biases against prostitute women, portraying them as women who needed rescue and reform rather than as political actors in their own right.

New Women's Organizations and the Sex-Exploitation of Women

The new feminist NGOs that came together in the early 1980s were interested in addressing grassroots women's needs rather than, like traditional elite women's groups, "sacrificing for the nation." However, the new organizations still operated from middle-class sensibilities and at some distance from grassroots women.[26] In many senses the groups picked up where feminist organizing during the 1973-6 period had left off. The new women's groups viewed prostitution as the product of the globalization of the economy and the increasing dependence of Thailand on the tourist industry as well as on women's lower status and sexual exploitation within a male-dominated society. The new groups were able to draw upon the increasingly sophisticated political economy studies produced by European Marxism and by survivors of the left in Thailand, but cooperation with unions was difficult in light of the continuing anti-communism of the period and the sustained infiltration of unions themselves. The new women's groups were also unique in bringing to the forefront previously unspoken issues of rape and violence against women. In challenging gender norms, these women's groups were often accused of being Western, particularly when they were seen as too anti-male or critical, even by other NGOs.[27] This resistance to gender issues put women's groups at an uncomfortable distance from the growing non-governmental, social justice movement and hampered their efforts to gain acceptance for gendered critique. Women's groups had to work carefully within the parameters of both Premocracy and the gendered order.

In 1980 a newly formed group, Friends of Women (FOW), agreed to focus on education and relief for poor women through providing an information centre, a magazine, research, and legal counselling.[28] The group mainly included young, university-educated, middle-class women and a few men (including trade union worker and former student activist Suparb Passa-ong).[29] Before the group could fully establish itself, the issue of sex tourism was dropped in its lap by Japanese and Filipina women's organizations protesting Prime Minister Senko Suzuki's tour of the Association of South-East Asian Nations (ASEAN) countries in early 1981. Times had changed since the student protest of Japanese goods in the late 1960s however, and criticism of the Japanese prime minister was seen by the government, the elite, and business groups as threatening to Japanese investment in Thailand. FOW, along with several other NGOs, sent a letter to the Japanese prime minister outlining the problem of Japanese sex tours to Thailand. The letter did not attack the tourism industry per se, stating only that Japanese tourists should focus on Thailand's other attractions rather than on Thai women. It was careful not to "blame" Japanese men:

> True enough, Japanese male tourists do not constitute the sole factor for the rapid growth of the sex trade. In a male-dominated society, such as Thailand, women have limited opportunities to share economic and political power and are shamefully considered as "second class" citizens. Consequently in time of crisis, such as the present economic crisis, women are singled out as easy "sacrifices." Such sacrifices involve low wages and the marketing of their bodies as commodities.[30]

While the group clearly incorporated a reading of gendered and global economic inequality into their analysis of prostitution, cooperation with groups concerned with labour issues was difficult. Trade union representatives slowly left the group because they considered "women's issues" – such as the sex trade – to be distinct from "labour issues." Other members of FOW also felt uncomfortable with the union presence because the unions might be more concerned with workers' issues than women's rights and, one suspects, too closely associated with the radical politics of the 1970s.[31] The split reflected both the problems of the unhappy marriage of feminism and socialism and the growing illegitimacy of labour issues in 1980s Thailand. The split greatly hampered the possibility of establishing a labour rights approach to prostitution.

The new FOW organizers felt unprepared to deal with the growing complexity of the prostitution issue. The initial campaign had exposed the international sex tourism trade, and there was growing evidence of Thai women working overseas as prostitutes. Siriporn Skrobanek conducted further research into the condition of Thai women in the sex industry abroad. Siriporn's work situated prostitution (both of Thai women overseas and in Thailand) within the context of global capitalist exploitation of the Thai economy as the capitalist elite, both global and local, exploited the labour of poor Thai women through the sex tourism industry.[32] She argued that, within the globalized economy, Thai women are relegated to secondary status as workers, finding work in foreign countries in exploitative factory work, prostitution, or the "monopolized labour" of marriage. Siriporn linked the transnational exploitation of Thai women's sexuality and labour to the sexual division of labour and the maintenance of peripheral capitalism – as women's work generated profit for international capital at the same time as their remittances helped cushion the effects of lower pay in the periphery. Rural Thai families could depend upon their daughters' work overseas to supplement their incomes, and capitalist industry could therefore continue to underpay its workers. The impoverishment of the countryside during the 1960s pushed women into the urban labour market, where the prevailing gender ideology forced them to work in jobs that were based on assumptions about their "feminine" characteristics.[33] Thus, Thai women in prostitution at home and abroad, according to Siriporn, needed to be seen as part of the world system of capitalist patriarchy. Siriporn and a few women colleagues formed the Women's Information Centre (WIC) to inform women of the dangers of going to work abroad and to provide other information and counselling to poor women.[34] WIC eventually became part of an independent group known as the Foundation for Women (FFW). The FFW was also headed by Siriporn and focused upon issues of women's labour, prostitution, and violence against women.

While Siriporn's own work carefully pointed out that women in prostitution were not mere passive victims, in these early years of organizing the new women's groups tended to view prostitution as inherently wrong, as something no woman could possibly choose freely. Instead of seeing prostitute women as "bad girls" or "soft-headed," the new groups insisted that prostitute women were victims, forced into the trade through economic and sexual exploitation. While such a portrayal drew swift attention to the unfairness of the economic burden being foisted upon women during the Thai economic miracle as well as to the sexual power of men, it also tended to reinforce an understanding of women as inherently sexually passive. The victimist approach was much more acceptable within the political climate of the time than was any approach that granted agency to prostitute women. Much as in the 1960s, by clearly aligning themselves on the side of "good" women, these women's organizations hoped to maintain some legitimacy in a society that viewed their demands for women's rights as "foreign." In the early campaigns, for example, women's groups emphasized the exploitation of women within an illegal trade. As one organizer recalls:

> [At first] we always [saw] the bad side to this kind of business, that women have to serve as sex objects for money, [are] oppressed by men, [are] oppressed by brothel owners ... and it's illegal. So far as I remember, the campaign that we made at that time was – even some of the posters said [it] – that prostitution is illegal. The caption [was] to attract the public, so that the people can see "oh it is illegal, it's against the law, it's not good to [be] involved"[35]

Such campaigns served to reinforce the idea that prostitute women were involved in something that was harmful to society and themselves and that, therefore, they required punishment or reform.

It was not the groups' intention, however, to increase punitive measures against prostitute women. Research by concerned groups uncovered a pattern of deception and fraud with regard to the entry of women and girls into prostitution (e.g., agents who promised good work in the city only to drop women off at a brothel or parents who sold their daughters to agents in order to pay off a debt). Mistreatment and abuse by bar or brothel owners and pimps also appeared to be common. The groups worked to draw attention to the cases of women who had been forced into the trade. A 1982 seminar entitled Measures to Address Legal Measures Related to Prostitution estimated that 10 percent of the women working in prostitution had been deceived and forced into the trade.[36] One hundred and fifty representatives of study groups gathered at the police department on 9 March 1982 to submit a petition demanding action on cases of deception and coercion of women into prostitution; they also offered a four-page report on such cases.[37] A fire in a brothel in Phuket in 1984 that killed six young women brought national attention to the problem of force in prostitution.[38] The Phuket fire became a potent symbol of women's sexual victimization in the prostitution trade. The women were reported to have been unable to escape because they had been chained in their rooms or "chained to their beds." The practice of locking workers into the workplace was and is a fairly common labour practice in industrial and manufacturing sectors in Thailand (the same practice resulted in the deaths of scores of women in the Kader toy factory fire in 1993). The imagery of women chained to their beds, however, which was picked up in many international and feminist recountings of the fire, made the practices pertaining to prostitution appear to be particularly lurid and failed to link them with labour practices faced by Thai workers more generally. The emotive force of the Phuket deaths did help to draw attention to the prostitution issue. The women's groups held memorials, exhibitions, and workshops on the trafficking of women who were taken out of the rural areas and placed into the sex trade within urban centres both at home and abroad.[39]

The new women's groups also supported international efforts against trafficking in women, which condemned prostitution as a human rights abuse against women and portrayed women as victims of male sexual violence. An international conference in 1982 led by American radical feminist Kathleen Barry, and attended by Siriporn, highlighted the abuse, deceit, and violence that was assumed to be an inherent part of prostitution. While Thai women's groups, such as the FFW and the Global Alliance against Trafficking in Women, were in later years to distance themselves from Barry's organization, in these early years organizers shared Barry's views on the need to abolish prostitution as inherently exploitative of women. In later years a number of these organizations came to realize that prostitute women's own demands could not be met through an abolitionist stance.

Highlighting the victimization and abuse in prostitution was the growing evidence of the involvement of children in the Thai prostitution trade. A 1983 study completed after a raid on a Bangkok teahouse found a number of children between thirteen and fourteen years old.[40] The Social Welfare Department also reported an increase in the number of children (under the age of fifteen) among its charges, up from 2.5 percent in 1978 to 6.3 percent in 1981. Children were believed to be sold into prostitution by their parents for advances or to pay off debts. A number of children's protection groups were formed throughout the 1980s and 1990s as concern over the prostitution of children increased. Again, however, the numbers involved were often imprecise or misleading. In the early 1980s, for example, the fact that the majority of women in prostitution were found to be between the ages of sixteen and twenty-one was viewed as evidence of children's involvement, even though it was unclear how many of that number were actually under eighteen.[41] The conflation of children's exploitation in prostitution with women's involvement in prostitution, however, presented women *as* children, as being in need of protection and as unable to make their own choices.

Nonetheless the focus on the victimization, abuse, and exploitation of women was clearly necessary in order to draw attention to the negative impacts of the rapid economic growth under way in Thailand. It also sought to address complacent attitudes over male sexual privilege, as women's groups fought to have rape and child sexual abuse addressed as serious social issues. (At the time, marital rape was legal and the age of consent was set at thirteen years, so there was little protection from male spousal abuse or child abuse.)[42] The victimization focus undermined the portrayal of Thai women, in both domestic and foreign advertising, as easily available sexual playthings – a portrayal that increased the acceptability of the sexual harassment to which women were subject. It was particularly uncomfortable for upper- and middle-class, non-prostitute women who travelled overseas and often faced ridicule, discrimination, and harassment on the assumption that they, as Thai women, must be prostitutes.[43] Finally, of course, there were cases of deceit and force within the prostitution industry that required redress. In their understandable concern to address these issues, therefore, women's groups often emphasized women's victimization in prostitution rather than their agency. However, the generalization of worst case scenarios to the industry as a whole denied the possibility of women's agency in prostitution and encouraged protective and patronizing responses. Indeed, it finds a frightening echo in the language of sex tourism itself, wherein sex tourists justify their behaviour by portraying themselves as "sugar-daddies" who are providing an income for poor Thai girls.[44] Even if some analysts acknowledged that not all women were purely victims in this process, the tendency for active groups to focus only on cases of abuse and deceit meant that women's demands for workers' rights were ignored. Thus, portrayals of prostitution as inherently exploitative, along with demands for its abolition, undermined prostitutes' efforts to organize for better working conditions and pay.

Thus, in those early years, the focus on force and victimization in prostitution put some distance between prostitute women and feminist organizers. According to research carried out in the late 1970s by Pasuk Phongpaichit, prostitute women viewed themselves as workers and wage earners. Pasuk's work was one of the first in-depth studies of women and girls migrating into the Bangkok prostitution trade from the North and the Northeast. Her study challenged traditional understandings of the women as psychologically "unfit" and "sexually overactive" by clearly situating the trade within the uneven economic relationship between rural and urban Thailand. But her analysis left room for women's agency in the prostitution trade. She pointed to how lucrative the trade was relative to other available wage labour and insisted that, given limited opportunities, migration into prostitution had to be understood as an "entrepreneurial move": "[Prostitute women] were engaging in an entrepreneurial move designed to sustain the family units of a rural economy which was coming under increasing pressure. They did so because their accustomed position in that rural society allocated them a considerable responsibility for earning income to sustain the family."[45] Indeed, her initial interest in the subject had been piqued by a newspaper article in the late 1970s that related the story of a local post office running out of money with which to honour all the remittances to be paid to local families.[46]

Pasuk's study, however, was greeted with some criticism from those women's groups that felt that her analysis did not draw sufficient attention to the patriarchal culture that encouraged women's sexual service. As Pasuk saw it, however, it was perhaps more important, given the economic situation, that prostitute women at least not be subjected to the kind of cultural condemnation that occurred in other countries. She relates:

> But I was also criticised by people on the feminist side that I paid too much attention to the economic imperative ... [and] not enough attention to social factors. Often the argument I heard was there must be a social acceptance, that's why it has proliferated. And in a way there is to some extent. The way people cope with prostitution here is certainly different from, say, in India. And that's the difference. [But] a lot of people then from there jump to say that the proliferation must be explained by social/cultural factors. My argument is that I don't think in terms of numbers – the openness here yes, women don't have to be locked up – but in terms of numbers I doubt if we have more than in Indonesia or in terms of percentage than in India. But the openness is a plus, at least these girls still can have a relationship with their family, with whoever in their subculture. But in those societies where it is closed, the slave-like trade is much more pronounced. I think it is worse than here.[47]

At the same time, activists like Sukanya Hantrakul warned that the continued focus on forced prostitution was avoiding the larger cultural and economic place of prostitution in Thai society. Sukanya felt that the focus on the "evil foreigner," in both the anti-tourism and the anti-trafficking campaigns, had encouraged feelings of nationalistic machismo among men. At the same time it had neglected to address the larger issue of a "sexual culture" within which "sex is harnessed to an economic end," whether through marriage or prostitution.[48] Sukanya also felt that the focus on the victimization of women in prostitution failed to challenge the sexual role assigned to women. She pointed out that, in earlier years, by drawing a picture of

> innocent young girl[s] being "corrupted" and "destroyed" by males – local and foreign – the conservative reformer as well as the feminist succeeded

in arousing people's rage against male vice. Women were in turn urged to be more virtuous, obedient, [and] non-assertive especially in sexual relations. The anti-vice campaign had always come to mean the repression of the vicious woman and imposed guilt conscience on both the prostitute and her client and finally became nothing but a power instrument of certain agencies under different labels.[49]

By campaigning against prostitution, seen only as the sexual abuse of women, some feminists, according to Sukanya, were denying women the right to sexual activeness and, instead, reinforcing control over, and repression of, women's sexuality:

> Although a number of concerned people ranging from women's groups, social reformers, human rights advocates to the authorities, have shown their feelings of anxiety over forced and child prostitution, they could not help showing their feelings of repugnance toward the pervert woman who allows more than one man to gain access to her body. For them, as well as for more repressive moralists, the desire to protect innocent women is largely overshadowed by an impulsive wish to impose a certain moral code of conduct.[50]

Indeed, in these early years of women's organizing against prostitution, the focus on rural women's migration into prostitution either in urban centres or overseas reinforced the role of elites and government in protecting peasant women by disciplining them into proper cultural behaviour as well as proper sexual behaviour.

The campaigns against prostitution tended to draw from and reinforce the wider political discourse of the decline of rural Thai identity in the face of foreign influence, particularly in the form of increasing tourism. Even though the majority of the prostitution trade remained focused upon local brothels servicing local men, the public eye was firmly fixed upon the tourism trade serviced by rural women. This discourse around prostitute women reinforced the link between women's sexual purity and the purity of national identity, which echoed the critiques of the student movement. In the era of Premocracy and the reconstitution of national identity as rural identity, the focus was upon rural women's bodies and their protection. The rural roots of the women involved played a key part in underlining the innocence and victimization of women who could not be expected to have known any better. A Foundation for Women report linked, in particular, forced prostitution to rural women, stating that "[it] is mostly innocent, ignorant, young girls from rural areas who are lured into forced prostitution."[51] Again, within this discourse prostitute women's self-interpretations as workers and family wage earners are rendered mute, and their calls for better working conditions are rendered illegitimate, drowned out by calls for protective and rehabilitative measures that will restore village culture to its idealized form, mainly as envisioned by the urban middle and upper classes.

The focus upon the movement of women out of the country into the city, where they prostituted themselves to foreigners, reignited some of the defensive nationalism of the 1970s. The progressive newspaper the *Nation,* born in the 1970s, echoed the nationalism of the student movement in a political cartoon that depicted Japanese sex tourists as kamikaze pilots diving into a woman's breasts (representing Thailand's sex industry).[52] That the women entering the trade were rural women deepened the sense of cultural crisis because the peasantry was rapidly being established as the root of Thai culture through the efforts of the National Identity Board and other government and elite organizations.

While the mainstream media increasingly accepted that poverty was the driving factor behind prostitution, tourism and foreigners were understood to be the source of the demand. The fire in Phuket – a major tourist destination – also intensified the spotlight on the role of the tourism industry in prostitution. In the wake of the fire a panel on tourism and prostitution was held by the Friends of Women, the Women's Information Centre, the Child's Rights Protection Centre, and the Northern People's Relations Group. Panellists pointed to the growing tourism in the northern provinces, the decline of traditional ways of life, and the growth in prostitution. Propote Sritet of the Northern People's Relations Group argued: "Since tourism has reached the North, my part of the country, we can claim that there is practically no village void of girls in prostitution."[53] The follow-up article in the *Nation* reported that "tourism ... has altered the way of living of local people, especially the northerners. Girl prostitutes from the North have been the most popular and desirable, with the new trend favouring the hill-tribe girls."[54] The growing involvement of peripheral societies such as the hill tribes – who were widely viewed as a backward but colourful part of Thai culture – highlighted the threat to Thai nationhood.

Increasing this sense of national anxiety, numerous reports of Thai women working overseas as prostitutes also began to appear in the media. The concern over protecting women from foreigners was made clear in a 1978 law that required any foreign man proposing to marry a Thai woman to obtain an affidavit from his embassy stating his occupation and income, along with two letters of reference from referees living in his home country. The change was prompted by the growing concern over the practice of European men taking Thai women abroad as their wives but then forcing them to work in prostitution.[55] In 1977, the director of the Department of Social Welfare estimated that 1,000 Thai women were working in West Germany as prostitutes, either "voluntarily or involuntarily." The director's rescue of a deaf-mute woman who was lured to Germany with the promise of marriage and then forced into prostitution created a stir in the newspapers.[56] In December 1982, 154 Thai women were sent home from Singapore for practising prostitution there. The Department of Labour also estimated that 5,000 women were in Hong Kong working as prostitutes.[57] In the wake of the anti-sex tourism campaign against Japanese men, the number of Japanese tours had decreased; however, the number of women going to Japan had increased concomitantly. Another 5,000 Thai women were thought to be working as prostitutes in Japan by 1984. Thai women were also working in Switzerland, Germany, Greece, Cyprus, and the Middle East. Reports of the mistreatment of Thai women abroad and their growing numbers appeared frequently in the media during the early 1980s.[58] By 1984 the Parliamentary Social and Cultural Committee reported that, at approximately 16,000, Thailand had the region's highest number of overseas prostitutes.[59]

Official Response: Prostitution Law in the 1980s
With regard to women, the response of officials, as Sukanya Hantrakul had predicted, was protective (and restrictive). In the language of territorial border guarding, the director of the Phayao provincial primary education office (a province noted for the number of women involved in the Bangkok trade) established a project for the "defence and 'blockading' of northern women to prevent them from becoming prostitutes."[60] In 1982, changes were made to the Penal Code to increase the penalties for procurers of girls under the age of eighteen and to address the problem of trafficking by punishing those who used "deceitful means, threats, violence, unjust influence" or "coercion by any other means" to obtain a woman for an indecent act. The government's intent to control women rather than clients or procurers, however, was made clear in a 1982 Cabinet regulation that stated that if the foreign ministry suspected that a woman who had made a passport application had a "dishonest motive for travel," then the matter could be referred to the Department of Welfare, which would investigate the woman's status and records. Although the measure was seldom used, the potential for increased difficulties in obtaining a passport increased the cost of bribes and, therefore, the debts that women incurred to recruitment agents.[61]

The government also made special arrangements with foreign governments to prevent trafficking. Such measures effectively curtailed women's self-determination and freedom of movement, making them, "for their own good," objects of state control. For instance, the Thai government made arrangements with the Hong Kong government for both governments to screen Thai women travelling to Hong Kong. Several hundred Thai women were turned away from Hong Kong immigration or deported from that country each year during the early 1980s. That these border control measures primarily affected uneducated, lower-class, and peasant women is indicated in the sorts of differentiations made by the Singaporean government in weeding out "acceptable" (i.e., non-prostitute) and "unacceptable" Thai women on the basis of their English language skills.[62] Such standards obviously reflected a class-based differentiation between women who were likely to be educated (and, presumably, therefore capable of independence and "moral behaviour") and those who were not. For women who were already working overseas in prostitution, the restrictions on visas and the crackdowns on illegal migrants that came out of these campaigns meant that they were unable to visit home for fear that they would not be allowed to return to their country of work.[63]

In the mid-1980s, the Thai government also introduced a new bill on prostitution, which sought to increase punitive measures against pimps and procurers. Public support, particularly among women, for increased punishment of pimps and procurers had been on the rise since the Phuket fire.[64] The government's proposed bill was particularly harsh in dealing with owners and managers who were found to have children working as prostitutes, and, in an attempt to address the enslavement of women in the trade, it strengthened punishments for confinement for prostitution purposes.[65]

Harsher measures against pimps and procurers were unlikely to be of help to many prostitute women, however. Stronger criminal enforcement and greater police attention had traditionally worked to their detriment. In the early 1980s a series of brothel raids had been carried our to assuage public opinion. The raids had resulted in a number of women being arrested for prostitution while owners and procurers conveniently managed to escape.[66] Whenever stronger measures against prostitution were enforced, it usually resulted in harsher realities for prostitute women. Kickbacks to police officials increased costs to the brothel owners, who, in turn, penalized prostitute women. Brothel raids were often arranged in advance so that prostitute women who were no longer "profitable" could be arrested. Indeed, the fear of arrest kept many women from reporting abuse or deceit on the part of brothel owners and/or procurers, and it led them to cooperate with owners in order to avoid police interference.

While women's groups were generally pleased that the government was taking the matter of prostitution seriously, there was some hesitation over fully accepting these new measures. Elite women in the House found the continued criminalization of prostitute women unacceptable as long as men's role as clients continued to be ignored. Elite women's groups had begun to use their position as leaders in development to criticize male behaviour more openly. A 1985 conference hosted by the Girl Guides and the Association for the Promotion of the Status of Women (APSW) on "men's development for women's development" concluded: "A major cause of women's plight in the service sector is the attitude and conduct of men. Most evidently, the prostitution problem in Thailand has grown in proportion partly because there is a ready market for prostitutes, with men as the consumers. Moreover, trafficking of women and profiteering from this trade, coupled with lax enforcement of laws on prostitution, are often due to the activities of certain men." If men were the cause of the problem, therefore, then addressing male behaviour was a key part of the solution. As the report went on to state: "If one is to curb such problems, then one must address oneself to how men can help in finding solutions. The solutions depend not only upon a re-orientation of men's attitude and conduct as the consumers, but also a more responsible role on the part of men as the law enforcers."[67]

MP Dr. Yupha Udomsak went so far as to have the issue of punishment for clients raised in the House. Although she convinced the House Committee on Social and Cultural Affairs, which she chaired, that punishment for clients should be included in the new bill, she found that it was "unacceptable to the majority of the National Assembly because the overwhelming majority of MPs are men. Only thirteen are women."[68]

Unable to achieve some sort of fairness in punishment in the bill, Dr. Yupha and some fellow legislative members put forward a new bill: "Insofar as we cannot do anything to change the national economic situation, we may have to accept the existence of prostitution. Laws should be made, therefore, in order to protect them and render justice to them."[69] The proposed bill gave some recognition to the view that prostitute women were more victim than perpetrator and called for the abolition of the 1960 act, which viewed prostitutes as criminals. The bill provided that "prostitutes would not be harshly dealt with" as long as they were not "loitering with intent" or "soliciting." At the same time, a special investigative force would be established to inspect suspected brothels and to root out forced prostitution while providing medical aid to prostitute women.[70] While this alternative bill leaned more closely towards regulation – which also increased state intervention in the lives of prostitute women, often for the benefit of male clients rather than the women themselves – it also offered some recognition of the agency and independence of sex workers. Most important, the proposed bill also allowed women to choose whether or not they would go into rehabilitation. At a 1985 workshop attended by a number of NGOs as well as by Dr. Yupha, it was reported that most women charged with prostitution in Chiang Mai fled while awaiting trial not because of the 200 to 500 baht fine but, rather, because they were afraid of being sent to the rehabilitation centres whose disciplinary measures and behavioural training were greatly resented.[71]

The agency of prostitute women and their resentment of punitive and reformative measures was also slowly becoming clear to women's groups like the FFW. As we shall see in Chapter 7, as the restrictive measures against trafficking in women resulted in more prostitute women being sent home to Thailand from overseas, FFW members were faced with more and more migrant prostitute women who, rather than conforming to the role of victim, insisted upon returning to work overseas in order to pay off debts or to build up savings. Critics like Sukanya Hantrakul, who had sought out and talked to prostitute women over an extended period of time, continued to insist that what needed to be addressed was the working conditions of prostitution rather than prostitution per se and that the agency and independence of women in the sex trade needed to be recognized and supported. She even opposed measures to punish clients, arguing that "prostitutes must be decriminalized. Clients who have never been subject to legal punishment must remain to be so. It would be most repressive thing to see 'moral police' whose duty is to regulate people's sexuality by punishing both the woman and the man in the deal."[72] Only measures that supported prostitute women's own efforts to organize and demand better working conditions could, according to Sukanya, address the abuse women faced in the trade.

While other middle-class women were less supportive of prostitute women's rights per se, they were increasingly suspicious of the role of state officials in policing and protecting prostitute women. What had become blatantly obvious to women's groups in their research on the contours of the prostitution trade was the extent of the involvement of corrupt police and state officials. NGOs had begun to realize that the failure of police to take action despite the blatant operation of the industry and the extremely light penalties handed down to operators (in the rare cases when they were actually apprehended) was due less to official unconcern than to deep official involvement. By the mid-1980s reports of police corruption and collusion in the industry were becoming commonplace. After the Phuket fire, an article in the popular newspaper *Thai Rath* pointed out that, although the fact that the brothel kept women in confinement was well known to police, officials, and politicians, no arrests had been made before the fire because of police involvement with the brothel.[73] The *Nation* reported that officials responsible for hill-tribe development projects were involved in bringing young hill-tribe women into prostitution.[74] In 1983, allegations by women working in Greece that the Thai consulate general was involved in the trafficking of women were confirmed by the foreign ministry.[75] In 1982 the Women Lawyers Association took up a case that involved sixty-two young women who were rescued from a hotel after one of them sent a letter to the Crime Suppression Division saying that they were being held against their will. When the case was transferred to the police force in the district where the hotel was located, all the women were sent back to work. The association took over the case, with the result that several high-ranking police officers were transferred and five people (who were accused of holding the women) were prosecuted.[76]

Police themselves admitted that corruption on the force was a major problem. A police colonel who, in 1974, wrote a master's thesis on the prostitution problem admitted that police were involved in pimping women.[77] In a 1981 article in *Business in Thailand*, a police general also admitted that, "often, the police can't do anything because they know that the men behind the operation of some brothels are those whose pictures are frequently seen in the newspapers, attending big parties with top ranking policemen or government officials."[78] Another general, in a study entitled "The State Control of Prostitution," outlined four main "points of connivance" between police and the prostitution industry: first, many policemen have "some relationship with the owners of the establishments or in many cases are the owners of establishments themselves, honest policemen of lower rank have been prevented from doing their duty for fear of their superiors' harassment"; second, where arrests are made they involve the women rather than the operators; third, during investigations little attempt is made to search for the operators, and, if they are caught, then they can bribe police to release them; and, finally, whenever operators are arrested for forcing women into prostitution they "negotiate with the women and their families to pay compensation. Even though these are crimes against the public which cannot be settled by the individual parties, the police mediate and set these people free."[79] A senior police officer commented that the special force to inspect brothels suggested in the 1986 MPs' bill could itself end up as being just another group of "bloodsuckers."[80] In the face of such corruption, women's groups realized that only the decriminalization of prostitution (through the abrogation of the Prostitution Suppression Act) would "prevent brothel proprietors, pimps and corrupted policemen from intimidating women who are willing to take up this profession."[81]

In the end, however, even the small steps proposed in the alternative bill were defeated in the face of the opposition of the extremely conservative, and powerful, Ministry of the Interior. Throughout Prem's leadership, the ministry was headed by either a bureaucrat or a soldier as part of the prime minister's pact with the military.[82] While the ministry housed the newly reconstituted National Commission on Women's Development, it had continued to oppose equal employment measures for women in the bureaucracy and the military as constituting a "threat to national security."[83] Predictably, the national commission lacked independence and authority, and it backed the ministry's call for harsher penalization of procurers and pimps while increasing control over prostitute women by giving courts the power to remand prostitutes to rehabilitation rather than referring them to the Department of Public Welfare (let alone recognizing the agency of the women themselves).[84] The measure suggested that the ministry continued to see prostitutes as criminal offenders rather than as victims of economic or social forces.

The Cabinet version of the bill, in the style of Premocracy, reflected a compromise between the two drafts. The bill's preamble recognized that "prostitutes are not criminals" and that many were forced into prostitution by economic and social pressure in conjunction with a lack of education. Nonetheless, the bill provided for punishing prostitutes with fines and jail terms. It also extended the provision for rehabilitation to include private NGOs, which could establish vocational training centres, as well as the Department of Public Welfare.[85] Thus, despite growing evidence that police and officials were themselves deeply involved in the prostitution trade, the government continued to support increased state control over prostitute women.

Conclusion

In the aftermath of the 1970s the issue of workers' rights was extremely difficult to raise. The unions were infiltrated and weakened, and the government championed rapid growth at the expense of workers. While prostitute women made demands for better working conditions in the growing brothels and bars, their efforts were often ignored by the women's groups who sought, instead, to draw attention to the victimization of women in prostitution. Such a focus was an important counterweight to the language of government and tourism agencies, which presented Thai women as freely available sexual objects. However, it presented prostitute women in a light that strengthened the notion that they required re-education and guidance in order to maintain their cultural identity. In other words, such representations were easily co-opted within the Premocratic state, which sought to establish itself as a legitimate state that reflected social needs and inputs rather than as an authoritarian state and, in so doing, helped to consolidate elite power, particularly the power of elite women. The emphasis on force and victimization, particularly in relation to rural women and the thriving tourism industry, also drew upon, and reinforced, newly consolidated notions of national identity. Again, such representations invoked relations of power, specifically the restoration of a "proper Thai identity" to rural peasant women by elite women. While some women's organizations later came to argue for treating prostitution as a problem of labour conditions, within the context of the 1980s there was little or no political space to make such an argument. Unfortunately, this also meant that prostitute women's own political actions and demands were often ignored. In the end, despite growing reservations on the part of women's groups about the appropriateness of using criminal laws to combat prostitution, new criminal laws were proposed – laws that threatened prostitute women with greater instability and loss of control.

5
The Politics of Prostitution and the "New Man": The 1996 Prostitution Law, International Image, and Middle-Class Masculinity

In an ironic twist of fate, the new prostitution bill brought forward in 1986 by the Prem government (1980-8) died on the order papers in the face of the fractious politics of an increasingly corrupt legislature. Rapid economic growth had been accompanied by the rise of "unusually wealthy" political figures who were able to manipulate the system to their advantage, frequently frustrating the aspirations of the new middle class in the process. The political climate of the late 1980s and the 1990s was marked by this struggle between the corrupt "old politics" of a military-godfather alliance and the new forces of the middle class. International criticism and growing middle-class frustration with corruption in government leant weight to elite women's arguments for the need to reform male behaviour and attitudes. For years in Thailand the model of masculinity was the military man (head of the military-bureaucratic state) complemented by his beauty queen wife. This was illustrated most clearly in the Phibun-Sarit era of the 1940s and 1950s, but it continued among the elite into the current era. A new discourse of masculinity emerged in the 1990s, one that emphasized rational, technocratic governance and responsibility to family as opposed to the military discourse of male sexual prerogative and state power. This chapter analyzes the rise of this new discourse on masculinity, its link to concerns over international image, and its effects on prostitution policy.

The new discourse on masculinity emerged within the context of growing dissatisfaction with how the government was dealing with such problems as prostitution. Measures to combat prostitution had been continually defeated in the face of vested interests, government corruption, and government instability. As the middle class grew in size and economic power, it became more insistent upon efficient and rational government and increasingly resentful of corruption and the government's inability to deal with the problems of rapid modernization. It was also very sensitive to growing international concern over prostitution in Thailand, particularly the involvement of children in the sex trade and the threat of AIDS (which became apparent in the late 1980s). Failure to deal with these problems led to European Union and American threats to boycott Thai products as well as to a potential drop in tourist numbers as the AIDS threat grew. These concerns were articulated as the "image problem" in the 1990s, when the international community trained its spotlights on Thailand. This chapter draws upon a wide variety of sources – from American news magazines to websites – in order to provide a general picture of the kinds of representations of Thailand that were prevalent within the international arena.

The growth of a modern middle class occurred quickly in Thailand. In Bangkok, this class numbered nearly two million by 1986, up from 200,000 in 1960.[1] In the boom period beginning in 1986 their numbers increased even more rapidly. Pasuk estimates that the middle class accounted for over five million people by the end of the 1980s.[2] Increasingly, this urban middle class, with its dependence upon international business and global money markets, connected the need to project a rational and efficient image to economic survival in a globalized era. The "internationally embarrassing" aspect of various government failures was consistently played up in the press, signalling the importance attached to a good international reputation and the potentially disastrous economic results of not having one. The potential political repercussions were clear. As one Western diplomat argued in the wake of the economic collapse of 1997, "with the global markets voting no confidence in Thailand ... there is a sense that they can't afford a bunch of slimy politicians running the country anymore."[3]

The language of the image problem was deeply gendered. The Thai state was presented as not being properly masculine and, for this reason, as having failed to efficiently deal with its problems. Elites concerned with addressing the problem of prostitution were able to draw upon the image problem to argue that efficient and rational government required a change in male attitudes and behaviour. A properly masculine state, according to this view, must protect and provide for the (feminine) nation by protecting Thai culture and national identity (embodied in women) rather than selling them to foreigners or abusing them. A "new man" was needed to address Thailand's problems. This new man was considered to be a thoroughly modern Thai, dressed in a business suit rather than the *chut kharachakan*, or uniform of the military-bureaucracy. The new man was faithful to his wife and cared for his children. He applied rational, technocratic reason to governance rather than seeking self-enrichment or self-aggrandizement. This concern over image became powerful enough in the mid-1990s to allow for changes to the prostitution law, which, for the first time, would provide for the punishment of clients (in particular, for the clients of child prostitutes). Most important, the focus on children allowed for a discussion of men's roles as fathers. The 1990s was, however, a period of struggle over competing discourses of the state and masculinity.

Prostitution and the Image Problem

The protests against sex tourism in the early 1980s had brought both national and international attention to the militarized masculinity of the Thai state. Even as some state representatives sang the praises of sex tourism (as a development scheme) and many profited from it, there was awareness that Thailand's image was under fire. The out and out acceptance of prostitution, through such measures as registration, was continually avoided. Both in 1981 and in the aftermath of the Phuket fire, the registration of prostitutes was raised as a possible measure to address the prostitution problem, and both times it was rejected by the government.[4] Police representatives were in favour of registration, but the government was opposed to the idea because it would "damage the country's image."[5] A government/private subcommittee set up by the Prime Minister's Office in 1984 (staffed entirely by men) recommended a cordon sanitaire approach to prostitution. The committee proposed that the sex industry areas of Bangkok and Pattaya be demarcated as red-light zones controlled by the Bangkok Metropolitan Administration and Pattaya City along with the public health ministry's Department of Infectious Disease Control in order to ensure "peace, order and hygiene."[6] Tourism officials were more concerned, however, with protecting tourists, and so ensuring the continuation of the tourism industry, than in the well-being of prostitute women.

At the same time, the committee showed grave concern with the problem of Thailand's image and suggested addressing it by ensuring that officials "mention only good things about the country in seminars or meetings held abroad."[7] The team also proposed legal action against the "shameless promotion" of the tourism industry and the "unscrupulous entertainment places which offer sexual services and shows for tourists." As well, the committee report outlined such public relations measures as providing handouts to Thais travelling abroad (these would "carry[ ] suggestions about the duty of Thais to help promote their country's image") and meeting with the press to "point out the damage to Thailand caused by certain news reports which were blown out of proportion."[8]

In the 1990s, the government became increasingly sensitive to portrayals of Thailand and the Thai government in the international media. A few limited incidents drew a great deal of attention and concern because they were felt to reflect a wider image problem. In 1993, *Time* magazine ran an article on prostitution – complete with a cover photo of a Thai bar girl – that claimed there were some two million prostitutes in Thailand.[9] Also in 1993 there was the famous Longman's Dictionary Incident, in which the

entry "Bangkok" included the description: "a capital city with many prostitutes." A loud and indignant government protest led to its withdrawal. In
1995, however, a Microsoft CD-ROM encyclopaedia described Bangkok as
a "flesh trade centre where there was danger of contracting AIDS."[10] A BBC
production on Thailand identified the country as a dangerous tourist destination, particularly because of the threat of contracting AIDS.[11] The Thai
government was concerned about these representations not so much
because they led to the blatant global reproduction of sexist and racist
images of Thai women, or because they constituted vulgar generalizations
pertaining to Thai people; rather, it was concerned about these representations because they brought into question its ability to govern in a modern,
responsible way.

Indeed, representations of the prostitution problem in Thailand often
focused upon the Thai government's complicity in the sex trade and its
ineffectiveness in shutting it down. These representations echoed the colonial constructs of the Thai state as effeminate and as unable to rule in a
proper, responsible, and (gentle)manly manner. One of the articles that
appeared on the issue in 1991 in *Rolling Stone Magazine* made the connection between Thailand's "unmanly" attitude and the prostitution problem:
"Why is Thailand the whorehouse of the world? The 'land of smiles'
is famously *compliant,* a crossroads country that has survived and kept
its independence by *accommodating* itself to the vagaries of power."[12] The
language clearly suggests that Thailand (a monolithic entity) lacks the
strength to stand up for itself. It is weak, but worse, it is willing. Targeted
at an American audience that pictured the American government's role in
international relations as decisive and powerful, the message was one of
blaming the victims for their unmanly behaviour. Further, like the prostitutes themselves, the Thai state was pictured as having acquiesced in its
own powerlessness. The blame was squarely shifted onto the shoulders of
the Thai government and people, and the context of their choices – the
limitations they face within a globalized market, for instance – was rendered
invisible. This move effectively erased the imbalanced power relations
between Thailand and the developed West. Bishop and Robinson have documented many instances of international press coverage that follow the
same pattern of representation, always presenting Thailand and "the story"
of the sex trade in a decontextualized way so that "First World culpability
is reduced to deviant individual behaviour, effectively eliding broader
social analysis."[13] Such representations powerfully underwrite First World
intervention, with the other country appearing to require intervention for
its own good. By the early 1990s, the United Nations had placed Thailand
on a watch list for its failure to fully address child prostitution, and the
United States and the European Union threatened trade sanctions if policing efforts were not improved.[14]

In a familiar colonial construction of the masculinity of the other, Thai men were frequently characterized as sexually rapacious.[15] Again, such a representation placed the blame for the prostitution problem squarely on the shoulders of Thai culture. The author of the *Rolling Stone* piece claimed that Thailand was "committing sexual suicide" through its uncontrolled sexual activities. The author listed the percentages of Thai men who visited prostitutes, had sex with multiple partners, never used condoms, maintained minor wives, and so on.[16] There is a consistent sense of uncontrolled sexual excess, harking back to the colonial representations of Thailand as oversexed, dissolute, a repository of feminine excess (and potential infection). As Chris Lyttleton has also pointed out, there is an increasingly common construction of Thai manhood that is "predicated on images of unrestrained male libidinousness and sexual profligacy[, which] is considered a national character trait." Consider, for example, the frequent repetition of reports that at least 90 percent of Thai men go to prostitutes. In 1991 and 1992, reports to this effect appeared in the *New York Times,* the *Far Eastern Economic Review*, and *Newsweek*.[17] Such attention to Thai male behaviour underwrites the sense that Thai men are unable to care for their women and children and that they lack Western men's assumed ability to govern.[18]

The neocolonial construction of Thailand in the international debate over prostitution was also made apparent in the protests launched against child prostitution in Thailand. The *Don't!Buy!Thai!* website established in 1996 portrayed Thailand as reprobate and Thais as evil child traffickers. It counterposed the benefits of American justice to the obviously backward and evil Thai state. The site's homepage announced: "We want Americans to boycott anything made or manufactured in Thailand. Thailand sells its children like products. It traffics in the flesh of its own babies. For money. And the only thing that will stop it is the loss of money."[19] According to this representation, Americans, due to Thailand's moral backwardness, were justified in punishing Thais.

Tellingly, the site was supported by Dark Horse Comics, a company that had produced a comic book called *The Ultimate Evil*. In the comic, Batman does battle with a child sex-ring in a fictional Southeast Asian nation called "Ubon Khai."[20] Throughout the site's propaganda, Americans are pictured as the saviours of the innocent children of evil Thais. The Batman connection is no coincidence. The American public is called upon to be the world's "caped crusader," saving children from the inhumane (and monolithic) Thais. The imagery echoes the racially charged panic over the so-called White slave trade at the turn of the century. The warrior language is very clear: "If the formation of Don't! Buy! Thai! could be regarded as placing a gun to the country's collective head, the recent news of the downturn in the Thai economy and the resignation of Prime Minister Banharn [in October 1996] is confirmation that the gun is, in fact, loaded. And they know it."[21]

The Thai government protested both the comic and the website, emphasizing the Thai state's ability to respond to the problem of child prostitution. In a letter to the comic's author, Andrew Vachss, the Thai vice-consul in the United States wrote: "The Thai Government has not turned a blind eye to it but has instead tackled the problem with vigorous resolve."[22] In the same vein, the "Public Official Response" distributed to Thai embassies during the first administration of Prime Minister Chuan Leekpai (1992-5) stressed that it had been the Thai government that had raised awareness of, and drawn attention to, the problems of underage and migrant prostitution:

> The Thai Government has disseminated information relating to this illegal activity in order to make the public aware of this growing problem and *in no way has attempted any cover-up*. The Government has mounted a campaign and effort to redress the problem, which originated from sources outside the Thai Kingdom ... The foregoing problem *became public knowledge as a direct result of the campaign mounted by the Thai authorities to eradicate it*, especially the problem of child prostitution.[23]

Clearly, the government sought to establish its capacity and modernity in the eyes of the international audience.

The image question has become a very powerful political tool. Questioning the capacity and masculinity of the Thai state was considered to be an attack on the survival and security of the state. The government blamed Thai NGOs, which worked internationally to address the sex trade issue, for "damaging [the] Thai national image." The NGOs were accused of playing up the prostitution problem in order to increase their foreign support. The two million number quoted in *Time* magazine came under sustained attack as the product of a particular child rights group's attempt to obtain more foreign funding. This kind of dismissal of NGOs (i.e., as being foreign-backed and foreign-controlled) was common enough among the security-minded officials of the Thai state within the Ministry of the Interior and the Thai military. Similar views were also expressed by such "progressive" politicians as Prime Minister Chuan, who attacked groups working on issues of child prostitution and trafficking of women for "exaggerating the problems and tarnishing Thailand's image abroad."[24] By equalizing all threats to state image making as coming from "outsiders," those in power hoped to neutralize their effect (often making not so subtle references to the communist threat of the previous era). Chuan also made the connection between NGOs and foreign funders in 1993, when he said that NGOs had disseminated negative information about the country in order to obtain foreign aid. Chuan criticized the press for disseminating negative images and asked diplomats in the Asia Pacific region to try to improve Thailand's image by providing "accurate and clear explanations to the international media" in order to counter unfair representations.[25]

So seriously was the image problem taken that, in 1996, the Thai foreign ministry ordered an investigation into Thailand's image abroad. After several months of gathering media reports on Thailand from around the world the report was released in April 1997. The report found a mostly negative portrayal of Thailand in the foreign media. Prostitution figured largely in the coverage of Western media, and child prostitution was the key issue. The response from Prime Minister Chavalit Yongchaiyudh's secretary-general was anger that the foreign ministry would go so far as to publish this report.[26] When, in September 1996, during a non-confidence debate, the Thai-language daily *Matichon* published a report on foreign investors' views of the Thai government, a Cabinet member accused it of being a "traitor that is undermining the reputation of the country," saying further that "the press has gone too far in using the views of foreigners, let alone locals, to oust the Government."[27] Other coalition members were quick to distance themselves from Samak's comments. General Chavalit Yongchaiyudh (who became prime minister in 1996) approved the establishment of a media control committee to monitor press stories on Thailand. The press cried censorship, although it soon discovered that the activities of the committee consisted of a bank of computers with no one to monitor them.[28] Nonetheless, the representation of the Thai government by both foreign and local media has been a constant theme during the last two years of economic meltdown, as the government blames this coverage for "scaring away investors" by playing up certain stories about the government and the economy.[29]

In an effort to respond to the image problem, according to the *Bangkok Post* in 1994 the Tourism Authority of Thailand hired a private firm (for US$800,000) to polish Thailand's image.[30] The managing director of the firm argued that Thai hospitality might be misinterpreted by foreigners: "It is widely known that Thai women are unique for their hospitality and this may be regarded as submissive and easy by foreign cultures."[31] Of course, the use of Thai women to represent Thai hospitality remained. As the *Thai Development Newsletter* pointed out, a member of the House Standing Committee on Tourism said in 1994 that the country's image could be improved through a campaign promoting service and hospitality. A film starring Miss Thailand, entitled *Land of Smiles and Hospitality*, was to be filmed for CNN and STAR TV for overseas marketing of Thai tourism.[32]

International image had become a central concern of the government in the 1990s. Business and the middle class were globally linked, and foreign investment was a central part of the booming Thai economy. Thus, while few had spoken out against the military takeover in February 1991, which had been justified on the basis of the "unacceptable levels of corruption" in the Chatichai government, business and middle-class support began to fade when it became clear that the international markets were less than pleased with the move. The coup, however, had been initially acceptable to many because of the appointment of technocrat Anand Panyarachun, who promptly lived up to his reputation as a democrat by removing military figures from executive posts in state companies[33] and reforming the bureaucracy and political institutions. Anand also appointed "capable technocrats," who were considered progressive, to his Cabinet, including Thailand's famous population control advocate and public health expert Dr. Meechai Veeravaidhya and women's rights defender Dr. Saisuree Chutikul. Such steps were extremely appealing to a middle class that had grown tired of government corruption and ineptitude.

The New Middle Class, Government Capacity, and Local Notables
The 1980s were marked by growing corruption in parliamentary politics and by increasing dissatisfaction with this on the part of the urban middle class. Indeed, the rapidly changing balance of forces within Parliament ensured that the government's bill on prostitution would die on the order papers as, in 1986, yet another election was called. The bill's demise reflected the growing influence of "local notables" who profited from the prostitution industry. The dominant party, Social Action, headed by Kukrit Pramoj and originally an alliance between metropolitan business Boonchu) and liberal royalists (Kukrit), had dissolved into nine competing factions, thus reflecting the growing power of the local notables.[34] In what was to become a major and repetitive feature of Thai politics in the following decades, those factions that had not been awarded Cabinet seats manoeuvred to bring about the collapse of the government coalition and new elections.[35]

The local notables built their political influence through their links to military and police officials, their spectacular wealth, and the loyalty of the rural citizenry. They had made their wealth in illegal businesses such as smuggling, gambling, and prostitution, garnering protection by establishing connections with military and police officials both through bribery and family ties.[36] As well, military leaders had often recruited local businesspeople to build organizations like the Village Scouts in the anti-communist campaign, and this served to establish enduring ties of loyalty between rural villagers and local notables.[37] To the poor, the local notables offered a system of social support that they could not get from the official bureaucracy. One local notable explained:

People cannot rely on *kharatchakan* [bureaucrats]. *Kharatchakan* have only small salaries. But I have much and I can distribute much. Whenever I sit in the local *ran kafae* [coffee shop] people can come and consult with me. I am a man of the people already. I am more accessible than *kharatchakan*. On any matter where the *karatchakan* cannot help, I can. And I do it willingly and quickly. It's all very convenient for the people ... Most of what I do is about giving employment and improving the local facilities.[38]

Local notables gave money to the poor, sponsored weddings and funerals, and helped to find jobs for local people. In doing so they either garnered loyalty or enforced it when it was not forthcoming. Hired guns were used whenever their services were required, including when it came time to obtain parliamentary seats.[39] At first, local notables were content to fund the entry of business-based politicians into politics, using their connections to arrange vote-buying schemes. By the mid-1980s more and more local notables were entering the race themselves. Newspapers increasingly referred to *ittiphon meut* (dark influences) to suggest the involvement of local notables.[40]

The power of the local notables in Parliament increased in the 1986 Cabinet under the Democrats (led by Bangkok businessman Bichai Rattakun) when a number of provincial bosses were appointed to Cabinet while the Bangkok-based core of the party was largely ignored.[41] Their power increased further after the 1988 election, when Prem stepped aside as prime minister and General Chatichai Choonhavan (1988-91), leader of the *Chat Thai* (Thai Nation) Party, became the first elected prime minister since the "democracy period" of the 1970s. The Chatichai government, however, quickly became known as the "buffet Cabinet" for reaching new heights of *kin muang* (literally, eating the country, a common term for government and the kickbacks associated with it). The military overthrew the Chatichai government in February 1991 and installed Anand. Anand's moves to reform the bureaucracy and to move aside influential military men were widely applauded in Bangkok. After a general election in March 1992, however, General Suchinda reneged on his promise not to seek the prime ministership. In May, members of the Bangkok middle class took to the streets in protests. They were led by Chamrong Srimuang, the former mayor of Bangkok and leader of the newly founded Palang Dharma Party – a party devoted to anti-corruption and social progress. In the clashes between the military and the protesters at least fifty people were killed and many more went missing.[42] Dubbed the "cell-phone mob" for the prominent representation of businesspeople in the crowd, the protest showed that the middle class would no longer accept outright military rule, not so much on the principle of democracy (although this too was important to some) but, rather, because of the perceived need for rational and efficient government (which could not be provided by the military directly but which could be provided by such enlightened technocrats as Anand).

Increasingly, for the middle class, governance was about competence.[43] The middle class was rapidly growing weary of the shakedowns and the need for "connections" that blocked its path to professional and financial progress.[44] As one business writer noted concerning the new business class in Thailand:

> As "outsiders" in traditional business circles, it is in their interests for connections to play a decreasing role ... Many members of the middle class also believe that businesses based on individuals' ability are bound to be more effective than those based on personal connections. This conviction has been transposed from the business sector to the government. A company in which the managing director and executives are people of low administrative quality, brought in through rampant nepotism, would not last long in Thailand's competitive business sector. The Thai middle class is losing patience with a government similarly assembled.[45]

Significantly, it was the rural sector that appeared to be blocking the kinds of changes that the middle class wanted to see. The rural-military-dark influence connection was the subject of growing resentment by the urban middle class, which continued to see its political aspirations founder on the basis of rural voting power. Some 80 percent of the seats in the National Assembly were from the rural areas, and the vote-buying schemes and connections kept the "dark influences" and corrupt politicians in power. The middle class blamed the peasants, who sold their votes to these corrupt politicians, for the continuation of old-style politics and the failure to develop a modern, efficient public sector. May 1992 provided clear evidence that the urban middle class would no longer put up with either military rule or inefficient and corrupt government. It sought a reformed society and government that could address the growing problems (such as prostitution) associated with rapid modernization. Accordingly, the middle class – in line with elite women – challenged the military model of masculinity underlying the old style politics of the "devils" (as pro-military parties became known during the May 1992 incident). The new "angels" of democracy were also a new kind of man – efficient technocrats (like Anand) and morally upright generals (like Chamrong).

International Image and the New Man
Prostitution had become a central example of the kinds of masculine and political behaviour that were no longer acceptable (at least publically) to the new middle class. Progressive members of the middle class used the image question to challenge the government and press to make progress on

the prostitution problem. In 1996, the *Bangkok Post*'s own editorial argued that "turning the issue of prostitution in Thailand into that of national honour and dignity, the authorities have cleverly used nationalistic sentiments to their own advantage."[46] Another *Post* editorial emphasized that Thailand must get its "own house in order" and cease the "easy finger-pointing and foreigner-bashing that enable us to avert our eyes from the real problem." It pointed out that 60 percent of Thai men were revealed to have had sex with more than one partner "and that of those promiscuous men, *fewer than one-third* use[d] condoms." It argued further that: "If we are honest, we will admit that the vast majority of patrons of Thai brothels are Thai men ... These are difficult, searching questions that only Thai people – not foreign 'sex tourists'; not the editors of Longmans Dictionary – can and must answer."[47]

For the aspiring middle class, what was undermining the country's image – and, thereby, its economy – was the political ineptitude and corruption of political leaders. Vitit Muntarbhorn, a professor of law, children's rights activist (Special Rapporteur on the Sale of Children), and media commentator, was emblematic of this growing understanding. In his three-part series on Thailand's image abroad (published in the *Nation* in October 1996), he began by critiquing a political system dominated by military power and old-time pro-military politicians – a system that was stifling the development of a civilian, "transparent" political system. The military crackdown on pro-democracy demonstrators in May 1992, he argued, was a result of "the long-standing acquiescence or collusion between self-interested 'civilian' politicians and key military leaders."[48] May 1992 was, according to Vitit, a "blot" on Thailand's image.

Similarly, the post-election fiasco of 1996, during which government formation was stalled while coalition members fought over choice Cabinet seats, was decried as a shameful and embarrassing spectacle. In a *Bangkok Post* editorial (entitled "Enough Shame: End the Farce") written after the election, the editors commented:

> Thais are ashamed because of the foreign spotlights shining on the country. Our politicians are always the first to complain of harm to the country's image when we are criticised by foreigners. But their antics of the past week and their downright refusal to pick a new premier and get on with business is the worst image our nation can project ... It is natural that foreigners and their press are watching proceedings with interest. It is natural they are appalled by our politicians' actions.[49]

Part of this shame was linked explicitly to middle-class interests in an international, globalized world. The editors pointed out that Thais were particularly ashamed because the debacle had caused the postponement of an international meeting on the Growth Triangle as well as the cancellation of the foreign minister's appearance at the UN General Assembly annual meeting. In particular, the editors called on the Bangkok business class to demand that the government get on with the job of governing.

The new elite and middle class have drawn on Western images of masculinity to challenge old-style governance as representative of old-style masculinity. The political debate pitches the old man of Thai politics – the greedy, oversexed, military dictator – against the new man of the Thai middle class – the rational, efficient, and fatherly defender (rather than user) of women and protector of children. A political cartoon from the 1996 election clearly illustrated this characterization of the old order. It portrayed a bloated, lascivious General Chavalit as grasping after the prime ministership, which is depicted as a nubile young woman desperately trying to escape his clutches.[50] By contrast, Chuan, the usual champion of the middle class, was often depicted as a knight in shining armour. The construction clearly parallels the Western construction of self and other, where the self is a sexually-restrained, rational gentleman and the other an oversexed, uncontrolled savage.

The Chavalit cartoon hints that it is not only Chavalit's obvious greediness for the prime ministership that is unbecoming, but also his sexual rapaciousness. It reflects a changing consciousness among a certain segment of the middle class concerning proper male sexual behaviour, which is seen as consisting of monogamous marriage rather than (in contrast to elite men) of taking mistresses and minor wives and visiting prostitutes. It also links that behaviour to the ability to govern. In opposition to the political legitimation earlier leaders, such as Sarit, gained from their sexual exploits, political leaders in today's Thailand face approbation and loss of political acceptability, among the middle classes at least, for similar types of behaviour. Speculation about Chavalit's past wives and womanizing ways became a continuing theme in the media after his election, not only as titillating gossip, but also as a form of political criticism.[51] The appearance of one Cabinet minister's minor wife on the steps of Parliament demanding compensation provided further fodder for the media and opposition politicians.[52] Female politicians in the House accused two Cabinet ministers of maintaining former beauty queens as minor wives.[53] Chuan, on the other hand, appeared regularly on family outings with his wife and young son. The only other woman in Chuan's life upon whom the media reported was his mother, a market vendor in the South who was considered an icon of the "real Thai people."

Indeed, within the changing patterns of family life in the middle class, new expectations for male behaviour were formed. The "warm family" became a central theme in middle-class family values. Not reliant upon their children's labour (as are families in the rural areas), the middle-class family could adopt the values of extended and protected childhood. The discourse of men's role within the family was also changing. Increasingly, middle-class women were demanding adherence to monogamy.[54] The discourse of middle-class families emphasized the warm (monogamous, committed) family. Mary Packard Winkler has argued that monogamy – and the images of the warm family with a helpful committed husband – is becoming a "fashionable ideology" for the middle class.[55]

The Seventh National Development Plan (1992-6) was the first plan to formally recognise the importance of the family in maintaining social values. A National Committee for the Family was formed in 1991, and it produced television broadcasts, radio spots, and essay and art competitions promoting the family and, in particular, male roles as husbands and fathers. The latter roles encouraged men to "take a greater share of the household chores and responsibility for child-rearing, and to remain faithful to their wives. (Particularly in view of the spread of HIV/AIDS)."[56]

With the discovery of the rapid transmission of HIV among noncommercial heterosexual partners in the 1990s, the need for men to change their sexual behaviour became clear. In 1993, Dr. Weerasit Sitthitrai, deputy director of the Red Cross Programme on AIDS and an adviser to the Prime Minister's Office on AIDS during the Chuan administration, argued that addressing the AIDS problem in Thailand would require a complete change in attitudes and behaviour: "Men should look at buying sex as the most disgusting thing in the world. All about chauvinism and power."[57]

Favourite corruption fighter, police lieutenant General Seri Temiyavej (a champion to the new middle class for fighting corruption in the police force and battling local notables like Kamnan Pho) exemplify the new manhood. In an article in the *Nation,* Seri characterized his difference from his fellow officers: "I never accept bribes, gamble nor commit adultery like the others."[58] Changing attitudes among young men became apparent in a 1997 poll of nearly 4,000 men in their late teens and early twenties at high schools, vocational colleges, and universities. Over 60 percent of those polled felt that it was "not OK" to have sex with sex workers, although almost half of them had in fact done so. Fewer still, 29 percent, felt that it was "good to have your first sexual experience with sex workers, in order to learn about sex" – a common explanation for young men's visits to brothels.[59]

Men's role as fathers was also challenged by the warm family concept. In the middle-class media of 1990s Thailand, new men, like academic and popular television host Pinthong Chermsak, praised the joys of fatherhood,[60] and advertisers began to target "house-husbands" for the sale of household products.[61] New men have spearheaded the children's rights organizations (e.g., Vitit Muntarbhorn [Special Rapporteur on Child Slavery to the United Nations and head of Child Rights Asianet], Koson Srisang

[End Child Prostitution in Asian Tourism], Sanphasit Kumpraphan [Centre for the Protection of Children's Rights], Wanchai Roujanavong [Coalition to Fight against Child Exploitation], and Sompop Jantranka [Daughters Education Project]). Sanphasit was the subject of a full-page feature article in the *Bangkok Post* in September 1996. The article depicted him as a champion of children's rights and outlined his tireless work for children, his own commitment to wife and family, and his condemnation of men's behaviour: "Men's promiscuous behaviour can greatly damage a marriage. Some men say they can't control their sexual desire so they have to visit a brothel or sleep around." He admitted that when he accompanied friends to brothels as a youth, "I would wait for them outside. I felt too guilty to go in. If you don't even know a woman, why sleep with her just for sex?"[62] Many elite men, including the editor of *Krungthep Thurakij* (*Bangkok Business*), continued to defend traditional male sexual practices but obviously felt themselves to be under attack. In sympathy, the editor wrote in an open letter to Chavalit in the wake of his latest minor wife scandal: "Mr. Prime Minister you have my sympathy. I am, after all, a real Thai man like you sir."[63] In March 1993, the governor of Songkhla province in the south of Thailand suggested that prostitutes should be prevented from returning to their home villages during the Thai New Year celebrations so that they could participate in Songkhla's parade. They "would make the procession more colourful, particularly when they are in Hawaiian dress or scantily clad ... I think they will attract foreign tourists."[64]

Nonetheless the ideal of the new man continued to gain political force. The decision by the conservative middle-class newspaper, the *Bangkok Post*, to halve the size of the Trink column – a regular feature dealing with what's new in the sex-trade scene – attests to the fact that the new men are gradually gaining ground in the media world. Rather than seeking to reassert his masculinity in the face of Western hegemony through his possession of women, the new Thai man asserts a "technocratic," "controlled," and "rational" masculinity, which is seen to be the key to membership in international society.[65] Within this discourse, only such a man will resolve Thailand's political and economic problems and move the country into a new era of rational governance and prosperity as well as international respectability. This representation clearly sought to differentiate middle-class, new-style men from the Thai men characterized by the international press.

Prostitution Policy in the 1990s: Disciplining Men

The rejection of attempts to control prostitution through registration in the late 1980s and early 1990s reflected the growing strength of the new middle class. The issue of most concern to government was the rapid rate of HIV transmission. In the late 1980s and early 1990s the rapid spread of

HIV infection in Thailand grew to rates that threatened a national crisis. At a 1990 meeting, entitled The Role of Government and Non-government Organizations in Preventing and Correcting Sexual Business Service, Dr. Meechai quoted extremely high rates of HIV infection among prostitutes in the northern city of Chiang Rai, which was known for its high concentration of prostitutes. Fifty-six percent of the total population of prostitutes was infected with HIV, up from 35 percent in 1989 and from less than 1 percent in 1988.[66] Meechai, whose name has become synonymous with condoms in Thailand and who has mass public appeal, also supported the World Health Organization's estimate that some 300,000 Thais carried the AIDS virus and that, by the year 2000, two to four million Thais would be infected.[67] (In reality, by the year 2000 the number of people infected was well under one million thanks to a sustained AIDS prevention program.)

The response of senior officials within the Ministry of Public Health was to call for the arrest of infected prostitutes, who would be sent to the Department of Welfare's retraining program.[68] Green cards were to be issued to prostitutes who tested negative. Less senior officials within the ministry, however, exerted strong pressure for more education rather than for punitive measures. Even as the ministry moved towards cooperating with brothel owners to mount condom distribution campaigns, it also pushed for Draconian legislation that would empower public health officials to enter private homes to force AIDS victims to enter treatment and that would compel entertainment facilities to provide medical services for their employees and to ensure that their clients used protection. Any sex establishment that did not use condoms (which was assumed to be evidenced by whether or not its sex workers visited clinics) would be temporarily closed.[69] The proposed legislation was strongly opposed by Meechai as well as by a number of NGOs for its authoritarian measures. The bill targeted "promiscuous people" for enforced testing and pressured medical workers to reveal to the ministry the identities of those who tested positive. The NGO Coalition against AIDS also objected to the green card idea, arguing that it was ineffective, particularly since it would likely lead to a false sense of security among clients who would then become careless in their use of protection. The group working most closely with women in prostitution, Education Means Protection of Women Engaged in Recreation (EMPOWER), objected to targeting prostitute women rather than their clients.

The objections to the bill forced the ministry to put it to more extensive parliamentary debate, and it died on the order paper with the 1991 coup.[70] The rejection of the bill reflected a growing resistance to authoritarian government among the urban middle class. The *Nation* had run an editorial decrying the "'strong-man' approach to the spreading pandemic [which] is politically attractive because it gives officials the appearance of taking action. It also satisfies the sensitive moralities of those who still cling to the illusion that Aids [sic] affects only 'bad' or 'sexually promiscuous' people, who should be 'punished' for their depraved lifestyles."[71]

Indeed, former strongman Thanin Kraivixian had been a major supporter of the bill, arguing for "strict control of 'irresponsible' people such as prostitutes, homosexuals, drug addicts and prisoners."[72] Strong international criticism was also aimed at the government's measures. For example, an international conference on AIDS in Bangkok (where the bill was promoted by the Ministry of Public Health) was boycotted by many international delegates and the World Health Organization.[73]

The vocal criticism of the bill was evidence that, while the new middle class wanted decisive action on the prostitution problem, its was not willing to accept authoritarian measures or the abrogation of fundamental rights. The appointment of Anand by the coup makers quelled any fears that personal rights would be in fundamental jeopardy. Indeed, the Anand government took several progressive steps in ensuring and furthering women's rights.

The end of the Prem premiership, and the gradual loosening of the hold of the military over the government, reopened space for women's lobbying in 1989. MP Khunying Supatra Masdit (later minister to the Prime Minister's Office) was able to lobby the Chatichai government to restore the National Commission on Women's Affairs (NCWA), this time as a permanent advisory and coordinating body under the Prime Minister's Office, where it remains today.[74] On 25 February 1992 the law on citizenship was changed to grant equal rights to women and men with regard to transmitting Thai citizenship to their children.[75] The government also extended maternity leave in the public sector to sixty days (from thirty) with an optional extra thirty days.[76] The suggestion that parental leave be extended to men as well was rejected in Cabinet; however, one reporter found a "lukewarm" reaction to this idea among the men she interviewed.[77]

While the Anand administration proposed a legalization bill, there was little support for it from the new democratic forces. The bill would have provided legalization measures for prostitute women over the age of eighteen who worked voluntarily and had their health checked regularly. The bill's position reflected that of a number of elite women on the NCWA anti-prostitution committee, which, in the face of continuing male sexual prerogative, resistance to decriminalization or punishment of clients, and the growing AIDS threat, considered legalization the only viable alternative. However, as one participant in the Cabinet debate notes: "I said, well, in a way, *pachot* – okay if you want to do it, let's do it [legalization] – and suddenly General Chamrong and his group, the Buddhist people, said no, no this is a Buddhist country you cannot do that. We can't do that because that means you're approving it."[78] The legalization bill, however, was lost in September 1992 with the end of the Anand administration and the election of Chuan Leekpai to the prime ministership.

Advisors to the Chuan government began a campaign to reform prostitution law, particularly in order to protect children. In line with growing concern over these problems, the legalization bill had sought to enforce stronger measures against child and forced prostitution.[79] The NCWA also recommended that the Chuan government focus its efforts on child prostitution.

In 1990 the Centre for the Protection of Children's Rights announced that it estimated that there were two million prostitutes in Thailand, 800,000 of whom were children. While the government vehemently denied that the numbers were accurate, the announcement heightened public awareness of the child prostitution problem.[80] Reflecting this concern, the Seventh National Economic and Social Development Plan (1992-6) acknowledged some of the negative effects of economic growth. For example, it noted that child prostitution was caused by children being "influenced by improper social values with regard to consumption and sexual relationships. Many are forced or misled to serve business interests or the [sex] entertainment industry. Law enforcement, as well as measures to protect, prevent, guard and supervise children ... are not efficient."[81]

Also in 1992 the NCWA outlined its program to prevent prostitution, which included a "campaign to change undesirable sexual values and create sexual morality, especially to discourage men from visiting prostitutes" and to discourage parents from selling their children into prostitution.[82] The NCWA's campaign to stop men from visiting prostitutes included a poster competition, with the captions on the winning entries reading: "My father does not visit the prostitute" and "Father, please come home tonight. Please don't go to the prostitute."[83] Increasingly, the NCWA emphasized the failure of fathers to create a warm family as a cause of prostitution. In a 1995 article, government advisor Saisuree Chutikul emphasized that prostitution was caused by a number of interrelated factors, including the economic irresponsibility of fathers towards the family, divorce, and family violence, all of which led children to run away. She also blamed the "unrestricted sexual freedom" of so-called traditional male sexual behaviour.[84]

The NCWA made it clear that changing Thailand's international image would require reforming male behaviour in order to effectively address prostitution. In its 1994 report to the Beijing meeting, the NCWA pointed out that the continued operation of sex businesses had undermined the international image of the country. In its twenty-year plan for women's development, the NCWA declared: "Prostitution is seen as a part of Thai culture resulting in damages to reputation of the country and to the dignity of Thai women."[85] The child sex trade was deemed to be particularly damaging. In 1996 the NCWA introduced a National Policy and Plan of Action for the Prevention and Eradication of the Commercial Sexual Exploitation of Children: "Tolerating children in the commercial sex industry has made the country a target of attack from local and foreign media. It affects inter-country trade and plays a part in tarnishing the country's image. There has been condemnation from abroad, so much so that it has damaged the dignity of Thai women and Thailand."[86] In his final article on Thailand's image, Vitit Muntarbhorn similarly stressed that the lack of effective law enforcement concerning prostitution, particularly child prostitution, had resulted in Thailand's lack of credibility within the international arena.[87]

The NCWA's National Policy and Plan of Action for the Prevention and Eradication of the Commercial Sexual Exploitation of Children called the commercial sex business a "social crime detrimental of human value and dignity ... against decent morality, tradition" and the "people-focused" Eighth National Economic Plan. It outlined government policy, which included the total elimination of entry into the commercial sex business by children (of both sexes) under eighteen; the prohibition of luring, threats, exploitation, and acts of violence in the prostitution business; and the "imposition of punishment to all persons with a part in bringing children into the commercial sex industry and punishment to officials negligent in, or choosing to ignore, their duty to enforce compliance with relevant policies, laws, rules and regulations."[88] The plan was introduced at the 1996 World Congress against Commercial Sexual Exploitation of Children as evidence of Thailand's commitment to ending the child sex trade.

Accordingly, both Chuan's and his successor's Cabinet introduced new legislation to combat prostitution that would include punishment for clients of children involved in the sex trade. Chuan was widely viewed as a clean politician and as a new man for a new age, and he was widely trusted by the urban middle class and progressive elites. Complaints from the United Nations and from the US Congress over Thailand's failure to address child labour and child prostitution pushed Chuan's announcement (in November 1992) of a crackdown on child prostitution. Provincial governors were told that they must "take responsibility and give special attention to child prostitution and child labour abuse." That same day a woman who had escaped a brothel in Songkhla and sought protection from the police was found murdered in the town hall. Initial reports that the woman was actually under eighteen were used to support the government's anti-child prostitution campaign.[89] Very soon, however, it became clear that not only was the "girl" a "woman," but also that the negligence of welfare officials and police had led to her murder.[90] In an attempt to restore the government's credibility, Chuan's minister of the interior – and future prime minister – General Chavalit Yongchaiyudh announced that he wanted all

brothels closed down within the next two months.[91] The campaign, however, was not nearly as successful as was promised, and the government
came under heavy fire for its failure to carry it out. The central weakness
of the Chuan administration was often cited as Chuan's being too slow
to bring about the reforms demanded by the middle class. As one prominent scholar noted, the Chuan Cabinet failed to "develop their reputation
as efficient administrators."[92] The importance of such a reputation was
becoming clear both within national and international circles.

Chuan's government was brought down in 1995 after a scandal erupted
over a land reform scheme in Phuket – the resort town and key prostitution
venue – that was designed to divide land resources more equitably. It was
soon discovered, however, that, under the scheme, the wealthy husband of
the local Democrat MP, and secretary to the minister in charge of land
reform, was the recipient of some of the land.[93] The scandal merely built on
previous disappointments, including Chuan's own deputy finance minister, Boonchu Trithong, being caught hosting an end-of-Parliamentary-
session party that included providing prostitutes to fellow MPs.[94] Chuan's
efforts to establish an effective special task force to combat prostitution
was rife with problems. In a July 1993 raid in Bangkok, the Crime Suppression Division (CSD) arrested eighty-nine girls and women holding fake
Thai identity cards, and it discovered account books listing protection pay-
ments to Thai government officials (including special police task units,
immigration officials, and the CSD policemen).[95] Once again, with the
proroguing of Parliament new prostitution legislation died on the order
papers.

The results of the election appeared to be a disaster for middle-class aspirations. In 1995 the Chat Thai Party, headed by the godfather of Suphan
Buri, Banharn Silpa-archa, formed a coalition government. It was believed
that "much more money was used in this election than in previous ones"
and that there was a good deal of party switching by MPs attempting to
garner Cabinet seats.[96]

While the Bangkok-based middle class was sorely disappointed with the
election of the Banharn government, the pressure for the reform of prostitution law and, with it, male behaviour was strong enough that the anti-
prostitution legislation was reintroduced. Concern to present a modern
and rational image to the rest of the world led to high support for the bill
even within the Banharn Cabinet (an unstable coalition of local notables,
business, and former military people), despite its links to the old ways of
governance. Some argue that, in fact, the bill was passed during this government's tenure because the Cabinet needed, above all, to prove itself in
light of the credibility crisis of a government rife with corruption and facing divisions within its own ranks.[97] Indeed, the Banharn government was

the first to consider legislation that would have allowed a woman to obtain a divorce if her husband had committed adultery and to file suit to seek compensation from unfaithful fiancées and adulterous husbands.[98] It clearly sought to show its commitment to fairer gender relations.

Nonetheless, debate over the prostitution bill was extensive, most significantly because, for the first time, it provided for the punishment of clients of prostitutes under the age of eighteen. The debate pitted the old guard of masculine privilege against the reformists. Shepherding the bill through the House in 1996 took the concerted effort of female parliamentarians and advisors. Female MPs (who numbered only twenty-four in the 391-seat House) from the anti-corruption party Palang Dharma (Sansanee Nakpong) and the Democrat Party (Laddawan Wongsriwong) initiated drafts of the bill in the House. The importance of passing the bill was emphasized to new female parliamentarians at a reception given by the NCWT. MPs such as Kanchana Silpa-archa, daughter of then PM Banharn Silpa-archa, promised her support.[99] The focus on the protection of children gave elite women within the House unassailable ground from which to defend the bill. The protection of children is an important basis of legitimacy for female politicians – one to which Kanchana made frequent reference when she was dismissed as being in politics merely to support her father. Nonetheless, supporters of the bill faced recalcitrance from some members of the House. Commenting on the length of time that it took to get the bill through, one participant pointed out that it was

> not only the opposition, but the procedure, we changed the government so often, also the delay in process of getting from the Office to the Parliament to the King, that takes a long time. Then there are substantive issues, particularly, do you want to arrest the customers? Because most men will say, some said to me, you'll have to build all sorts of prisons because there might be 1.6 million men who are being arrested. But we're saying eighteen below, sometimes people don't understand that, that our priority group is eighteen below.[100]

Clearly, the focus on minors and clients of minors was a key component in building acceptance for the bill. Even then, the bill was delayed for some time in the joint committee as MPs argued for lowering the penalties for clients.[101] One male MP, who was an executive on the committee, said: "A lot of male MPs were shocked to learn of the harsher punishment to be imposed."[102] Other proponents, like Thongbai Thongpao, a well known human rights lawyer and media commentator, appealed to the character of the men in the House to defend the bill. In his weekly column he assured his audience that the bill would surely be passed despite the delays over the section penalizing clients and despite the male domination of the House because, "after all, these male MPs have morals and education. Most of them are Buddhists who also fear Aids." Thongbai argued further that, "for the sake of righteousness, virtues, humanity, principles and the pride of the nation[,] the new prostitution suppression draft ought to be passed" because Thai people are "notorious for prostitution all over the world."[103]

Some committee members argued strenuously for the higher penalties, pointing out that the bill targeted activities inside brothels only (although the definition of brothel, or "place for prostitution," has been expanded to include any places or establishments "used for contact between prostitutes and clients").[104] They were warned, however, that the bill would face veto in the House if the punishments were considered "too stern."[105] Although, as some MPs pointed out, the Penal Code already contained harsher penalties, others insisted that real change in attitudes would only come about when the prostitution bill was modified to bring it into line with that code. In the Senate, proponents of the bill faced male senators who argued that "sex was like food" for men – a basic requirement. One female defender of the bill answered quickly: "Don't you think we are hungry too? You should respect your wife and daughter ... also the women of Thailand likewise."[106] Nonetheless, the penalties were eventually lowered (to two to six years plus a 40,000 to 120,000 baht fine for obtaining the services of children under fifteen) in order to win wider support.[107] Thus the penalty for soliciting the services of a child prostitute remains lighter than the prison penalty for statutory rape.[108] Yet, for the first time, clients were to be punished for their role in prostitution.

Conclusion

The debate over what to do about the prostitution problem was part of a much larger debate about the shape of Thai society and statehood. By linking the question of prostitution to the failure of the state – and of the men who ran it – to modernize, to become efficient, and to protect women and children, proponents of changes to prostitution legislation were able to garner considerable support. In particular, the growth of a middle class whose interest lay in having Thailand seen as a modernized, globalized nation lent support to the campaign to reform masculine behaviour. Prostitution became increasingly viewed as the result of old-style Thai politics that were frustrating to the aspirations of the middle class. The middle class demanded a new kind of state and a new kind of man to run it. Only this, it argued, would lead Thailand into a new era of prosperity and international respectability. The discourse of the new manhood, however, clearly functioned to establish middle-class authority – both against the old-style military politicians/local notables and male peasants/male poor, who were not considered capable of adopting this new form of rational, modern masculinity. And, while middle-class women stand to benefit from the new model of masculinity that insists upon monogamy for men, they find themselves continuing to be responsible for the maintenance of tradition and morality. As we shall see in the next chapter, for prostitute women this has meant continued pressure to conform to particular standards of traditional female behaviour.

6

The Middle Class and the Material Girl: The 1996 Prostitution Law and the Disciplining of Peasant Women

The achievement of the 1996 Prostitution Prohibition Law was widely celebrated by its champions as a sign of the Thai state's commitment to addressing the prostitution problem and to reforming social attitudes, particularly male attitudes, towards women and children. It quickly became clear, however, that the price of this new measure to discipline men into proper modern, masculine behaviour was increased control and discipline over the peasant population and prostitute women themselves. The disciplinary measures laid out by the new legislation would have their greatest impact on lower-class men and on prostitute women, who continued to be penalized for engaging in prostitution.

The contradictory impact of the new law was largely the result of the changing attitudes of the new middle class. While this class increasingly championed the values of modernity – including human rights, democracy, and increased gender equality – it also sought to ensure the continuation of traditional Thai identity. It was clear, however, that the middle class did not see its own role as one of maintaining traditional identity; rather, this task fell, once again, to the peasantry and to women. For the middle class, prostitution was the result of the failure of these groups to maintain this "true" identity. Peasants and women had adopted the values of consumerism in opposition to the ideals of Buddhism and bucolic village life. The search for "easy money" and "nice things" had led country girls and women into a life of prostitution. Prostitute women, therefore, still needed to be disciplined into "correct" behaviour.

While this concern about the role of rising consumerism in leading women into prostitution was widely shared by the media, government, and NGOs, some women's organizations pointed to the economic exploitation of women and the poverty of the rural areas as the underlying causes of prostitution. Over the course of the 1980s these women's groups had begun to recognize the importance of addressing the working conditions surrounding prostitution rather than seeking to abolish prostitution itself. The punishment of prostitute women, they argued, only led to further exploitation and abuse of women who, rather than being "bad girls," simply represented a "new form of wage-worker" struggling to survive within an impoverished economy. The media and middle class, however, continued to present prostitute women as undeserving and greedy consumers rather than as women working to support their families. The legislation's penalization of prostitute women reflected this belief. This chapter explores how a nascent approach to prostitution as part of a politics of work was overridden by middle-class concerns over rising consumerism and the loss of traditional culture. These concerns justified the continued criminalization of prostitution.

Women's NGOs and Prostitution in the 1990s: Towards a Politics of Work

In the early 1980s, within a context of growing awareness of a global prostitution industry staffed by rural Thai girls, feminist activists in Thailand emphasized that many of these girls and women were unaware that they were going into the prostitution trade when they accepted offers from agents to work in the city or overseas. In doing this, feminists drew attention to the abuse and deceit suffered by many young women in the prostitution trade. By emphasizing that these girls were victims rather than bad girls, activists hoped to lay to rest the common patriarchal myths about women's willingness to work in prostitution. By the late 1980s, however, it had become increasingly clear that many women did know that their likely destination was the bars and brothels of Bangkok or abroad – although, as activists argued, they may not have known the conditions under which they would have to work. By the 1990s, tens of thousands of Thai women were believed to be working in prostitution overseas, while a growing number were working in Japan. Recruited by friends and sisters as much as by gangs or pimps, many women admitted that their chief concern was to take advantage of the financial benefits offered through prostitution work overseas. The chair of the Foundation for Women in Bangkok remembered that, as feminists did more work with prostitute women who had been deported from foreign countries, they discovered that, rather than being relieved to be back home, many wanted to return overseas as quickly as possible to try to make back the money it had cost them to go there in the first place. As the foundation chair pointed out, "the reason [the women try to go back] is that they want to find money to cover their debt and [hope for] the experience of some kind of job that can make money, a lot of money – if they are not controlled by anybody ... So, they try to go back."[1] Increasingly, organizations like the Foundation for Women had to admit that many women entered the trade because it was the best option available (admittedly within extremely limited circumstances) for making a relatively good income.

For some years critical feminist Sukanya Hantrakul had been arguing that viewing prostitute women merely as victims was unproductive and, in fact, harmful. Sukanya contended that addressing the prostitution issue would require addressing sexual control over women, particularly parental control of their daughters' sexuality and the insistence that girls become "dutiful daughters." Prostitute women, Sukanya argued, were not mere victims but "fighters." They had rebelled against the control of the state in, for example, trying to escape from the reform institutions and dared to throw off the moral restraints imposed on "good" women.[2]

Analysts like Sukanya tried to break the good girl/bad girl divide and sought to consult with prostitute women themselves. When several bar girls asked to be given English lessons in the early 1980s, Sukanya and others agreed to teach them. Sukanya quickly came to respect the prostitute women she met, seeing them not just as economic agents, but also as women who resisted the disciplinary gender structure and morality of Thai society. As she put it:

> Personally, I very much valued the spirit of struggle and the relatively independent and defying attitudes of the prostitutes I know which I rarely found in women who are not of their kind. They are women who have the spirit of a fighter – in sexual relations and others. While their middle-class sisters are being repressed by conservative values and the sexual double standards, they seem to have more autonomy in their personal and sexual lives ... Having marked themselves as whores, they have come out of their place – having broken so many repressive rules of good women, and developed the spirit of a fighter for survival and better living.[3]

Sukanya was particularly concerned to respect prostitute women's agency by, for instance, selling English lessons rather than offering them as a social welfare service. Sukanya argued that the majority of activities aimed at prostitutes – repression, rehabilitation, registration – were aimed at disciplining women into "proper sexual behaviour," to "make the prostitute recognise her crime of being promiscuous and repent"; "to control women's sexuality[;] to perpetuate women's sex roles"; and to restrict women's independence.[4]

Sukanya's approach was very much in opposition to the approach of those who sought to turn prostitute women back into good women, either through reform or punishment. It also diverged from the approach of most women's groups, which, while gradually accepting prostitution as a form of work aimed at survival, had greater difficulty celebrating it as a form of rebellion. Some elite women's organizations reacted with hostility to the idea of giving English lessons to prostitute women.[5] Elite organizations sought to abolish prostitution entirely, and it was felt that the English lessons encouraged rather than discouraged the trade.

Nonetheless, the English lessons gradually led to the development of a formal organization for prostitute women – Education Means Protection of Women Engaged in Recreation (EMPOWER). As one EMPOWER representative remembers, while at first she, too, saw prostitutes as bad women who could be helped by good women, she soon came to recognize them as "all women." Further, she realized that to treat prostitute women simply as victims would mean ensuring that they would not be able to help themselves.[6] EMPOWER continues today to provide English classes, health education, and career workshops, publishing a newspaper and producing dramas with and for women working in the sex trade. The organization aims to "protect bar girls' rights; to rebuild their sense of dignity and self-pride by finding ways to regain control of their lives; to encourage them to build a base for their next step in life; to provide information on health care and legal rights."[7] The organization, however, does not view itself as a prostitutes' rights organization; rather, it carefully differentiates between the situation of women in prostitution in Thailand and women in prostitution in the West on the basis that the former are "economically forced" to take up the occupation, pointing out that, if they were not, then they "would not want to be prostitutes."[8] Nonetheless, for EMPOWER, the most effective and empowering way to work for women in prostitution is to address their concerns while they are still working rather than to focus upon rescuing or removing them from the trade.[9]

Siriporn Skrobanek, founder of a number of women's groups in Thailand (most recently the Global Alliance against Trafficking in Women), also found that the more she met and worked with the women involved in prostitution, the more her understanding of prostitutes changed:

> I think at the beginning I also had the position like the abolitionists ... you would like to do something good for the women in prostitution but you cannot recognize this as a form of work yet. You think that it is part of patriarchy and as a feminist you have to dismantle it. But then later on, after working more with women who are in the trade, and exchanging information with people working on this issue, I gradually changed my position. Right now I think that we should recognize it, whether we like it or not, as a form of work. When we talk with women who are prostitutes they say they go to work. So I think we have to take that into consideration when we work on this. When you said that you would believe in this feminist patriarchal approach I think you should listen to them and then not just impose your ideas on what should be done ... And we should become more realistic in dealing with this problem. Certain women do

not have equal opportunities like others so they have to take up this form of work.[10]

In her research on Thai women working in prostitution in Europe, Siriporn emphasized that the women were not mere "passive victims" but, rather, that they fought back where possible. She considered prostitute women to be a "new type of wage earner[]."[11]

The importance of drawing attention to both the economic aspects of prostitution and women's agency in prostitution in the Third World was made very clear in the 1980s as international feminist campaigns against prostitution and the "traffic in women" took shape. In 1979 American radical feminist Kathleen Barry began a campaign to have the abolition of prostitution put back on the international agenda. Barry viewed prostitution as yet one more example of male sexual violence against women – along with rape, veiling, and female genital surgery.[12] After initially cooperating with Barry's campaign, Thai activists soon came to resent the fact that Barry's approach reduced the lives of all Thai women to that of victimhood. They also resented the failure of Western activists to recognize the role of the global economy in shaping (but not determining) the lives of women in Thailand. The echoes of colonialism in how Thailand appeared to be singled out for "mistreating its women," and in the portrayal of Thai women as passive victims, were heard clearly by Thai activists. They countered these Western representations with an insistence that Thai women in prostitution were active agents within limited circumstances. Most important, Thai activists emphasized that the women still acted and were not simply acted upon. As Siriporn has pointed out, in a way, organizations like the coalition put together by Kathleen Barry "argue from the 'third world' point of view – if you are in economic hardship then you have no other choice. You are forced to do that even though you get a certain income, but somehow the reason behind that is force. I think that there are many kinds of work that we do not like to do but we do not have any other choice – so we have to do that. So I think, in that sense, women in prostitution are not different from those in other occupations."[13]

The careful differentiation between "force," with its implications of passive victimhood, and "limited choices" – as agency within circumstances "not of one's own choosing," to paraphrase Marx – is upheld in much of the recent Thai feminist literature on prostitution. It reflects the desire of Thai feminists to prevent a paternalistic response to prostitution on the part of Western agencies and activists and to forge solidarity with prostitute women themselves. Siriporn, for one, has argued that focusing upon the economics of prostitution and sex tourism was the only way to act in concert with prostitute women:

Previous actions against sex-tourism conducted by women in the center of capitalism and in the periphery constituted a strategy from above and were directed only against one side of the coin, the exploitation of sexuality. This is more subtle, more complicated and less easily accepted by prostitutes than actions against economic exploitation. In order to avoid a hierarchical and patronizing approach, such actions should include Thai prostitutes, because they know more about their own problems and have already started to fight in their own way.[14]

Nonetheless, the activities of organizations such as the Global Alliance against Traffic in Women (GAATW) have not gone far enough for international prostitutes' rights advocates, who feel that the distinction between "forced" and "chosen" prostitution, which remains predominant, merely justifies focusing upon the victims and ignoring prostitutes' rights as workers.[15] Even EMPOWER, with its limited pro-rights stance, is held at a distance by other women's groups that target prostitution issues. The failure to challenge the good girl/bad girl division in much middle-class women's activism on prostitution has, as Nerida Cook has argued, resulted in a tendency for "Thai middle-class women [to] depict themselves as the prostitutes' saviours; as substitutes for the moral guardians a materialistic and venal world has failed to provide for young peasant women."[16] The increasing involvement of middle-class NGOs, including some women's groups, in the government's "rescue and rehabilitation" schemes attests to this underlying compulsion.

Nonetheless, feminist middle-class women's groups have come together to fight for the decriminalization of adult prostitution. In 1989 Friends of Women, Foundation for Women, EMPOWER, Association for the Promotion of the Status of Women (APSW), and the YWCA among others issued a joint letter to the government attacking its use of women to boost tourism and calling for the abolition of the 1960 act, which "treats prostitutes as criminals." Instead, the groups sought new anti-prostitution measures that focused upon youth, including a strictly enforced law not permitting girls under eighteen to work in the sex trade; punishment for customers and operators employing girls under eighteen; non-formal occupational training for rural young people to prevent them from entering the trade and for reskilling prostitutes seeking alternatives; and a public campaign warning rural villagers that they could be heavily punished for selling their children into prostitution.[17] Many of these demands were in line with the concerns of the new middle class over the involvement of rural youth and the behaviour of rural parents, which was seen to be the product of rampant consumerism among the peasantry. And, indeed, many of these concerns were addressed in the 1996 legislation, which was produced in consultation with the aforementioned groups. Nonetheless, Siriporn and others refused to support either the bill or the consultation process when it was discovered that, under it, prostitute women would continue to face penalties. And the growing realization of the effect that punitive measures could have on peasant parents and youth involved in the trade led many NGOs to criticize the bill.

Modernity and the Middle Class

While feminist activists had begun to accept that prostitution needed to be viewed as a form of work and that prostitute women's demands for better working conditions should be met, there was little support for this position among the expanding middle class. Just as women's groups were realigning themselves around a politics of labour in prostitution, society at large, particularly the rapidly growing urban middle class, was seeing prostitute women in a very different light. The association of prostitution with the arrival of foreigners, or with women going overseas, reinforced the notion that prostitution was a sign of the loss of traditional culture. In particular, in booming 1980s Thailand, prostitution was linked to the growth of materialism in what had been established (in the wake of the 1970s) as the very heartland of Thai culture – the rural areas. In truth, however, it was the rising fortunes of the new middle class itself that was provoking changes in consumption patterns and, accordingly, fears about the loss of culture.

The achievement of middle-class status by ever larger numbers of urban Thais in the 1980s and 1990s brought with it a shift in the practices of everyday life, of consumption, and of identity. According to Sukhumbhand Paribatra, the new Thai middle class is

> mostly young (ages 25-35); well educated (bachelor degrees or equivalent); exposed to "modern," Western-influenced culture; and employed in the professions in executive, managerial, administrative, or technical positions. A typical member of this class has a small family, a working spouse, and a two-bedroom house in a housing estate paid for with a long-term loan. He or she is predisposed to shop for food in modern supermarkets, travel, read newspapers and magazines, listen to radio and television, and if not already owning one, planning to own a car and credit card.[18]

By 1993, Thailand boasted the seventeenth largest car market in the world.[19] Shopping centres, department stores, and convenience and fast-food outlets dominated Bangkok. Shopping centres and department stores had become

> the parks of Bangkok, with fast-food outlets, mini-movie theatres, fashion stores and discount merchandisers providing much entertainment for the

population. As air-conditioned pleasure-domes, evening and weekends see them filled to overflowing with family groups and young people, dressed in the latest youth fashions, who meet in the fast-food shops. A recent survey has shown that 48 per cent of 21-30-year-olds prefer shopping in department stores rather than small shops or open markets.[20]

Older members of the middle class, who remember the days of nationalist student protests over the influx of Japanese products, are worried by young people's attraction to foreign goods and the decline of mom-and-pop shops and open markets. Indeed, the lifestyle of the middle class was a far cry, it seemed, not only from the ideal of the Thai village, of local trade, close-knit communities, and rural interdependence, but also from the Buddhist values of merit making and anti-consumerism.

This consumption of foreign goods, therefore, produces a great deal of middle-class anxiety over national culture and identity. Articles on the loss of Thai culture and the increase in cosmopolitan consumerism appear regularly in middle-class newspapers. In 1989, one group of newspaper analysts produced this anxiety-inducing summary: "The era of mass consumerism is upon us ... The globalization of consumerism transcends cultural differences and leaves the value of restraint as expounded by Buddhism a relic of the past. Consumerism puts the whole show on stage."[21]

Buddhism is one of the three pillars of Thai national identity, the other two being nation and king. If Buddhism is a "relic of the past," then perhaps nation and king are as well. Such dire predictions heightened middle-class fears over the decline of national culture and identity due to the onslaught of globalization.

"Consumerism" has become one of the watchwords of urban Thai society, being linked to the decline of Buddhist values and cultural identity. Kasian Tejapira argues that, unlike in the student era (when nationalism was linked to national commodity consumption), Thainess has now been "liberated" from any "specific national or ethnic commodity-referents":[22]

Thus Thainess becomes unanchored, uprooted, and freed from the regime of reference to commodities signifying national or ethnic Thai identity. Thainess is now able, as it were, to roam freely around the commodified globe, to coexist and copulate with Italian earrings, American fragrance, English wool [etc.] or any other un-Thai commodities and sundries. Its referential essence lies in mere spectral, amorphous, undefined Thai-Thai feelings in the spirit. Once liberated Thainess takes wing and turns into a free-wheeling, free-floating signifier.[23]

The anxiety over this development can only be assuaged for the middle class if there is a population that remains linked to national culture. The peasantry, already established as the backbone of Thai identity through the machinations of Premocracy (1980-8), became increasingly important in grounding what has become a free-floating identity for the middle class.

Contributing to this anxiety, a large part of the new middle class is Sino-Thai in background. Although most Sino-Thai families have actually been in Thailand and intermarried with Thais for several generations, the group "Sino-Thai" is often delineated for political purposes, making its claim to Thainess always uncertain. In the 1970s many tried to hide their Chinese background, but, in the 1980s, a "new Chinese modernity" emerged – a modernity that is less bounded to Thainess and more cosmopolitan. Christina Szanton Blanc argues that "it is this cosmopolitan modernity that Thailand's film industry is presenting to its rural populations when it portrays the modern homes and lifestyles of urban professionals and that both the Thai and the lower-class or petty bourgeois Sino-Thai are now increasingly striving to imitate, even though not everybody partakes of it equally, and some may even resent it."[24] Proving one's modernity (*than samay*) is a matter of consuming the right goods, renting "modern condo apartments not wooden houses," eating in Japanese restaurants, wearing international fashions, and playing golf with one's foreign counterparts.[25]

Despite the increasingly cosmopolitan character of the new middle class, however, the "thoroughly modern Asian" is still "primarily concerned with maintaining control over the large indigenous populations of his or her country."[26] One of the most powerful weapons of control is the manipulation of national identity discourse. Indeed, it is the classical role of the rising middle class to lay claim to a nationalizing or civilizing effort that legitimizes its claim to increased political power. National identity narratives, as Peter Vandergeest has made clear, render the village an object to be modernized and administered (or rescued and protected),[27] and the middle class just the group to do the job. The middle class in Thailand must lay claim to national identity in order to legitimize its claim to political (and economic) power, but to anchor this identity it turns to the peasant population, which is to act as the bearers (not the interpreters) of national culture. The effects of globalization on national identity production, therefore, are marked by class.

The growing distance between the middle and elite classes, on the one hand, and the peasant class, on the other, was marked by a growing anxiety over the "degradation" of rural culture (as defined by elites) and the peasants' presumed inability to maintain that culture. Although peasants had become icons of true Thainess, they were also viewed as the ones "most at risk of losing their culture and need[ing] to be policed to ensure that they not become Westernized."[28] This seeming contradiction reflects the dominant classes' belief that only they – with their education and insight – can correctly interpret national culture. For elite women, for instance, that culture included a strict sense of moral decency (as encoded in Buddhism) for both men and women, and a commitment to family (as espoused by the middle class). That national culture could simultaneously be embodied in the rural population (particularly its women) and yet not properly understood and maintained by this self-same population is no surprise, given feminist readings of national identity and how embodiment translates not into control but, rather, into its opposite. Even outside elite circles, where older versions of nationalism as state- or elite-based remained in the background, the peasantry was widely viewed as endangering Thai culture. This was true despite the celebration of rural culture and the peasantry as symbols of true Thai culture in what Vandergeest has called the "counter-narrative" to elite, modernization discourse. For the growing non-governmental movement, the real Thai culture of the rural areas was sharply opposed to the capitalist culture of the urban centres. Similarly, the reformist Buddhist school argued that the villages were the source of true religion, resisting the greed fostered by capitalism.[29] Indeed, consumerism goes against the central tenets of Buddhism – to free oneself from desire/greed in order to free oneself from suffering. Therefore, the presumed growth of materialistic values in the rural areas – particularly among those deemed most responsible for maintaining cultural purity (i.e., women) – was viewed with growing anxiety by a middle class that was itself increasingly removed from the values embodied within the rural areas.

This discourse of peasant inability to protect national culture underwrote the continuing political and economic power of the middle and upper classes and disempowered rural populations. The economic development that has made the middle class has resulted from the economic and environmental destruction of the rural areas. Massive logging for construction and export, and the construction of dams to generate hydro-electric energy for the urban areas, has resulted in the destruction of village ecosystems. The rapid economic growth of the 1980s and 1990s resulted in the widening of the gap between rural and urban incomes. By 1993, Bangkok, with 16.2 percent of the population, accounted for 55.4 percent of gross domestic product, while the more populous Northeast, with 34.3 percent of the population, accounted for only 10.6 percent.[30] The exploitation of rural women's labour in prostitution (as well as in factory and informal work) that made this urban economic boom possible was easily dismissed (and therefore perpetuated) by the attack on rural consumerism and loss of national identity. Once again, this had to do with the centrality of women as symbols of national culture.

The Material Girl
Even within the elite and middle classes there are clear gender differences with regard to the acceptability of this "modern, cosmopolitan identity."

While elite and middle-class women were certainly among those benefiting from the rapid modernization of urban Thai society – as the legal restrictions on their abilities were gradually lifted between 1989 and 1998 – the model Thai woman of the middle class continued to be "modern yet traditional." Thoroughly modern businesswomen, like the recipient of the 1995 Outstanding Business Woman Award, were profiled for their traditional charitable behaviour, in particular their religious, merit-making activities. The *Bangkok Post* profile opens: "Sriporn Suthipongse does not like to waste her time doing the rounds of parties in Bangkok. Instead, the executive chairman of Pergrine Nithi Finance and Securities prefers to spend her free time making merit through Thod Kathin – offering robes to monks during the 30 days following the Buddhist Lent, and through Thod Phapa – the off-season offering of robes and other needs to monks."[31] Women's role in the day to day maintenance of the Buddhist religion has remained strong, even in the urban areas. The strength of this role marks their continued importance in the maintenance of this key area of national identity.

The continuing flow of women into prostitution was seen by the urban middle class as a betrayal of this cultural role. As one *Bangkok Post* editorial read: "Art, tradition and culture are the root of society. Once the root is severed, people lose their knowledge of their own roots and rapidly accept a new culture, usually from the West, aggravating social problems such as prostitution."[32] Consumerism was seen as symptomatic of the influence of Western, capitalist, and un-Thai culture. The problem of consumerism, however, was mainly attached to the rural population and, in particular, to prostitute women themselves.[33] It was not blamed on the increasingly lavish lifestyles of urban men who could afford to buy ever higher-priced services, nor was it attached to the owners and procurers who were enriched through prostitution.

While reports – particularly within the middle-class press – on Thai women in prostitution overseas had become increasingly empathetic to the conditions they faced, the women themselves were often characterized as "gold diggers."[34] In 1983 the popular *Daily News* carried a front-page story that declared that Thai girls were "cashing in on the 'sex business'" and that "Thai prostitutes ha[d] been pouring into [Japan] to 'dig for gold.'"[35] It reported that two Thai prostitutes had claimed they had made 200,000 baht each in three months while working in Japan. Even a sympathetic chronicler like Chitraporn Vanaspong, in covering the yearly traffic of Thai women to Japan (where they can make some three million baht in a year), concluded: "Many women still flock to Japan as gold diggers. The potential for saving makes them overlook the negative side of the venture. Harsh treatment by pimps, *mamasans* and agents and the risk of AIDS mean nothing compared with the prospect of wealth."[36] As Marjorie Muecke has pointed out, "materialism is widely cited in the media as the primary incentive for their choosing prostitution as a career, just as it is for parents selling their daughters."[37] The governor of Phayao province, speaking of the town of Dok Kam Tai (a town infamous for sending women and girls into prostitution), reasoned that young girls were susceptible because, "when they saw their neighbours and friends coming back from Bangkok with money to maintain a more comfortable living, they could not resist that somehow they must reach that economic status as well [sic]."[38] Such characterizations, however, emphasized the need for elite guidance. According to the governor of Phayao, "we have to hold frequent seminars to inject into their way of thinking that prostitution is not the only solution. They have to be taught that such a profession is a degradation of the social value of women."[39] Materialism also accounted for middle-class women becoming prostitutes – as reports of government workers and college girls entering the trade grew over the years – but the central focus of the critique remained the rural population. While the consumerism critique clearly underwrote elite intervention and power, it was taken up by the new middle class, which sought to similarly distinguish itself from, and seek power over, the rural peasant.

The consumerism critique appeared in forms other than journalistic writing and even invaded the work of NGOs and women's organizations, despite their commitment to viewing prostitution as work. A flesh-trade seminar held after the fire in Phuket emphasized that "the media – with its heavy consumerism – had raised the aspirations of rural people, whose hopes simply could not be met. These aspirations were exploited by unscrupulous agents and operators." It recommended "greater emphasis on morality to fight materialism."[40] A study of prostitution and trafficking by the Foundation for Women in the late 1980s showed that "in the North, money earned through prostitution is normally used to build new and spacious houses for the families. A lump sum is commonly spent on consumer goods."[41] The report went on to say that "the villagers are *preoccupied* by materialism."[42] The term "preoccupied" conveys a sense of "obsession," a sense that something – "traditional culture" most likely – has been pushed aside and neglected. Similarly, the 1992-2011 women's development plan produced by the National Commission on Women's Affairs (NCWA) stressed the "impact of the growing materialism and consumerism of the past two decades. People have become more money conscious as a means to gain respect into the society [sic]. New values based on amounts of possessions has taken roots [sic] and have enticed poor women to look for ways to earn easy money. Prostitution offered such an opportunity ... Parents who were willing to sell their own children wanted money."[43]

Children's representatives argued that even children were "victims of luxury" since "many teenagers agreed to sell themselves for as little as a fashionable outfit." While many accepted that children were generally victims of the trade, their parents could be blamed for similarly material-istic sentiments. Prapote Sritet of the Northern People's Relations Groups estimated that 80 percent of prostitutes were sold by their parents, who wanted to "cut out the middlemen."[44] For Mattani Rutnin, who prepared an investigatory video on child prostitution in preparation for the con-ference, the parents who sold their children into prostitution were not victims of poverty but "calculating and business minded and reserved in their feeling of love and care for their children." Activists like Mattani insisted that discussions at the conference should focus on the "materialis-tic values of parents who followed the example of their neighbours and were willing to sacrifice their daughters." While the film's narrator, Sanit-suda Ekachai (among others), emphasized that the parents were driven by economic necessity and argued that putting the blame on rural parents would lead to legal measures that sought to punish the parents rather than the procurers, Mattani maintained that this failed to come to terms with parental responsibilities.[45]

This perspective on rural parents emphasized that they needed to be trained in "proper parenthood" by the elite rather than that the economic and political structure was stacked against them. This perspective, there-fore, underwrites elite and middle-class authority. This became clear in Mattani's later work when she scripted a drama as part of a community development project aimed at preventing prostitution. In her reasoning for the project she argued: "Human values have changed, and today's youth lack knowledge and understanding of traditional culture, a heritage handed down through many generations. To reach the young generation of today in an attempt to *reinstate the age-old traditional values, beliefs, and culture*, there is no better medium than the performing arts, which can be enter-taining as well as educational."[46]

Mattani's approach clearly reflected a concern to instil traditional values, which, presumably, were better understood by elites than by rural peas-antry and youth. The play depicts how village life is disrupted by the temp-tations to lead an easier life, which result in indebtedness. A mother is forced to sell her daughters into prostitution. The play's hero is the village leader who goes to Bangkok in search of the daughters and fetches them back to their mother.[47] The play suggests that it is the role of leaders to pro-tect the women and girls of the villages, returning them to their "proper" place within the family and the village.

The consumerism critique echoed the middle-class belief that the poor are, in part, responsible for their own poverty because of their lax spending habits and/or lack of moral fibre. The construction of "new and spacious homes" with what one's offspring made in prostitution became the focus of considerable concern. In the eyes of the middle class, new homes, along with refrigerators, televisions, and furniture, represented "little of productive value."[48] Of course, given the declining value and increasing costs of agricultural production, there was little point in investing in it. In the 1990s agriculture accounted for less than 20 percent of the gross domestic product.[49] Government development plans clearly aimed at encouraging the rural population to join the industrial labour force rather than to undertake subsistence farming.[50] It is more profitable to sell one's labour to local agribusiness or to migrate to the cities as a labourer than it is to farm, and one's daughters are increasingly valued, particularly in the North, as high-income-generating labourers in prostitution.[51] The income from prostitution is also dedicated to the education of siblings and children and is seen as an investment in future labourers or even as a step into the middle class. Meyer argues that the conspicuous consumption of the villagers, which they can display thanks to the money earned from daughters in prostitution, is a way of accumulating prestige and thus handling the stigma of prostitution.[52] Indeed, the more shunned prostitute women feel by society, the more pressure they feel to "hurry home with their money to show off their wealth by renovating their houses or buying electrical appliances."[53] More important, perhaps, the rural areas were trying to take part in the processes of modernization and economic growth from which their urban counterparts seemed to benefit so effortlessly.

Reinforcing this sense of "undeserved gain" was the frequent reference to "easy money" as one of the reasons for women entering the prostitution trade. The phrase suggests that the work of prostitution was illegitimate because it did not require any training or application of effort; rather, it was seen as women being paid simply for "having a good time." Not only does such a suggestion belittle the extraordinary amount of physical and emotional labour prostitute women must put into their work, but it also suggests that the poor should be happy to be "honest labourers" in the rice paddies of rural Thailand – to engage in hard work for little pay. Indeed, a number of prostitute women comment on the back-breaking labour of rice farming as being much less desirable than work in the bars.[54] Certainly the moral condemnation of prostitutes as having chosen to make easy money gives a sense of pride and superiority to lower-paid women, such as female construction workers and urban labourers, who have not taken that route. Kanchana Tangchonlatip and Nicholas Ford's research shows that, while female construction workers often were sympathetic to the reasons for becoming a prostitute (particularly poverty), they viewed prostitution "more negatively in terms of gaining a relatively high income without having to engage in hard work. The female construction workers (who derive from the same social strata as most sex workers in Thailand) were very clear in their minds that 'prostitutes preferred to be sex workers than construction workers' like themselves who earn little money in return for extremely arduous and often dangerous work."[55]

A 1996 study on prostitution conducted by the Foundation for Women discovered that the increased earning power of women in prostitution was, in fact, changing their status within the village community. The researchers pointed out that "women's increasingly obvious contribution to the improvement in the family's economic status through labour migration has changed [the decision-making power of senior males] somewhat. In some families, women are now considered the head of the household and women have a greater share of the decision-making power. Even parents have come to respect their daughters."[56] On the other hand, the more aggressive and self-confident attitude of returning women can be resented: there is a belief that local men will not marry them because they are too independent.[57]

Indeed, the independence of many women working in the prostitution industry, particularly those involved in the tourist-oriented trade, may be precisely what is being targeted by the consumerism critique. This "brazenness" contradicts the dictates of middle-class and elite society – that peasant women should be guided by their betters. Prostitute women have refused to stay within their proper roles, consorting with both the modern and the foreign outside the control of the elites who seek to guide them. By interpreting the agency of prostitute women merely as consumerism or greed, the consumerism critique effectively silences the complex realities of prostitutes' lives: either women are innocent victims or they are greedy consumers. The consumerism explanation of prostitution silences the structural issue of poverty by turning those who try to survive through prostitution into the "undeserving poor," suggesting that their suffering stems from their greed and improper attitudes rather than from the economic conditions in the countryside.

The idea that women would engage in prostitution simply for consumer goods erases the fact that, even though prostitution can provide a better income than factory or domestic work, the greatest percentage of the money generated from each transaction does not end up in the pocket of the prostitute; rather, it goes to owners and middlemen as well as to the officials who have to be paid off. Prostitute women themselves, particularly those from the North, often send the largest portion of their income back to their villages to support their families, thus fulfilling their roles as dutiful daughters. Indeed, rural women's consumption is more easily condemned than men's because of women's traditional responsibility to support the family. Men, on the other hand, are expected to be irresponsible and are given a great deal more latitude in their discretionary spending.[58] At the same time the consumerism critique repeats a stereotype of women from the North (who predominate in the prostitution industry), depicting them as being *jai on* (soft-hearted/headed) and in love with beautiful things. This characterization of Northern Thai women erases their underlying sense of duty, which involves providing for their families. In fact, this stereotype is precisely what lies behind Thai customers' demand for Northern women.

Further, characterizing prostitute women as consumer-driven undermines attempts to recognize the agency of young women in entering the prostitution industry by translating it into something misguided and self-ish – a betrayal of their cultural heritage and their role in preserving it. As Aiwha Ong has noted in the case of women factory workers in Malaysia: "By rivetting public attention on the female workers' consumption, the press trivialized women's work and helped divert discontent over their weak market position into the manageable channels of a 'youth culture.'"[59] Further, by viewing the consumption in which women did engage as part of a youth culture, such a reading erased their deliberate challenge to traditional definitions of identity and sexuality.[60] Similarly, young women in prostitution continue to be read as in need of guidance and/or punishment rather than as self-interpreting agents.

Thus, despite growing openness among some elite and middle-class women to the idea of decriminalizing prostitution, and the growing evidence that such a move would benefit prostitute women by enabling them to get out from under the hold of procurers, owners, and corrupt officials, most feel that Thai society is not yet ready for such a step. Hence, current legislation designed to address the prostitution problem focuses upon punishing both prostitutes and parents who sell their children into prostitution rather than upon the broader causes of prostitution and the demands of prostitutes themselves.

While a number of Thai organizations and commentators are now calling for the decriminalization of prostitution and the formation of self-help groups or unions as the only practical solution, the new act forecloses this possibility for the foreseeable future. Prostitute women's own voices were drowned out by the campaign to reform male behaviour and change Thailand's image to that of a paternal, protective, and effective state. For elite and middle-class women, however, the campaign has provided considerable benefits. For example, the various exemptions to the United Nations Convention for the Elimination of Discrimination against Women have been removed over the course of the 1990s as governments attempt to mend Thailand's image, starting with the removal of barriers to employment in government in 1990 and concluding with attempts in the late 1990s to address the only remaining substantive reservation on Article 16 – equality in family life and marriage.[61] At the same time, however, there is continuing pressure on women to act as defenders of tradition, particularly as male roles become increasingly modernized. Women's sexual behaviour remains an object of control, as in the new prostitution law, but now men are to be disciplined to adhere to the same standard. Prostitute women, therefore, remain in a precarious position in regards to the law, and young women face increased disciplinary measures (through education and training programs) to ensure proper moral and sexual behaviour. Most recently, the deputy education minister has instructed universities and colleges to step up their instruction on women's chastity in response to reports that university students were engaging in casual sex. According to the minister: "The traditional Thai way of life is girls must protect their virginity before marriage. Every [education] department must work towards restoring this original way of life."[62] In a similar vein, women at Chulalongkorn University were instructed to lengthen their skirts or face grade penalties. University officials argued that "short skirts go against Thailand's customs" and "damage Chula's dignity" as well as tempting men to commit sexual attacks.[63] Women remain responsible for ensuring that men adhere to moral restraints. Women's political power will remain limited as long as politics are considered a "dirty game" unfit for "proper women."[64] In accordance with this continued vigilance over women's moral and sexual behaviour, prostitute women remain targets of reform and rehabilitation.

Peasant Parents and the 1996 Bill

The other targets of the new prostitution legislation were, not surprisingly, peasant parents. As we saw in the previous chapter, the model of the new man had gained increasing acceptance among the middle class as the proper form of masculinity for Thai men. The new prostitution legislation was championed by those who sought to ensure the adoption of this model, and the strength of its international and middle-class appeal eventually led to the acceptance of punishment for clients of child prostitutes. However, the adoption of the bill was seen, in effect, to be proof that middle-class Thai men were already modernized new men and that the bill's disciplinary measures would be directed against other men – foreigners, old-style men, local notable types, and lower-class men. Thongbai Thongpao defended the bill on the grounds that, "above all, the law will protect our children who are usually abused by tourists, some [of] whom fly in solely for such a purpose at the expense of the welfare of Thai children and the country's honour."[65] Others argued that it was Chinese men who were the problem, arguing that the belief that sex with a child is rejuvenating comes from Chinese tradition and has led to a demand among Sino-Thai businessmen.[66]

Experts on child prostitution, however, note that a large percentage of customers of child prostitutes are Thai rather than foreign. Significantly though, it is poor men rather than rich men who appear to frequent child prostitutes. According to Dr. Sanphasit Kumpraphan, while "the rich will go to member clubs where women with university degrees are for sale,

... the low-income Thai will go to the back-street brothel and buy a child. These men are not paedophiles ... They would prefer sex with a woman but they cannot afford it."[67] The decrease in prison time and increase in fines suggests that the bill is indeed slanted in favour of the wealthier classes. Certainly, rural and working-class men are seen as less inclined to adopt the new-man attitude.[68] Less educated men are failing to adopt the new standards of behaviour, according to newspaper reports on, for instance, AIDS prevention. According to a 1995 report in the *Nation,* men with lower levels of education are "still visiting brothels frequently although the HIV infection rate among prostitutes is as high as twenty per cent."[69] The emphasis on brothel and child prostitution in the new legislation, therefore, will be most likely to catch poor men within its ambit. The new law acts as a disciplinary mechanism to force lower-class men into the new-man model of the middle class.

Poor men are also a target of the disciplinary ideology of the new man as father. Elites have pointed to the failure of proper fatherhood among rural, lower-class men as a cause of prostitution. Mattani Rutnin has argued that, according to her research, girls sold into prostitution "usually have fathers who are not strong financial supporters of the family."[70] According to a 1992 NCWA report on prostitution, the lack of "love and warmth" in the rural family is a result of the changes wrought by modernization. It is this lack of warmth that leads children to leave home and that leaves them open to being pressured or deceived into the sex business.[71] And, as we saw in the previous chapter, the rural peasantry is viewed as having sold out to materialist values and as in need of being redisciplined into traditional values. Hence, the bill also provided, for the first time, punishment for parents who knowingly sold their children into prostitution – parents who, again, were assumed to be among the rural poor.

Originally, the bill provided for the punishment of parents whether they sold their children knowingly or not. NGOs argued that it would be unfair to punish parents who were often unaware of what their children would be going into, having been told that they would be working as maids or waitresses in Bangkok.[72] Even with the insertion of "knowingly," human rights organizations were concerned that the "burden of proof [would] be on the parents." As one analyst points out, whether or not parents willingly and purposefully sell their children into prostitution is difficult to determine. Many parents face difficult economic and social conditions and may not be aware of the working conditions of their children: "If this section is passed under these terms, one may fear that it could later lead to many legal blunders where parents, some of them victims themselves, are systematically arrested and charged. If such a section is included, it should take into account the hardship that drives many people into committing this serious crime."[73]

However, elite proponents of the bill believed that the problem was the "backwards" attitude and morals of rural peasants rather than poverty. MP Laddawong Wongsriwong, one of the chief proponents of the bill, argued that parents in the North simply do not regard selling sex as immoral: "They just think that their children can make money by going into the profession." She claimed that parents often asked, "What's wrong with prostitution?" Laddawan argued that the news media needed to teach parents to be more aware of the negative effects of selling girls into the sex industry.[74] Once again, the peasantry were characterized as the backward "other" who needed instruction from the morally superior middle class.

Indeed, the middle-class opponents of prostitution were seen as better interpreters of true tradition than were the peasants who supposedly embodied it. For example, while some members of the House worried that the bill's provisions would damage the Thai tradition of gratitude to parents, commentators like Thongbai replied, "no Thai tradition has ever stipulate[d] that daughters sacrifice by committing an immoral deed which runs opposite to humanity and human rights. It is simply a hypocritical claim to exploit one's own children without moral support."[75] "Real" Thai tradition, therefore, was not that practised by the peasants; rather, it was what the educated classes decided that it was.

So seriously was the issue of reforming rural parents' behaviour taken that the punishments for parents were higher than those faced by procurers and clients (parents could be imprisoned four to twenty years and fined 80,000 to 400,000 baht).[76] Parents who sold their children or who conspired with others to allow their children to enter prostitution could also have their guardianship of them revoked.[77] Commentators pointed out that it would certainly be easier to penalize parents – especially those from marginalized hill tribes who do not speak Thai – than the operators who know how to "work the system."[78] Others were sceptical about the provision's ability to be helpful to the children:

> It's very difficult to prove the age of the girls. And the part ... that empowers authorities or NGOs to arrest the parents of the girls, in my opinion, will work negatively, it won't help the girls. The girls will be even more abused, more paralysed. There were some disagreements among some feminist groups and social workers who are working on women's issues and some NGOs who want to have some authority to do something with the parents because some parents are quite terrible. But, in my opinion, they may be targeting the wrong target, the weakest people. It's very easy to target parents instead of procurers. The girls will be more paralysed because the procurers or the owners of brothels will threaten them that if they run away or what not their parents will be arrested.[79]

Others worried that the bill increased the disciplinary power of the state over children and their parents:

> Actually we agree with their idea that the child should be protected from their parents selling them or allowing them [into prostitution] because we think it is exploitation of children. But to have a national committee to be responsible ... we were not sure whether this will work or not, I feel it's like, not only me but the NGOs working with children, it's like, if the ... children are taken out from brothels and the parents can not [be] involved, [and] if the court proved that they [were] sold, [then] the child has to be placed somewhere, in a home, that the national committee [has] sent them to. In my opinion it's a kind of "compulsory rehabilitation," you cannot choose.[80]

Further, the state was ill-equipped to play the role of foster parent: "And we worry about the institution that will come to take care of the children. Because so far in our law and in our practice we don't have yet that kind of structure or skills to take care of the young people to replace their parents. It will be government and NGOs shelters who are registered by the government so it will be more controlled in a way, by the government."[81]

The new act greatly expands the powers of the state and police vis-à-vis prostitution-related offences, despite the problematic involvement of police and other officials in the trade. In an attempt to counter corruption among officials the Senate did add a clause to Section 12, which levied a heavier penalty on administrative officials who committed the act outlawed in the new legislation.[82] In all, the new act greatly increases the penalties for pimps, procurers, and brothel owners, bringing them in line with the government's concern to crack down on child prostitution and to appear to be taking strong measures against its perpetrators.[83] Section 9 provides for the punishment of "whoever procures, deceives, or traffics the other person to commit the prostitution activity, with or without consent of the other person" with one to ten years imprisonment and a fine of 20,000 to 200,000 baht (and even stiffer penalties for trafficking in children under eighteen). And, for the first time, the advertising of sex services is punished.

The act also attacks the use of force in adult prostitution by penalizing procurers for using deceit, threat, physical assault, "immoral influence," or "mental coercion by any other means." The highest penalties specified in the act are for detention and assault for the purpose of forcing someone into prostitution. The death penalty or life imprisonment is the specified punishment if the victim is killed in the attempt to force her into prostitution.[84] This provision gave pause to some members of the House, who argued that the inclusion of the death penalty would be damaging to Thailand's image, given that it had been abolished in many countries on humanitarian grounds. Debate over the provision caused a second delay in the bill's passage.[85]

Other passages that would have increased the search and seizure powers of officials were scaled back. In the second reading in April, passages considered key by children's rights activists concerning search and entry were dropped from the bill. The provisions allowed officials, without a warrant, to "enter any place, night or day, if there is good reason to believe that there is confinement or forced prostitution, in order to assist the victims" and "[to] search any vehicle and persons in the vehicle, in cases where it is suspected that the vehicle is transporting persons to commit offenses under this act, in order to help the victims of such offenses." The new provision read simply: "The official shall have authority and duties as follows: (1) to enter into the entertainment place according to the law on entertainment places, both day and night, for inspection and monitoring the commission of the offenses in this Act."[86] Children's rights organizations were concerned that this greatly reduced the abilities of officials to act against procurers and owners.[87] However, sweeping powers for officials, as proposed in the original bill, would have been open to abuse.

The tendency to support dangerously expanded police powers in order to counter child prostitution and trafficking was also reflected in the proposed anti-trafficking bill put forward by the NCWA under PM Chuan Leekpai (1992-5). This bill would have empowered officials "to question and inspect women and children who travel abroad, at any time and without warrants" and to detain them for up to seven days without a court order.[88] Such provisions contravened women's right to travel freely, as per the United Nations Convention for the Elimination of Discrimination against Women, and were dropped before the bill's passage under the Chavalit government (1996-7).[89] In all, however, the new legislation ushers in several measures that will likely be used against rural parents and working-class men without respect to their weak economic and political position.

The Continued Criminalization of Prostitution
The ultimate price of these new measures to protect children and to discipline parents and clients is the continued disciplining of women. As mentioned above, a number of women's groups withheld support for the bill because it continued to penalize prostitutes rather than remove all criminal sanction (as these groups had requested). While the NCWA's development plan argued that "the way of dealing with the sex trade must be in the form of assistance/aid instead of arrest and punishment,"[90] according to one

insider the continued penalization of prostitute women was part of the price of getting the bill through. Male MPs were unwilling to accept penalization of customers if prostitutes themselves were to go unpunished.[91] Some elite women also felt that punishment of prostitutes was needed. MP Sansanee Nakpong (Palang Dharma Party), who initiated the bill, argued that, if prostitutes – including child prostitutes – were not punished, then they would return to the sex industry and that, in any case, the punishment was light.[92] However, the chief author of the NCWA plan for prostitution was also unhappy with the penalization of women, pointing out that men are punished only if the prostitute is under eighteen:

> I'm still not really happy about it, it still punishes the prostitute, and they didn't punish the man, they punish if [the men] use the young prostitute, eighteen down. But if [the women are] nineteen up, if they are caught in the sex industry, the sex workers will be punished. But what about the men? If they want to punish the prostitute they should punish the man, but if they don't want to punish the man they should not punish the prostitute, because it takes two.[93]

Section 4 of the new bill defines prostitution as "the acceptance of sexual intercourse, the acceptance of any other act, or the commission of any act for sexual gratification of another person in a promiscuous manner, in order to gain financial or other benefit, no matter whether the person who commits such act and the other person are of the same or opposite sex." The promiscuity of these acts presumably differentiates them from the acts performed by a minor wife. Prostitute women face a fine of up to 1,000 baht and/or one month's imprisonment for "benefiting from the prostitution activity." These punishments are lighter than the ones in the 1960 act, but they are not as light as was originally intended. The NCWA had originally agreed to drop all prison terms and had settled on a 500-baht fine. Under the new act, however, punishment for solicitation "overtly or shamelessly committed" has been set at a 1,000-baht fine.[94]

Unlike the 1960 act, Section 6 of the new act recognizes that if the prostitute is "forced" or "under an influence in which that person cannot avoid or resist, the offender is not guilty," thus recognizing women's groups arguments that women can be forced into the trade and held against their will and, therefore, should not be punished. On the other hand, the bill does not clearly recognize that women may willingly choose to work as prostitutes or enter into prostitution through a third party. While women are punished for their activities, all procuring activities are also punished "with or without consent of the other person."[95] This provision is in line with the UN Convention for the Suppression of Traffic in Persons and meets the objections of anti-trafficking organizations, which point out that women can be forced to consent. The section is also clearly part of the government's goal to stem the flow of women into the trade, which, throughout the act, is deemed to be unacceptable. Critics also point out that "several sections ... refer to the protection, education and care of offenders convicted under sections 5-6, but the wording of the sections only thinly disguise the corrections mentality from which most of the work to 'reform' prostitutes in Thailand has so far been undertaken."[96]

Those convicted under Sections 5 and 6 (and Section 8, which provides for traffickers) could be remanded to a rehabilitation shelter under the newly created Committee for Protection and Vocational Development, which includes both government organizations and NGOs. If the offender is eighteen years of age or less, then the court can decide, "after having examined the biography, behaviour, intelligence, education, physical health, mental health, profession and environmental surrounding of the offender," to send her to such a shelter. If the offender is over eighteen, then she can ask to go to a shelter if it is "appropriate in the opinion of the court." Presumably, the court will determine the "recalcitrance" of the character of the convicted person – whether or not she can benefit from vocational training and rehabilitation – which means that she either express a desire to leave the trade or claim victimhood. Section 38 of the act empowers officials, with the assistance of the police, to pursue and to return those who escape from the shelter.[97] The bulk of the act deals with setting up and overseeing the reform institutions, reflecting its main thrust, which is to discipline the women involved into correct behaviour.

However, at the April 1996 meeting of women's and children's NGOs, which was convened to discuss the bill, all the participants agreed that the new bill opened the way for further exploitation of women in prostitution through arbitrary enforcement and demands for protection money. It was feared that the new controls would force the trade underground, making it more difficult for NGOs to investigate sex establishments. And, once again, participating sex workers argued that what they wanted was protection under the labour law; legitimate work contracts specifying work hours and ensuring access to welfare, benefits, and medical check-ups; reduction of working hours; minimum wage guarantees; and access to education. Arrests and closures resulting from stricter enforcement have often meant greater difficulties for sex workers because bar owners often require them to compensate for lost revenues.[98] Thaanavadee Thajeen, chair of Friends of Women, called for the bill to be scrapped, arguing that better law enforcement, rather than a new law, was needed.[99]

Even some children's rights activists, such as Vitit Muntarbhorn, came to see the importance of decriminalizing adult prostitution.[100] For others, such as Sanphasit Kumpraphan, the chair of the Centre for Protection of Children's Rights, who does not support the liberalization of prostitution, the bill's harsh measures pose problems for victims and others coming forward to complain.[101] Sanpasit was also less sanguine about the bill's potential enforceability: "Who will enforce the law when almost every man was once a client including the judge, the police officer, the public prosecutor? The problem should be solved with social not legal measures."[102] One EMPOWER activist asked a similar question, pointing out that, during raids on brothels under the old law, the men were never to be found and that it was unlikely things would be any different under the new law. Indeed, in the three years after the passage of the new bill only one client – a foreigner – had been prosecuted for buying sex from a minor.[103]

Above all, the law fails to provide what prostitute women are asking for: safe working conditions. As an EMPOWER representative points out: "This law does not allow support to women while they are still working, they must wait until they are arrested. [As well] this law doesn't give these things [safe working conditions, education, health, and legal rights] to women – it doesn't give them a salary so they can gain pride and dignity and decide for themselves when they will leave voluntarily."[104] Further, "trying to negotiate with government to help people they call victims will [only result in their] being re-victimized."[105]

Indeed, a number of feminist organizers feel that the continued criminalization of prostitution defeats what many now consider to be the only practical solution for women in the industry – organizing among themselves. As a Foundation for Women representative expressed it: "I think that women themselves in the sex business [should] get organized, but under this bill that says prostitution is illegal how can they speak out that I am a prostitute and I want this and this?"[106] Indeed, the hoped-for soft-pedalling of the illegality of prostitution for those over eighteen has not materialized. Prostitute women continue to face arrest by police who ignore or remain ignorant of the new legal provisions and charge women under the old act.[107] Thus, through this continued criminalization, the new legislation further silences the voices of prostitute women.

Conclusion

The condemnation of prostitute women as being driven by consumerism is a reflection of the current era's anxiety over the apparent loss of traditional culture and national identity. Women often have a symbolic role as bearers of national culture, and this can result in their activities being closely circumscribed. Prostitution is particularly threatening because it signals women's failure to stay within their prescribed roles, thereby endangering the "reproduction of the nation" both physically and socially. The "discovery" of prostitution as a social issue in Thailand occurred within the context of the American military presence, resulting in it being presented as an attack on traditional culture as embodied in Thai women.

While, traditionally, women are considered to be bearers of national culture, with the globalization of the middle class, peasants have taken on an increasing importance in the Thai national imaginary. The sudden expansion of the middle class in an age of globalized consumption has gone hand in hand with a growing sense of loss of culture and identity. As the middle class enjoys the fruits of the cosmopolitan and the modern, it seeks to anchor Thai identity in the rural peasantry. Following the upheavals of the 1970s, the government established the peasantry as central to the maintenance of Thai identity. Nonetheless, without the guidance of their betters, the peasants are not trusted to have the education/intelligence to maintain traditional culture while also engaging with modernity. The middle class found ample evidence of this as it saw its political and social goals frustrated by the rural areas. If there were men who needed to be made modern, then they were lower-class and peasant men who refused to conform to middle-class standards. Further, if men were to be made modern, then women would need to be made more traditional in order to maintain national culture and identity. As peasant women, therefore, prostitute women are doubly marked as bearers of national culture. Their clear refusal to play their proper roles and to follow the direction of the middle/elite classes provokes anger and anxiety among the latter, who feel that these women should be disciplined into so doing. The accusation of consumerism legitimizes such discipline by silencing the complex realities of prostitutes' lives and their demands for control over them.

This discussion clearly indicates the complex ways in which globalization and modernization shape political identities in peripheral countries. The price of modernization is downloaded onto peripheral groups – women and peasants – not only in economic terms, but also in terms of identity. But, again, this is not simply a process involving the suppression of local cultures through the dispersion of mass culture; rather, it is a drive to demarcate and to preserve a "true" national identity and tradition in the face of globalization. This is what limits the possibilities of progressive politics for both women and peasants. This is not to say that resistance to globalization is self-destructive but, rather, that the identity politics of globalization work in a more complicated manner than we assume, provoking a defensive and restrictive reaction. The restrictive and punitive implications of such identity politics are evidenced in Thailand's policies towards prostitution.

7
The Politics of Prostitution: Gender, Class, and Nation

The prostitute is a symbol that powerfully evokes the limitations of acceptable female behaviour. It is an important tool, therefore, in disciplining female identity. Rather than assuming that there is "a" reality to prostitute women's lives, this study asks how prostitutes are constructed and understood within particular historical locations and how certain interpretations come to shape state policy on prostitution. It is these policies – criminalization, reform, re-education – that have posed the most immediate problem for prostitute women and have increased state power over women in prostitution rather than empowering them as political actors.

Therefore, instead of assuming that the prostitute is, by definition, a powerless actor, I examine how she is rendered powerless as a political actor by specific interpretations of prostitution. Analyses that assume that the prostitute is indeed powerless serve only to legitimize the operation of power; that is, they invoke protectionist and restrictive responses that further limit the lives of women in prostitution and, in many ways, simply echo the worldview of the powerful. By turning the usual assumption about prostitute women inside out, we expose the complex workings of discursive power and challenge its operation. In this study, we have seen how the discourses of gender and national identity intersect to construct the prostitute and to determine policy by rendering her as an object of re-enculturation rather than as a political actor. Women's bodies have become powerfully connected to the reproduction of the nation – both literally and symbolically – particularly since the colonial era. Western practice and discourse established that gender identity and sexual behaviour grounded a national identity. Particular forms of gender and sexuality grounded claims to "civilization" and "modernity" and, therefore, to national independence. In Thailand, women's identity and proper behaviour were in many ways linked to women's role in the maintenance of national identity and tradition. This link, however, was differently constructed in different periods and was subject to manipulation by political actors.

The International and the National: The Global Politics of Representation

The historical discussion of prostitution policy illustrates that gender and sexual standards were always a part of international relations. Western gender identities were used to establish the "essential" differences between civilized and uncivilized. The seeming failure of Siamese masculinity and femininity to meet up with Western gender norms was given as evidence of Siamese inability to govern themselves properly. In the semi-imperial era, reforming women's behaviour to meet international gender standards – particularly in the form of the abolishment of the harem and the institutionalization of anti-prostitution legislation – was a key part of establishing Thailand's civilized status. At the same time, however, gender roles were a site of resistance to Western demands. The practice of polygamy became, for a number of male elites, a matter of cultural identity rather than a state practice. Women's sexual service to men was institutionalized further in the form of legalized prostitution. Once the traditional bonds of slavery were undone, state leaders, particularly Chulalongkorn, attempted to incorporate lower-class males into the modernizing state through the military. A militarized masculinity, whose sexual prowess indicated political power, remained a central, if contested, model of elite Thai manhood well into the present day. Many elite men, therefore, resisted efforts to abolish prostitution. Despite this resistance, both polygamy and prostitution were, eventually, officially banned, as was required in order to meet Western standards of civilization and modernity and so enable Thailand to gain full international status.

This historical discussion shows both the importance of the construction/representation of self/other identities in international politics and the importance of gender in anchoring this construction/representation to relations of power. In this light we also begin to understand Thailand's modern-day concern with international image and its gendered aspects. While such concern has tended to be dismissed as the "Asian concern with saving face," this misses an important aspect of international power, one that is quickly recognized within non-Western contexts – the power of representation. As was made clear during the semi-imperial era, the constructions of Thai gender identities and sexual behaviour were key in establishing Siam/Thailand as "unmanly" and, therefore, as "other," or "lesser," and as a site for Western intervention and dominance. These same constructions were activated in the modern era, when Thailand was criticized for its failure to appropriately address the issue of prostitution. Such representations, once again, invoked and enabled relations of dominance between the West and Thailand, underwriting possible boycotts and sanctions as well as threatening Thailand's status in the world market due to the fact that its governments were judged weak and inefficient. The Thai middle class was able to use these constructions to push for changes in modes of governance and male behaviour. By championing a new ideology of modernized masculinity as the appropriate basis of governance – one that was in line with Western ideals – new middle-class actors were able to legitimize their claims to authority and power. That they were able to do so reflects the authorizing power of Western constructions of identity. The modern debate over international image, therefore, reflects the central role of representation in international relations of power. As in the colonial era, the construction of the other as backwards, or traditional, underwrites the imposition of relations of dominance and has real political effect in countries such as Thailand.

Analysts and activists have often ignored these aspects of international power and, thus, have failed to thoroughly understand how power works in a gendered and globalized world. For example, in Thailand in the 1990s, as masculinity became increasingly modernized, femininity became increasingly traditional. In a reflection of women's importance to the nation, men's rescripted role as modern leaders of a modern state demanded women's closer adherence to tradition. Thus the international pressure to reform Thai masculinity to conform with Western standards has, ironically, meant increased restrictions on women in general and greater control over prostitute women in particular. In other words, unreflective Western criticism of Thailand's failure to deal with prostitution has undermined prostitute women's chances for political self-determination.

Thus, Western reluctance to interrogate the operation of power in representations of identity has blinded Western analysts to how power works. It is for this reason that Thai feminist groups, for example, have sought to draw attention to this aspect of international power. As Sanitsuda Ekachai argues: "One thing that's troubling me is the reporting of prostitution in Thailand overseas as a moral problem. That Thailand is a land of immoral people, a land of parents who sell their children – it's very sensationalist stories. But it's only part of the story, and a big part of it is the income gap around the world that enables people to buy sex and all that, which goes unreported. It stresses [the] superiority of the rulers and that's troubling."[1]

Activists like Sanitsuda seek international relations within which the West is critically aware of its own power. Such activists are very well aware of the inequality of the sexual and economic relations between the North and the South, and they resent the continued assumption of power implicit within international views of the sex trade in Thailand. As one representative of Friends of Women argues, the focus upon Thailand, and Thai women, as "the problem" is inappropriate:

When I went to Germany that time I said why do you talk about Thai women problem because Thai women don't have any problem, it's very clear, we don't have money – bad economics – and we came here. So why do you say it's Thai women's problem? It's a German men's problem. Because we can't explain why they marry with Thai women – they don't marry with German women, what happened in their society? What about the power relationship between men and women in their society? ... And men exploited some who are disadvantaged. This is a very complicated problem so in Thai women it's very clear, we want money ... It's their society's problem. So now it turns back to me, now there are many prostitutes from Burma, from China from Laos, so what about Thai men? [2]

International solidarity among women as well as other groups clearly requires a reflexivity concerning the West's discursive as well as economic power (although this can be extended beyond the West, as the above quote shows). This study, therefore, has paid close attention to the fact that the construction of identity – national, gendered, or otherwise – takes place within a global context and is strongly shaped by the power of Western discursive representations. This is not simply a cry of Western cultural imperialism. The relationship is not a mere matter of the imposition of Western culture upon a traditional society; it is neither so simple nor so one-sided. Indeed, the West is not so simply unified or powerful, although one can safely state that its long hegemonic position within international affairs has given it a certain structural advantage in reproducing relations of power. The point is that politics in countries outside the hegemonic West are fundamentally shaped by the need to contend with – to resist or respond to – Western discursive power. This is particularly clear in the construction of national identity within non-Western contexts.

Sex and Borders: Gender, Class, and the Nation

The above discussion has explained that national identity building is a globalized process; however, it is also clear that it is a thoroughly gendered process. Throughout the historical period under discussion here, the understanding of the "prostitute" and "prostitution" was constructed in terms of a link between feminine sexual behaviour and the nation. While prostitution was at first construed as a necessary service to the male citizen-soldier, it was gradually reconfigured as a sign of national decline. This reconstruction reflected the changing role of the state between 1850 and 1980 as it moved from a monarchical sphere of influence to a modern nation-state. The nation was at first elite-based, constructed through the official nationalisms that interpolated elite women's bodies as symbols of the modernity and civilization of the nation. While elite women's purity and marital fidelity were closely guarded – in law and practice – from the era of absolute monarchy on, the sexual behaviour of lower-class women was only gradually brought within the ambit of the state. As the state broadened its reach under Chulalongkorn, lower-class women were made available to sexually service male citizenry and elites. After the fall of the absolute monarchy, leaders such as Phibun and Sarit sought to extend the disciplinary mechanisms of the state to lower-class women through the reversal of previous practices and the criminalization of prostitution. Such attempts, however, lacked legitimacy and depth. The 1960 law that extended the sexual discipline of the elite to all classes of women was viewed as a response to international pressure. It was nearly immediately reversed by the 1966 law, which continued to regulate certain forms of prostitution.

It was only with the middle-class nationalism of the 1960s that the nation expanded to incorporate peasant women's bodies as the key locus of national identity. The middle class, both in the form of the student revolution and the later pro-democracy push, sought the institutionalization of a disciplinary rather than an authoritarian state. Subjects were to become citizens, integrated into the state's ambit through the inculcation of national identity and loyalty rather than force. The student movement was the first sign that the middle class "imagined" a larger nation. For the reformist state, peasant unrest had demonstrated that the peasantry, in particular, had to be educated into this national identity. The postrevolutionary reformist state interpolated the peasantry as the "backbone of the nation." Through this process, peasant women's bodies were established as icons of national identity. For the middle class, which sought the benefits of globalization and modernity, national identity was anchored in the peasantry. Prostitute women, who, significantly, were also peasant women, came to symbolize the threat to national identity and culture posed by the American presence and growing Westernization. As symbols of cultural decline, prostitute women were denied voice and agency. The importance of national identity construction and maintenance drowned out the voices of prostitute women's own interpretations of their lives and their political demands (e.g., for better working conditions). Instead, the response to prostitution was determined by the concern to restore proper cultural identity among peasant women. This discursive construction of peasant and prostitute women, as with the peasantry more generally, erased the agency and resistance of the women themselves and established the disciplinary authority of elite and middle-class women.

The predominance of national identity, and women's embodiment of it, in the universe of political discourse in Thailand, however, did not prevent women from being political agents; rather, various women sought to engage in the political process, in interpreting and reinterpreting political reality to further women's interests and to promote women's equality. Elite women, in particular, were able to draw upon their position as guarantors of national identity in order to make claims for women's equality. In doing so, however, they strengthened the disciplinary hold of national identity over other women, particularly prostitute women. Elite women gained political voice through their role in disciplining other women (i.e., peasant prostitute women) into the "correct cultural role." By shifting the burden of tradition onto peasant women, first elite, and then middle-class, women were able to move out of more restrictive roles. Thus, while women's role in national identity maintenance is a double-edged sword – giving women a political voice but just as surely restricting their behaviour – it is also a role that is cathected by class, which allows the burden of restrictive behaviour to be carried by one class while freeing up another. It is the peasants who are now viewed as both the embodiment of national identity and the ones most at risk of losing that identity. The authority and legitimacy of the elites and the middle class depended upon the construction of an "other" in the form of the peasantry, who required elite/middle-class guidance to maintain national identity. Just as masculine modernity has required feminine traditionality, so middle-class modernity has required peasant cultural purity. Prostitute women – as women who defy the norms of female behaviour and as peasants who engage with the modern – are at the centre of these concerns over the loss of traditional identity and culture and are the object of disciplinary measures.

This discussion, therefore, also highlights the role of class in the politics of national identity. Indeed, despite the belief that the rise of the middle class heralds the onset of democracy, the attitude of much of the new middle class in Thailand towards the peasantry and the lower class (as indicated in their attitudes towards prostitute women) does not bode well for the development of a full democracy that incorporates the poor on their own terms. Nonetheless, these class barriers can be, and have been, forded. Along with the growing numbers of NGOs championing peasant causes, a number of the women's groups that formed in the 1980s have taken up the argument for the decriminalization of prostitution and have defended prostitute women's political and social agency. These feminist organizers have taken the time and effort to meet with and listen to prostitute women. They have recognized the process of discursive domination that results in prostitute women being characterized as "victims" (which is similar to the process by which Western feminist discourse ends up characterizing Thai women in general as victims). They have, therefore, taken up a two-pronged critique that demands both (1) that the global economic exploitation of women in prostitution be recognized and addressed and (2) that prostitute women's right to work in prostitution under safe conditions be recognized.

These groups, however, have found their appeals drowned out by middle-class anxiety over the decline of national culture as symbolized in prostitute bodies – an anxiety that the members of these groups sometimes share.

Even after the 1997 economic meltdown, which sent more women into the prostitution industry, the construction of the prostitute as consumer continued to delegitimize claims to prostitution as a form of work for survival. The government of "new men" elected in the aftermath of the financial crisis has, in fact, turned its attention to those who are construed as the "real victims" of prostitution – Burmese and Chinese women who are believed to be trafficked into Thailand, and who engage in prostitution under what are sometimes slavery-like conditions. The new government also threw itself into anti-child prostitution campaigns and crackdowns, proving to the world its commitment to human rights and modern, democratic government. These campaigns for the protection of children and migrant prostitutes, which will only lead to more difficult circumstances for prostitute women, have not been accompanied by a sustained defence of the rights of Thai women in prostitution; instead, Thai women continue to be viewed as material girls who deserve to suffer for their folly. The new middle-class democracy in Thailand comes at the price of the continued disenfranchisement of prostitute women.

The Globalization of Gender: Or, the Gender of Globalization
These processes, of course, are not confined to the borders of Thailand; rather, they reflect a global pattern of the gendered reconfiguration of national identities (and state power) in response to transnational forces. Or, to put it another way, they reflect a global pattern of responding to transnational forces *through gender*. Thus, gender is the central discursive mechanism through which the contending forces of globalization and nationalism are managed and resolved. In particular, the nation is gendered female under the direction of the modernized, globalized masculine state. The result has been the circumscription of women's agency and power (albeit resisted and differentially experienced) and the enhancement of (particularly upper- and middle-class) male power. Therefore, the construction of gender and the resulting imbalance in power are not simply national or cultural processes; rather, they are processes in which Western societies are involved and for which they must take some responsibility.

This process of responding to transnational forces through gender dates back to the earliest from of modern globalization – colonialism – and has occurred throughout the colonial and postcolonial world. For instance, Partha Chaterjee's work on nationalism in India argues that, in responding to imperialism, anti-colonial nationalism marked out a territory of acquiescence, "a domain where the West had proved its superiority and the East had succumbed ... [where] Western superiority had to be acknowledged and its accomplishments carefully studied and replicated" and a domain of resistance, an "inner," "spiritual" realm that bore "the 'essential' marks of cultural identity."[3] This demarcation was gendered in that it was the inner realm, the domain of resistance, that was understood to be the realm of women, or women's bodies. And, while Chatterjee does not state this explicitly, we may conclude from this study and venture that the outer realm, the realm of acquiescence (which Chatterjee describes as including the practices of statecraft, the economy, science, and technology) was, and is, the realm of masculinity.

Chatterjee does, however, describe the inverse relationship between the two realms: "the greater one's success in imitating Western skills in the material domain ... the greater the need to preserve the distinctness of one's spiritual culture."[4] Thus, success in modernization in the masculine realm has come at the price of the increased control over women's bodies in the feminine realm. Indeed, the importance of this process in postcolonial societies has been precisely this growing circumscription of female power by the (masculine) state. As Ong and Peletz have pointed out in their introduction to a collection of studies on body politics in Southeast Asia, the inscription of state power on female bodies has been a central task of the postcolonial state: "The postcolonial state, in its varied tasks of building a national identity, meeting challenges from communally-based interest groups, and representing itself as a modern nation, is continuously engaged in defining the composition and form of political society. This making and patrolling of the body politic is an ongoing struggle that often entails the inscription of state power on women's (and to a lesser extent, men's) bodies."[5] Both Suzanne Brenner's and Evelyn Blackwood's work on discourses of gender in Indonesia have uncovered the ways in which local, alternative discourses of gender (which grant women social power) are being increasingly sidelined by state-led, nation-building discourses. Typically, these discourses reconfigure women's roles as "house-wives" ("ibu-ism") or draw on Islamic interpretations of women as lacking in self-control and, therefore, spiritual potency.[6] As Brenner points out, the resultant "dominant ideologies of male potency serve to legitimate male control over women and over the society more broadly."[7] Women's sexual, reproductive role is of particular concern to the nation-building state, as is indicated by Heng and Devan's essay on reproductive policies in Singapore. The Singaporean state has overtly sought to manipulate the class and racial make-up of the body politic by figuring Chinese women's "failure" to reproduce in sufficient numbers (along with Malay and Indian women's "over"-reproduction) as a threat to Confucian culture. This feminine failure, in turn, demands and justifies the increasing intervention and power of the patriarchal state (power that, as Heng and Devan point out, is operationalized precisely through the adoption of Western instruments of "definition, selection, and control").[8] The result throughout Southeast Asia, and in other postcolonial societies, has been a tighter disciplining of female sexual behaviour (in line with the need to police national culture) and a concomitant restriction of women's social, economic, and political power and manoeuvrability.

Women have not simply been victims of these processes of course, and one can look for ways that they have manipulated nationalist imagery to their own advantage (e.g., as elite women in Thailand did) as well as how women at the margins negotiate among the various discourses of gender. Nonetheless, the thrust of these developments has generally been to undermine women's claims as workers and political subjects. Ironically, therefore, this call to protect national culture in the face of global economic and cultural forces through the disciplining of women has served the interests of international capital well. Indeed, those self-same government leaders who are calling for the protection of culture through the restriction of women's power (as well as that of the peasantry more broadly) and, therefore, their rights as workers, benefit enormously from global investment and profiteering.

The flip side of this process has been a concomitant increase in the power of middle-class and elite men. This point leads us back to examining the globalized construction of masculinity. This global structuring of masculinity has been even less the subject of investigation than has the reconfiguring of feminine identities; however, it has been key to the formulation of the anti-colonial movement and the postcolonial state. Nandy and Fanon have uncovered the process of "hypermasculinization" in national movements – an aggressive remasculinization in response to the feminizing of the other under colonialism.[9] Lily Ling sees the modern process of "hypermasculine developmentalism" in East Asia, including support for the sex industry, as a reaction to the West's feminizing of Asian societies.[10] While this appears to be a masculinity that differentiates itself from the West, in fact, it is Western masculinity in an exaggerated form and, therefore, receives some grudging respect from the West. The new man that we saw in Thailand, and that we can see elsewhere throughout the world, is most clearly a global creation. He is the product of the boardrooms and backrooms of, for example, the World Bank, the United Nations, and the World Trade Organization, where proper masculinity and its twin, proper forms of rule, are performed, standardized, and disciplined. While this form of masculinity may at first glance appear to be a kinder, gentler, and more equitable gender construct than hyper-masculinity, it is precisely this new man who, in the name of protecting national culture, "protects" and, therefore, limits women while simultaneously profiting from the ensuing intensification of globalized profit.[11] Clearly, this new masculinity is a fundamentally globalized masculinity.

It is not only in the postcolonial world that, in response to globalization, gendered images are being employed to reshape societies. The image of the prostitute that opened this study is a globally reproduced image. It is employed in the service of Western states in ways that enhance the power of a particular form of masculinized state vis-à-vis not only women, but also other (by implication, less masculine) states. For instance, the re-emergence of the panic over trafficking in women relies on a series of powerful images about prostitute women – particularly as misguided/victimized waifs who require protection or, alternatively, as "greedy girls" who require punishment. Neither of these images give credence to demands by migrant and non-migrant prostitute women for protection of their rights as workers; rather, both of these images justify a protectionist stance on the part of wealthy nations who wish to block further "economic migration" to their comfortable shores. In doing so, these states enhance their image as caring and protective (or "fatherly") states – certainly more caring (and, therefore, more legitimate) than the states that produce these women (which would include not only the traditional sending states of Southeast Asia, but also the former Eastern Bloc countries). Thus national and global legitimacy are enhanced even as these same states further weaken the position of women within their own borders by, in the Canadian case, for example, declaring that to grant prostitute women rights would open the floodgates to traffickers and migrant prostitutes. In other words, the state declares that certain women (and therefore, I would argue, all women) must be denied rights *in order to protect the national society from the negative consequences of globalization.* This is a precise echo of the arguments put forward by postcolonial states. Even Western states, therefore, use gender as a mechanism for managing the clash of the local and the global.

Together, the two central themes of this book – that national identity construction is a global process and that it is a gendered process – point us towards understanding that global processes are gendered and that gender is itself a global process. Such gendering does not happen simply at the material level of the distribution of the burdens and benefits of globalization but, rather, in the very discursive construction of what is national/local and what is global. States (and other political entities) configure their responses to global processes *through gender,* as well as class, and this has very different, and unequal, consequences for actual men and women. Further, this means that gender cannot simply be viewed as the product of a particular culture. Thus, while gender is by no means universal, it is global in that the process of cultural, and therefore gender, construction is itself embedded within the process of globalization (in differentiating self from other, local from global). The failure of Western analysts to recognize this process is itself a denial of the West's power and its involvement in this process. Paying closer attention to this intertwined construction of identities is the jumping off point for the new international relations demanded by Thai activists (among others) – relations that entail the West being reflexive about its own power.

Conclusion

Throughout this book, looking at politics as a struggle over meaning, and at prostitution as a contested category of identity construction, has allowed us to see the political struggle over prostitution policy – the attempts to "do something about it" rather than to see an a priori capitalist/patriarchal interest in the maintenance of prostitution. Prostitution is a constructed category that reflects the social desire to police female behaviour. To understand prostitution policy, therefore, we need to understand how prostitution is understood and how prostitute women are constructed. In Thailand, where the construction and maintenance of national identity has been of primary importance to state survival since the era of colonialism, female identity has been viewed in terms of cultural and national identity. Prostitute women, as women who do not conform to proper modes of behaviour, have come to symbolize cultural decline. They are therefore viewed as requiring state intervention and discipline rather than as being capable and self-determining political actors. Prostitute women's own interpretations of their lives as, for example, wage earners and family supporters are silenced by dominant interpretations that focus on their cultural symbolism. Therefore, prostitution policy, even as written by a progressive, pro-democratic middle class, continues to penalize prostitute women rather than to focus upon their demands for decriminalization. In the end, such an approach only works to further undermine the position of women in general and of prostitute women in particular. If the mistreatment of women in prostitution and elsewhere lies in constructions of gender that position women as objects rather than as subjects, then the continued treatment of prostitute women as incapable of voicing their own demands only reinforces the gendered imbalance of power. Thus, it is only by giving prostitute women a political voice and the ability to make their own political demands that the class-based, gendered power that underlies the institutionalization of prostitution will be addressed. By uncovering the ways in which the prostitute and prostitution are constructed within particular historical locations and in relation to particular structures of power, such as gender and national identity, we can understand – and change, it is to be hoped – the relations of power that vocalize particular interpretations of prostitution while silencing others.

Appendix
Chronology of Historical Events, 1850-1997

1851-68	Reign of King Mongkut (The Fourth Reign of the Chakri Dynasty).
1855	Bowring Treaty.
1868-1910	Reign of King Chulalongkorn (The Fifth Reign).
1905	Slavery abolished.
1910-25	Reign of King Vajiravudh (The Sixth Reign).
1932	Overthrow of the absolute monarchy.
1935	Polygamy abolished.
1938-44	Phibun Songkhram government.
1939	Siam renamed Thailand.
1941-44	Thailand occupied by Japan.
1948-57	Phibun's second government.
1957-63	Sarit Thanarat government.
1960	Prostitution Prohibition Act.
1963-73	Thanom Kittikachorn/Praphat Charusathian government.
1964	American military bases established in Thailand.
1966	Entertainment Places Act.
1973	Student uprising. Overthrow of Thanom-Praphat dictatorship, beginning of democracy period. Prof. Sanya Thammasak elected PM.
1975	M.R. Kukrit Pramoj elected PM.
1976	Return of military dictatorship. Thanin Kraivixien becomes PM
1977	Gen. Kriangsak Chomanand becomes PM.
1980	Gen. Prem Tinsulanond becomes PM. Period of "guided democracy" begins.
1988	Free elections held. Gen. Chatichai Choonhavan elected PM.
1991	Military overthrow of Chatichai government. Anand Panyarachun acts as PM.
1992	Gen. Suchinda Kraprayoon declares himself PM. Uprising against military rule (in May). Democracy restored, Anand returns. Chuan Leekpai elected PM (September).
1995	Banharn Silpa-archa elected PM.
1996	New Prostitution Prohibition Act.
1996	Gen. Chavalit Yongchaiyudh elected PM.
1997	Chavalit steps down, Chuan Leekpai becomes PM.

Notes

Introduction

1 The terms "Western" and "non-Western" are, like the terms "First World" and "Third World," problematic in their seeming characterization of overlapping and complex realities as monolithic and mutually exclusive. I use the terms here as a shorthand for global relations of power that have, since the age of imperialism, typically involved the predominance of Euro-American countries (in all their complexities) and of a Euro-centric point of view.

2 This point was emphasized to me over and over again in interviews with both government and non-government representatives in Thailand in 1996.

3 See Chandra Mohanty, "Under Western Eyes: Feminist Scholarship and Colonial Discourses," in *Third World Women and the Politics of Feminism,* ed. Chandra Mohanty, Ann Russo, Lourdes Torres (Bloomington: Indiana University Press, 1991), 51-80.

4 Cited in Saisuree Chutikul, *Children in Especially Difficult Situations: I (Thailand),* report to UNICEF (Bangkok: National Youth Bureau, Office of the Prime Minister, June 1986), 38.

5 See Morris G. Fox, "Problem of Prostitution in Thailand," in *Social Service in Thailand* (Bangkok: Department of Public Welfare, Ministry of the Interior, 1960), 141.

6 Saisuree, "Children," 38.

7 Thahn-dam Truong, *Sex, Money and Morality* (London: Zed, 1990).

8 Wathinee Boonchalaksi and Philip Guest, *Prostitution in Thailand,* IPSR Publication No. 171 (Bangkok: Institute for Population and Social Research, Mahidol University, 1994), 10.

9 Pasuk Phongpaichit and Chris Baker, *Thailand: Economy and Politics* (New York: Oxford University Press, 1995), 80.

10 Pasuk Phongpaichit, *From Peasant Girls to Bangkok Masseuses* (Geneva: ILO, 1982), 8.

11 S.D. Bamber, K.J. Hewison, P.J. Underwood, "A History of Sexually Transmitted Diseases in Thailand: Policy and Politics," *Genitourinary Medicine* 69 (1993): 153; Bhassorn Limanonda, "The Demographic and Behavioural Study of Female Commercial Sex Workers in Thailand," Institute of Population Studies Publication No. 210/93, Chulalongkorn University, October 1993, 1.

12 See, for example, Maria J. Wawer et al., "Origins and Working Conditions of Female Sex Workers in Urban Thailand: Consequences of Social Context for HIV Transmission," *Social Science and Medicine* 42, 3 (1996): 454.

13 Cornelia Ann Kammerer et al., "HIV Infection among Hilltribes in Northern Thailand," in *Culture and Sexual Risk: Anthropological Perspectives on AIDS,* ed. Han ten Brummelhuis and Gilbert Herdt (Amsterdam: Gordon and Beach, 1995), 59.

14 See Hollie Shaw, "Legal Whip Set to Crack in Domination Case," *Globe and Mail,* 9 October 1998, A5.

15 See Eric Cohen, "Thai Girls and Farang Men: The Edge of Ambiguity," *Annals of Tourism Research* 9 (1982): 403-28.

16 Kamala Kempadoo, "Introduction," in *Global Sex Workers,* ed. Kamala Kempadoo and Jo Doezema (New York: Routledge, 1998), 14.

17 See Gail Pheterson, "The Whore Stigma: Female Dishonour and Male Unworthiness," *Social Text* 37 (Winter 1993): 39-64.
18 Denise Riley, *"Am I That Name?" Feminism and the Category of "Woman" in History* (Minneapolis: University of Minnesota, 1988), 3.
19 Mohanty, "Under Western Eyes," 54.
20 Ibid., 54. Mohanty here points out that this critique is not simply aimed at "Western feminists" but at anyone who uses the techniques that she criticizes.
21 Ibid., 54 and 63. See also Note 7.
22 See, for example, Khin Thitsa, *Providence and Prostitution: Image and Reality for Women in Buddhist Thailand* (London: Change International Reports, 1980).
23 See Chatsumarn Kabilsingh, *Thai Women in Buddhism* (Parallax Press: Berkeley, 1991).
24 See Penny van Esterik, *Materializing Thailand* (Oxford: Berg, 2000), 65-90.
25 Nicola Tannenbaum, "Buddhism, Prostitution and Sex: Limits on the Academic Discourse on Gender in Thailand," in *Gender and Sexualities in Modern Thailand*, ed. Peter A. Jackson and Nerida M. Cook (Chiang Mai: Silkworm, 1999), 252.
26 See, for example, Siriporn Skrobanek, "The Transnational Sex-exploitation of Thai Women," master's research paper, Institute of Social Studies, The Hague, March 1983.
27 Truong, *Sex, Money and Morality*, 46.
28 Siriporn, "Transnational Sex-exploitation," 55, 61-2.
29 Sukanya Hantrakul, "Spirit of a Fighter – Women and Prostitution in Thailand," *Manushi* 18 (October-November 1983): 32.
30 Kumari Jayawardena, *Feminism and Nationalism in the Third World* (London: Zed, 1986).
31 Floya Anthias and Nira Yuval-Davis, *Woman-Nation-State* (New York: St. Martin's Press, 1989), 7.
32 Deniz Kandiyoti, "Identity and Its Discontents: Women and the Nation," *Colonial Discourse and Post-Colonial Theory: A Reader*, ed. Patrick Williams and Laura Chrisman (New York: Columbia University Press, 1994), 377.
33 Anne McClintock, "Family Feuds: Gender, Nationalism and the Family," *Feminist Review* 44 (Summer 1993): 62.
34 John Girling, *Thailand: Society and Politics* (Ithaca: Cornell University Press, 1981), 21.
35 Ibid., 21-9. See also Truong, *Sex, Money and Morality*, 142-6.

Chapter 1: Gender, Prostitution, and the "Standards of Civilization"
1 See Thongchai Winichakul, *Siam Mapped: History of the Geo-body of a Nation* (Chiang Mai: Silkworm Books, 1994), chap. 1.
2 Simon de la Loubère, *The Kingdom of Siam* (New York: Oxford in Asia Historical Reprints, Oxford University Press, 1969 [1697]), 74.
3 Anthony Reid, *Southeast Asia in the Age of Commerce, 1450-1680*. Vol. 1: *The Land Below the Winds* (New Haven, Yale University Press, 1988), 156.
4 Barbara Watson Andaya, "From Temporary Wife to Prostitute: Sexuality and Economic Change in Early Modern Southeast Asia," *Journal of Women's History* 9, 4 (Winter 1998): 23.
5 de la Loubère, *Kingdom of Siam*, 74.
6 Ibid., 52.
7 Randolph Trumbach, "Sex, Gender, and Sexual Identity in Modern Culture: Male Sodomy and Female Prostitution in Enlightenment London," in *Forbidden History: The State, Society and the Regulation of Sexuality in Modern History*, ed. John C. Fout (Chicago: University of Chicago Press, 1992), 91.
8 Susan Hekman, *Gender and Knowledge: Elements of a Postmodern Feminism* (Boston: Northeastern University Press, 1990), 114-6.
9 Jeffrey Merrick, "Sexual Politics and Public Order in Late Eighteenth-century France: The *Mémoires secrètes* and the *Correspondance secrète*," in *Forbidden History: The State, Society and the Regulation of Sexuality in Modern History*, ed. John C. Fout (Chicago: University of Chicago Press, 1992), 187.
10 R.W. Connell, *Masculinities* (Berkeley: University of California Press, 1995), 186-7; Ruth Perry, "Colonizing the Breast: Sexuality and Maternity in Eighteenth-century England," *Forbidden History*, 113.

11 Craig Reynolds, "A Nineteenth-century Thai Buddhist Defense of Polygamy and Some Remarks on the Social History of Women in Thailand," paper prepared for the Seventh Conference of the International Association of Historians of Asia, Bangkok, 22-6 August 1977, p. 16.
12 Abbot Low Moffat, *Mongkut, The King of Siam* (Ithaca: Cornell University Press, 1961), 135.
13 Gayatri Spivak, "Can the Subaltern Speak?" in *Colonial Discourse and Post-Colonial Theory: A Reader,* ed. Patrick Williams and Laura Chrisman (New York: Columbia University Press, 1994), 93.
14 Nigel J. Brailey, *Two Views of Siam on the Eve of the Chakri Reformation* (Whiting Bay, Scotland: Kiscadale Publications, 1989), 37.
15 Cited in Ronald Spector, "The American Image of Southeast Asia, 1790-1865," *Journal of Southeast Asia Studies* 3, 2 (September 1972): 301. Emphasis added.
16 Andaya, "From Temporary Wife to Prostitute," 21-2.
17 Cited in Margaret Strobel, *Gender, Sex and Empire* (Washington, DC: American Historical Association, 1993), 13.
18 Suwadee T. Patana, "Thai Society's Expectations of Women, 1904-1935: An Approach to Women's History," paper presented to 12th IAHA Conference, University of Hong Kong, 24-8 June 1991, p. 23; Gail Omvedt, *Women in Popular Movements: India and Thailand during the Decade of Women* (Geneva: UNRISD, 1986), 44.
19 Reynolds, "A Nineteenth-century Thai Buddhist Defense," 21-2.
20 See Water Vella, *Chaiyo! King Vijiravudh and the Development of Thai Nationalism* (Honolulu: University of Hawaii Press, 1978), 53.
21 Ibid., 155-7.
22 For accounts of the movement to repeal the Contagious Diseases Acts in England, see Judith Walkowitz, *Prostitution and Victorian Society: Women, Class and the State* (New York: Cambridge University Press, 1980); on the White slavery panic, see Deborah Gorham, "The 'Maiden Tribute of Modern Babylon' Re-examined: Child Prostitution and the Idea of Childhood in Late-Victorian England," *Victorian Studies* 21, 3 (Spring 1978): 353-80.
23 Deborah Stienstra, "Madonna/Whore, Pimp/Protector: International Law and Organization Related to Prostitution," *Studies in Political Economy* 51 (Fall 1996): 191.
24 Ibid., 192, 195.
25 Suwadee, "Thai Society's Expectations," 12-3
26 Ibid., 13.
27 Sukanya Hantrakul, "Prostitutes and Human Rights in Thailand," (N.p., 1982), 7.
28 League of Nations Commission of Enquiry into Traffic in Women and Children in the Far East, *Siam: Internal Conditions Relating to Traffic* (Report to the Council) (New York: League of Nations, 1933), 313-4.
29 By regulating brothels the government made it illegal for women to operate independently as prostitutes and to move in and out of the trade. While there is little information on how the trade operated at this time, evidence from other countries has shown how licensing regulations have usually worked to decrease women's independence and to delimit a particular identity as that of "prostitute" (rather than prostitution being viewed as a sometime occupation or occasional exchange). See Walkowitz, *Prostitution and Victorian Society.*
30 Suwadee, "Thai Society's Expectations," 9.
31 "Summary of the Control and Prevention of Venereal Disease Act R.S. 127, 1909," in Morris G. Fox, "Problem of Prostitution in Thailand," *Social Service in Thailand* (Bangkok: Department of Public Welfare, Ministry of the Interior, 1960), Exhibit A, 147-8.
32 Thanh-dam Truong, *Sex, Money and Morality: Prostitution and Tourism in Southeast Asia* (London: Zed, 1990), 155; Stienstra, "Madonna/Whore," 192.
33 Vella, *Chaiyo!,* 122-4; Gerrit Gong, *The Standard of "Civilization" in International Society* (Oxford: Clarendon Press, 1984), 231-7.
34 Gong, *Standard of Civilization,* 236-7.
35 League of Nations Commission of Enquiry, "Siam," Annex II, "Extracts from the Traffic in Women and Girls Act, B.E. 2471 (1928)," 325.
36 Ibid., 316. Along with Siam, France and the United States (and their colonies) maintained

a system of licensed brothels, arguing that they were an internal rather than an international affair and that they were more humane and "civilized" than abolitionism. On the other hand, the French considered the traffic in women a product of Asiatic culture, which could be modified through the influence of a French culture, which is "so respectful of the rights of women and children." Truong, *Sex, Money and Morality,* 83-6.

37 League of Nations Commission of Enquiry, "Siam," 308, 313.

38 Gail Hershatter, "Courtesans and Streetwalkers: The Changing Discourses on Shanghai Prostitution, 1890-1949," *Journal of the History of Sexuality* 3, 2 (1992): 247.

39 Response of the Thai delegate, *League of Nations Bulletin,* 1 July 1936. Cited in Kenneth Perry Landon, *The Chinese in Thailand* (New York: Russell and Russell, 1977), 95.

40 Minutes of the Committee for Considering the Abolition of Licensed Brothels and the Welfare of Women and Children, 1937 and 1938. Cited in Fox, "Prostitution in Thailand," 41, 49; Exhibit B, "Proposal for Venereal Disease Control in Thailand, B.E. 2481 (1938)."

41 See "Proposal for Venereal Disease Control in Thailand, B.E. 2481 (1938)," in Morris G. Fox, "Problem of Prostitution in Thailand," *Social Service in Thailand,* Exhibit B, 149.

42 League of Nations Commission of Enquiry, "Siam," 313.

43 Landon, *The Chinese,* 96-7; Victor Purcell, *The Chinese in Southeast Asia,* 2nd ed. (Kuala Lampur: Oxford University Press, 1965), 136. The increased charges were part of a program of increased taxes and tariffs aimed at the Chinese merchant class.

44 *Bangkok Chronicle,* 10 January 1940. Cited in Landon, *The Chinese,* 97.

45 Health officers were to be further empowered to order anyone with a venereal disease to seek treatment, including (and, according to the committee, most important) prostitute women. See Fox, "Prostitution in Thailand," Exhibit C, 151-2.

46 The British sent Lord Mountbatten with troops to "open relations" with Thailand in March 1944. M.R. Seni Pramoj, a senior statesman, felt that accepting the terms set down by Lord Mountbatten would result in colonization. The American government was suspicious of British motives: "In their eyes Mountbatten, a great-grandson of Queen Victoria with close relatives in most of Europe's royal families, looked likely to have as his main objective the restoration of the British empire in the Far East ... Fears were expressed too that, with Mountbatten in command of this theatre, Britain would seek to expand its empire to encompass Thailand." See Judith Stowe, *Siam becomes Thailand: A Story of Intrigue* (London: Hurst and Co., 1991), 271.

47 Chief Secretary to the Cabinet to Wichit Wathakan, 8 June 1939. Cited in Kobkua Suwannatha-Piat, *Thailand's Durable Premier: Phibun through Three Decades, 1932-1957* (New York: Oxford University Press, 1995), 153-4, note 26.

48 Scot Barmé, *Luang Wichit Wathakan and the Creation of Thai Identity* (Singapore: Institute of Southeast Asian Studies, 1996), 158.

49 Kobkua, *Thailand's Durable Premier,* 126.

50 Sir Anthony Eden, Cited in ibid., 129.

51 Thamsook Numnonda, "Pibulsongkram's Thai Nation-Building Programme during the Japanese Military Presence, 1941-1945," *Journal of Southeast Asian Studies* 9, 2 (September 1978): 238.

52 Kobkua, *Thailand's Durable Premier,* 115.

53 It is perhaps of no small importance that it was in 1944 that Anna Leonowans' 1850s writings on harem life in Siam were revived and republished (by none other than the wife of Kenneth Landon, representative of the US State Department in Thailand) and, in 1951, produced as the Rogers and Hammerstein musical *Anna and the King of Siam.* The musical then became an internationally popular film and was immediately banned in Thailand for its portrayal of King Mongkut as a cruel and backward despot (and, no doubt, for its portrayal of Thailand as "uncivilized"). Even today *Anna and the King of Siam* meets with hostility in Thailand. In 1998 the government refused to allow filming of a new version to take place on Thai territory. See "Shall They dance? Probably Not in Bangkok's Backyard," *National Post,* 7 December 1998, D4.

54 Kobkua, *Thailand's Durable Premier,* 127.

55 Thamsook, "Pibulsongkram's Thai Nation-Building Programme," 240.

56 Ministry of Foreign Affairs, *Statements by Chairmen of the Delegations of Thailand at the*

Second to Fortieth Sessions of the UNGA (1947-1985) (Bangkok: Ministry of Foreign Affairs, International Organizations Department, 1986), 14.

57 Stienstra, "Madonna/Whore,"195-6.

58 Article 16, *United Nations Convention for the Suppression of the Traffic in Persons and of the Exploitation of the Prostitution of Others.*

59 United Nations, Department of Economic and Social Affairs, *Study on Traffic in Persons and Prostitution (Suppression of the Traffic in Persons and of the Exploitation of the Prostitution of Others* (New York: United Nations, 1959), 21.

60 United Nations, *Study on Traffic,* 30-1.

61 "Prostitution in Selected Countries of Asia and the Far East," *International Review of Criminal Policy* 13 (October 1958): 50.

62 Ibid., 53.

63 National Identity Board, *Thai Life: Thai Women* (Bangkok: National Identity Board, Prime Minister's Office, 1983), 41.

64 Fox, "Prostitution in Thailand," 162.

65 Ibid., 145.

66 Centre for the Protection of Children's Rights, "Case Study Report on Commercial Sexual Exploitation of Children in Thailand" (Bangkok: Centre for the Protection of Children's Rights, October 1996), 12-3.

67 Fox, "Prostitution in Thailand," 140-1, 163. In a move designed to discredit his close rival General Phao, who had been caught in an opium smuggling scandal, Phibun also vowed to close the opium dens by 1957. It was in this political climate that Phibun and Lady Laiad supported new measures be taken vis-à-vis prostitution.

68 Ibid., 143.

69 Vibul Thamavit and Robert D. Golden, "The Family in Thailand," in *Aspects and Facets of Thailand,* ed. Witt Siwasariyanon (Bangkok: Public Relations Department, 1958), 2.

70 Ibid., 8.

71 Ibid.

72 See Frank C. Darling, *Thailand and the United States* (Washington DC: Public Affairs Press, 1965), 146-53.

73 Vibul and Golden, "The Family in Thailand," 8-9.

74 Fox, "Prostitution in Thailand," 142, 144-5.

75 Ibid., Exhibit G, 162.

76 In 2001, 10,000 baht was the equivalent to approximately Cdn$350.

77 Section 13, "Prohibition of Prostitution Business Act, BE 2500 (1957) in Fox, "Prostitution in Thailand," Exhibit F, 160.

78 The 1956 Penal Code punished procurement for sexual purposes with one to ten years imprisonment *and* a fine of 2,000 to 20,000 baht, with even steeper fines for procuring those under eighteen. See Centre for the Protection of Children's Rights, "Case Study Report," 13.

79 Pasuk Phongpaichit and Chris Baker, *Thailand: Economy and Politics* (New York: Oxford University Press, 1995), 72.

80 Thak Chaloemtiarana, *Thailand and the Politics of Despotic Paternalism,* Social Science Association of Thailand, Thai Khadi Institute (Bangkok: Thammasat University, 1979), 338-9.

81 Ibid., note 3, 336-7, and 338-9. During an investigation into the terms of Sarit's will it was also discovered that he had used government funds to maintain his mistresses. Ibid., 337.

82 Charles F. Keyes, *Thailand: Buddhist Kingdom as Modern Nation State* (London: Westview Press, 1987), 81.

83 Thak, *Thailand,* 324-5.

84 Between 1960 and 1970, the ratio of men to women migrating to the city shifted from 131:100 to 115:100. See Darunee Tantiwiramanond and Shashi Ranjan Pandey, *By Women, for Women: A Study of Women's Organizations in Thailand* (Singapore: ISEAS, 1991), 18; see also Pawadee Tongudai, "Women, Migration and Employment: A Study of Migrant Workers in Bangkok" (PhD diss., New York University, 1982).

85 Bruce London, *Metropolis and Nation in Thailand: The Political Economy of Uneven Development* (Boulder, CO: Westview Press, 1980), 90.

86 Thak, *Thailand,* 214-5.
87 Ibid., 197-8.
88 Ibid., 198.
89 Ibid., 163.
90 "Act for the Abatement of Prostitution B.E. 2503," *Royal Thai Government Gazette* 2, no. 212, 28 November 1960, 562-3. For the first time, legislation on prostitution did not distinguish according to sex: both male and female prostitution are covered in the act. Fox's report had mentioned some incidents of male prostitution in Bangkok. See Fox, "Prostitution in Thailand," 143.
91 Also in the 1909 act. See Sukanya Hantrakul, "Prostitution in Thailand," paper proposed to the Women in Asia Workshop, Monash University, Melbourne, 22-4 July 1983, 6.
92 "Act for the Abatement of Prostitution," Section 5 (2), 561.
93 Ibid., Sections 8 and 9, 562.
94 Ibid., Section 11, 562.
95 Sukanya, "Prostitution in Thailand," 19.
96 Ibid., 21.
97 Ibid., 18.
98 Ministry of the Interior, cited in Sukanya Hantrakul, "Prostitution in Thailand," in *Development and Displacement: Women in Southeast Asia,* ed. Glen Chandler, Norma Sullivan and Jan Branson (Clayton, Australia: Centre of Southeast Asian Studies, Monash University, 1988), 125.
99 Ibid.
100 Sukanya, "Prostitution in Thailand," 18.

Chapter 2: Peasants, Prostitutes, and the Body Politic

1 Pasuk Phongpaichit and Chris Baker, *Thailand: Economy and Politics* (New York: Oxford University Press, 1995), 75.
2 Ibid., 189.
3 Chris Lyttleton, "The Good People of Isan: Commercial Sex in Northeast Thailand," *Australian Journal of Anthropology* 5, 3 (1994): 266.
4 Eric Cohen, "Thai Girls and Farang Men: The Edge of Ambiguity," *Annals of Tourism Research* 9 (1982): 405; See also J.F. Embree, "Thailand: A Loosely Structured Social System," *American Anthropologist* 52, 2 (1950): 186; Sukanya Hantrakul, "Sexual Culture of Thai Women," *The Nation,* 2 September 1996, A4.
5 Mary Beth Mills, "Rural Women Working in Bangkok: The Rocky Road of Social Change," Final Report to the National Research Council of Thailand, n.d., 4.
6 Pasuk Phongpaichit, *From Peasant Girls to Bangkok Masseuses* (Geneva: International Labour Office, 1982), 14-8. In the early study Pasuk discovered that most of the women she interviewed remitted one-third to one-half their wages to their families. Pasuk, *From Peasant Girls,* 22-5.
7 Mills, "Rural Women in Bangkok," 5.
8 Lenore Manderson, "Public Sex Performances in Patpong and Exploration of the Edges of Imagination," *Journal of Sex Research* 29, 4 (1992): 451-75. See also Walter Meyer, "Beyond the Mask: Toward a Transdisciplinary Approach of Selected Social Problems Related to the Evolution and Context of International Tourism in Thailand" (PhD diss., University of Geneva, 1987), 337, on go-go dancing as "a ritual of protest."
9 Thak Chaloemtiarana. *Thailand and the Politics of Despotic Paternalism* (Bangkok: Thammasat University, 1979), 255.
10 Ibid., 264.
11 Cited in Bruce London, *Metropolis and Nation in Thailand: The Political Economy of Uneven Development* (Boulder, CO: Westview Press, 1980), 96.
12 Pasuk and Baker, *Thailand,* 74-5.
13 Ibid., 291. John Girling, *Thailand: Society and Politics* (Ithaca: Cornell University Press, 1981) 115, 252-6.
14 Pasuk and Baker, *Thailand,* 294.
15 Ibid., 294.

16 Benedict Anderson, "Introduction," in *In the Mirror: Literature and Politics in Siam in the American Era*, ed. Benedict Anderson and Ruchira Mendiones (Bangkok: Duang Kamol, 1985), 19.
17 Girling, *Thailand*, 177.
18 Robert J. Muscat, *Thailand and the United States: Development, Security and Foreign Aid* (New York: Columbia University Press, 1990), 193.
19 Pasuk and Baker, *Thailand*, 186-7.
20 Ibid., 188.
21 Ibid., 198.
22 Benedict Anderson, "Withdrawal Symptoms: Social and Cultural Aspects of the October 6 Coup," *Bulletin of Concerned Asian Scholars* 9, 3 (July–September 1977): 17-8.
23 Pasuk and Baker, *Thailand*, 321, note 9; Kevin Hewison, *Bankers and Bureaucrats: Capital and the Role of the State in Thailand* (New Haven: Yale University Southeast Asia Studies, 1989), 107.
24 Ross Prizzia, *Thailand in Transition* (Honolulu: University of Hawaii Press, 1985), 190.
25 Pasuk and Baker, *Thailand*, 300-1.
26 According to one observer, the crowds included the bar-girls themselves. See David Van Praagh, *Thailand's Struggle for Democracy: The Life and Times of M.R. Seni Pramoj* (New York: Holmes and Meier, 1996), 149.
27 ISOC was originally CSOC – the Communist Suppression Operation Command – established in the mid-1960s "under US auspices to co-ordinate counter-insurgency." See Pasuk and Baker, *Thailand*, 307.
28 The Red Gaurs refers to a type of wild boar, while Nawaphon translates literally as "Ninth Power," which is thought to refer to the current monarch (the ninth king of the Chakri Dynasty).
29 Girling, *Thailand* (Ithaca: Cornell University Press, 1981), 193.
30 CIA influence is also believed to be behind these groups, particularly Nawaphon, which was formed by a Thai student who had been studying in the United States and who claimed to be linked to the CIA. See Pasuk and Baker, 307-8; David Morell and Chai-anan Samudavinjia, *Political Conflict in Thailand: Reform, Reaction, Revolution* (Cambridge, MA: Oelgeschlager, Gunn and Hain, 1981), 239.
31 Pasuk and Baker, *Thailand*, 307.
32 In April 1975 Saigon fell to the communists, as did Phnom Penh. The spectre of communist takeover on its borders lent credence to fears of communist advance in Thailand – particularly through a linkage of students, peasants, the CPT, and the new communist regimes. See Pasuk and Baker, *Thailand*, 306.
33 Thongchai, "The Account of an Eyewitness," *The Nation*, 5 October 1996, A4. Thongchai records the conversation thus: "'Definitely, they must be the *Yuan* (Vietnamese),' one suggested. 'Of course they are Yuan. Otherwise why couldn't they speak Thai at all?' the other seconded." Another senior police officer (and famous author) Manas Sattyarak excused the death of one student by saying: "His complexion is so white. Perhaps he is a *Yuan*." See Thongchai, *The Nation*, 5 October 1996, A4. Other people on the scene in October 1976 also remember this kind of reference. See, for example, the memoir of a mother who went looking for her son after the massacre: "I saw [soldiers] burning the students. Those children were still squirming in the flames. They [the right wing] kept saying that they weren't students, but *Yuan*." Lek Wittayaporn, quoted in Pennapa Honthong, "Living with Memories of a Lost Son," *The Nation*, 6 October 1996, A9.
34 Thongchai, "Struggle," A5.
35 Pasuk and Baker, *Thailand*, 309.
36 Katherine Bowie, *Rituals of National Loyalty: An Anthropology of the State and the Village Scout Movement in Thailand* (New York: Columbia University Press, 1997), 19.
37 A 1964 police department report stated that "there were 426,908 'special service girls' of various occupations out of which 171,973 persons or about 40.28 percent of this group were clearly 'prostitutes.'" See Saisuree Chutikul, *Children in Especially Difficult Situations: I (Thailand)*, report to UNICEF (Bangkok: National Youth Bureau, Office of the Prime Minister, June 1986), 38.
38 Cynthia Enloe, cited in Katherine Moon, *Sex among Allies: Military Prostitution in U.S.–Korea Relations* (New York: Columbia University Press, 1997), 11.

39 Another important aspect of the displeasure expressed by townspeople with the American presence was the number of mixed-race children produced through these unions. See Jeffrey D. Glasser, *The Secret Vietnam War: The United States Air Force in Thailand, 1961-1975* (Jefferson, NC: McFarland, 1995), 103. Nearly 2,000 such children were born between 1964 and 1970 (Anderson, Introduction to *In the Mirror*, 24, note 20). In 1996 the Pearl S. Buck Foundation, which helps fatherless Amerasian children, estimated that it had helped nearly 6,000 children since 1967. See Carole Fane, Francoise Joaquin, and Wendy Madrigal, "Mixed Fortunes," *Asia Magazine*, 24 August 1996, 11. Mixed-race children were treated with contempt and tended to display corresponding behavioural problems, although today mixed-race (particularly White/Asian) young people are in the forefront of the entertainment business (several Miss Thailands have been *luk krung* [half and half]) to the point where there is some concern over the imposition of Western standards of beauty. See Fane et al., "Mixed Fortunes," 11.

40 See the account of one such wife in Dave Walker and Richard S. Erlich, *Hello My Big, Big Honey: Love Letters to Bangkok Bar Girls and Their Revealing Interviews* (Bangkok: Dragon Dance, 1992), 92-8.

41 Glasser, *The Secret Vietnam War* (Jefferson, NC: McFarland, 1995), 103.

42 Nigel J. Brailey, *Thailand and the Fall of Singapore* (Boulder, CO: Westview Press, 1986), 25. The racist/sexist attitude towards women this entailed is well documented in accounts of military behaviour in Vietnam.

43 Glasser, *The Secret Vietnam War*, 103.

44 Ibid., 103, 104. In 1965, 76,000 prostitutes registered their medical records with government offices. See *Thai Development Newsletter*, 27-8 (1995), 87.

45 Malee Pluksponsawalee, "Women and the Law," in *Women in Development: Implications for Population Dynamics*, ed. Suchart Prasith-rathsint and Suwanlee Piampiti (Bangkok: National Institute of Development Administration, 1982), 158.

46 The term "special services" was created by the police department in the early 1960s. See Thahn-dam Truong, *Sex, Money and Morality: Prostitution and Tourism in Southeast Asia* (London: Zed, 1990), 157, note 4.

47 Wathinee Boonchalaksi and Philip Guest, *Prostitution in Thailand* (Bangkok: Institute for Population and Social Research, Mahidol University, 1994), 20-1.

48 Ibid.

49 Truong, *Sex, Money and Morality*, 161; Wathinee and Guest, *Prostitution in Thailand*, 8.

50 Truong, *Sex, Money and Morality*, 161.

51 Ibid., 118-22, 172.

52 Ibid., 167.

53 Ibid., 172.

54 As the director of the Tourism Authority of Thailand explained to the *Far Eastern Economic Review* in 1976: "Yes, we have to admit that we have prostitution, but it is the same in every country ... It might be partly true [that tourism encourages prostitution], but prostitution exists mainly because of the state of our economy, because everyone needs to earn their income. If we can create jobs, we can promote per capita income and do away with prostitution." Cited in Truong, *Sex, Money and Morality*, 179.

55 Truong, *Sex, Money and Morality*, 179.

56 See Katherine Moon, "East Meets West: Sex Industries in East Asia," paper presented at the Annual Meeting of the International Studies Association, Toronto, 18-22 March 1997, for a discussion of the sex trade and postcolonial masculinity.

57 See Sukanya Hantrakul, "Prostitution in Thailand," paper proposed to the Women in Asia Workshop, Monash University, Melbourne, 22-4 July 1983, 34. Sukanya further points out that most prostitution in Thailand takes place in "traditional brothels," which "play a more vital role in the continuation of prostitution in the country. Not only because they are more ancient but also because they have maintained popularity and access to massive [numbers of] Thai males of average middle class and lower economic class." See Sukanya, "Prostitution in Thailand," 12. In 1981 Pasuk argued that about half of the clients in high-class massage parlours were Thai. See Pasuk, *From Peasant Girls to Bangkok Masseuses*, 17.

58 Sukanya, "Prostitution in Thailand," 34.
59 Brock and Thistlewaite argue that "the military is notorious for its use of the sex-trade to break in new recruits and for its frequent use of brothels." See Rita Nakashima Brock and Susan Brooks Thistlewaite, *Casting Stones: Prostitution and Liberation in Asia and the United States* (Minneapolis: Fortress Press, 1996), 61.
60 Pasuk, *From Peasant Girls to Bangkok Masseuses,* 37.
61 This was the dominant interpretation of cultural nationalists such as Sulak Sivaraksa, as we shall see below. It was, however, challenged by intellectuals such as the neo-Marxist scholar Nidhi Aeusrivongse, who praised Sulak for "having the courage to raise the issue of the bad influences exerted by the American bases," and pointed out "that the Thai have been absorbing Western influence for more than a century." See Anderson, "Introduction," 27.
62 Pasuk and Baker, *Thailand,* 69.
63 Ibid., 76.
64 The backup dancers provide an interesting cultural continuity between rural girls and Patpong dancers. While some have marvelled at the ability of "traditionally modest" and body-conscious rural girls to take up topless dancing in go-go bars, the similarity between the back-up dancer and the go-go girl style is quite remarkable. In my own field research in Chiang Mai in 1996 I was struck by the similarity between the body movement and expression of the back-up dancers in performances at a local political rally and those of go-go dancers in Patpong. Mary Beth Mills also noted that, in a travelling show in the Northeast in 1988, "A troupe of maw lam singers (a song style associated with the Northeast but increasingly popular nationally) performed in front of a chorus line of scantily dressed dancers. The young girls changed costume (under the portable stage) between numbers, adding to the titillation of the excited young men in the audience. This format echoes the presentation of maw lam stars on popular television broadcasts seen nationwide." See Mary Beth Mills, "Rural Women Working in Bangkok: The Rocky Road of Social Change," final report to the National Research Council of Thailand, n.d, 18, note 12.
65 Pasuk and Baker, *Thailand,* 78-9.
66 The extent of an actual communist insurgency is still unknown, and it was certainly much less than was claimed by counter-communist forces. (At the height of the reaction even moderate conservatives such as Kukrit Pramoj were termed communists by the far right.) However, villages soon discovered that claiming to be subject to a communist insurgency would lead to an influx of aid and services from the military and the government. Today, therefore, analysts believe some of the reported numbers were inflated.
67 Donald Kirk, *Wider War: The Struggle for Cambodia, Thailand and Laos* (New York: Praeger, 1971), 71; Nigel J. Brailey, *Two Views of Siam on the Eve of the Chakri Reformation* (Whiting Bay, Scotland: Kiscadale Publications, 1989), 250.
68 Movement for the Independence of Thailand, 1964. Cited in Donald E. Weatherbee, *The United Front in Thailand: A Documentary Analysis* (Columbia: Institute of International Studies, University of South Carolina, 1970), 31.
69 Thailand Patriotic Front, 1965, Cited in ibid., 38.
70 Ibid., 52.
71 Ibid., 38.
72 Glasser, *The Secret Vietnam War,* 103.
73 Cited in Weatherbee, *The United Front in Thailand,* 38.
74 Ibid., 710.
75 Communist Party of Thailand, 1968. Cited in ibid., 69.
76 Pasuk and Baker, *Thailand,* 304.
77 Sulak Sivaraksa, "Siam versus the West," 1970, reproduced in Sulak Sivaraksa, *Siam in Crisis* (Bangkok: Kamol Keemthong Foundation, 1980), 202.
78 Anderson, "Introduction," 45.
79 Suchit Wongthes, "Second Nature," in *In the Mirror: Literature and Politics in Siam in the American Era,* ed. Benedict Anderson and Ruchira Mendiones (Bangkok: Duang Kamol, 1985), 98-9, 103 note 8.

80 Suchit, "Second Nature," 98-9 and 103, note 8.
81 Pasuk and Baker, *Thailand,* 304
82 Anderson, "Withdrawal Symptoms," 18.
83 Sulak, "Siam versus the West," 202.
84 Thanks to Sukanya Hantrakul for pointing this out.
85 Cited in Morell and Chai-Anan, *Political Conflict in Thailand,* 165.
86 Cited in Anderson, "Withdrawal Symptoms," 23, note 19.
87 Mattani Rutnin, *Modern Thai Literature: The Process of Modernization and the Transformation of Values* (Bangkok: Thammasat University Press, 1988), 74-5.
88 Yuangrat, "Current Thai Radical Ideology," 198-202.
89 Cited in Craig J. Reynolds, *Thai Radical Discourse: The Real Face of Thai Feudalism Today* (Ithaca: Cornell University Press, 1987), 134.
90 Cited in Reynolds, "A Nineteenth Century Thai Buddhist Defence of Polygamy," 57.
91 Cited in Yuangrat, "Current Thai Radical Ideology," 100.
92 Cited in Kirk, *Wider War,* 183.
93 Ibid., 183.
94 See Rachel Harrison, "The 'Good' the 'Bad' and the Pregnant: Why the Thai Prostitute as Literary Heroine Can't Be Seen to Give Birth," Proceedings of the 6th International Conference on Thai Studies, Chiang Mai, Thailand, 14-17 October 1996, 31-44.
95 Ko'n Krailat, "Let Me Alone Be the One to Have Feelings." Cited in Rachel Harrison, "The Writer, the Horseshoe Crab, his 'Golden Blossom' and her Clients: Tales of Prostitution in Contemporary Thai Short Stories," *Southeast Asia Research* 3 (September 1995): 143.
96 Cited in ibid., 139-40.
97 Mattani, *Modern Thai Literature* (Bangkok: Thammasat University Press, 1988), 117.
98 Cited in Yuangrat Wedel, *Radical Thought: Thai Mind: The Development of Revolutionary Ideas in Thailand* (Bangkok: Assumption Business College Administration, 1987), 143.
99 Harrison, "The 'Good' the 'Bad' and the Pregnant," 39.
100 Harrison, "The Writer," 145.

Chapter 3: Elite Women, the Reconstruction of National Identity, and the Prostitution Problem

 1 Pasuk Phongpaichit and Chris Baker, *Thailand: Economy and Politics* (New York: Oxford University Press, 1995), 346.
 2 Yuangrat Wedel, "Current Thai Radical Ideology: The Returnees from the Jungle," *Contemporary Southeast Asia* 4, 1 (June 1982): 12-4.
 3 John Girling, "Thailand in Gramscian Perspective," *Pacific Affairs* 57, 3 (Fall 1984): 396-7.
 4 Pasuk and Baker, *Thailand* (New York: Oxford University Press, 1995), 312.
 5 Katherine Bowie, *Rituals of National Loyalty: An Anthropology of the State and the Village Scout Movement in Thailand* (New York: Columbia UP, 1997), 350.
 6 David Morell and Chai-anan Samudavanija, *Political Conflict in Thailand: Reform, Reaction, Revolution* (Cambridge, MA: Oelgeschlager, Gunn and Hain, 1981), 242-3; Pasuk and Baker, *Thailand* (New York: Oxford University Press, 1995), 309.
 7 Television coverage was far-reaching by the end of the 1980s. Television reached more than 90 percent of urban households by the mid-1980s and over 70 percent of rural households in the late 1980s. See Pasuk and Baker, *Thailand,* 315-6.
 8 Ibid., 314-5.
 9 Darunee Tantiwiramanond and Shashi Ranjan Pandey, *By Women, For Women: A Study of Women's Organizations in Thailand* (Singapore: ISEAS, 1991), 30.
10 Pasuk and Baker, *Thailand,* 314. These were the key ingredients in the establishment of Premocracy in the 1980s. Saiyud's move to Poll Watch (an impressive-sounding, if highly ineffectual, organization, which is best known for failing to prosecute the well publicized practice of vote-buying) nicely encapsulates this change in tactics.
11 Charles Keyes, *Thailand: Buddhist Kingdom as Modern Nation State* (London: Westview Press, 1987), 101; Pasuk and Baker, *Thailand,* 313.
12 Craig Reynolds, "Introduction: National Identity and Its Defenders," in *National Identity and Its Defenders,* ed. Craig J. Reynolds (Chiang Mai: Silkworm Books, 1991), 14.

13 National Identity Office, "Thailand in the 1980s." Cited in Pasuk and Baker, *Thailand,* 319.
14 National Identity Office, cited in ibid., 319. Emphasis added.
15 Reynolds, "Introduction," 18. The government also produced *Thai Life* in English "for the consumption of foreign visitors [which] suggests something else about the government's promotion of Thai culture, namely, the connection between Thai culture and tourism. The marketing of Thai culture domestically and to foreign visitors subsidizes or underwrites the cost of efforts to preserve Thai culture seen to be under threat by Western ways." See Reynolds, "Introduction," 15.
16 See Hamideh Sedghi, "Third World Feminist Perspectives on World Politics," in *Women, Gender and World Politics,* ed. Peter R. Beckman and Francine D'Amico (Westport, CT: Bergin and Garvey, 1994).
17 Craig Reynolds, "A Nineteenth Century Thai Buddhist Defence of Polygamy and Some Remarks on the Social History of Women in Thailand," paper prepared for the Seventh Conference of the International Association of Historians of Asia, Bangkok, 22-6 August 1977, 29.
18 Suwadee T. Patana. "Thai Society's Expectations of Women, 1904-1935: An Approach to Women's History," paper presented to Twelfth IAHA Conference, University of Hong Kong, 24-8 June 1991, 23.
19 Gail Omvedt, *Women in Popular Movements: India and Thailand during the Decade of Women* (Geneva: UNRISD, 1986), 44.
20 Robert Lingat, *Le statut de la femme au Siam* (N.p., 1959), 283.
21 Amara Pongsapich, "Women's Social Protest in Thailand," *Journal of Social Research* 10 (1987): 6.
22 Wichit Wathakan, "On Propaganda," 1 February 1943. Cited in Kobkua Suwannatha-Piat, *Thailand's Durable Premier: Phibun through Three Decades, 1932-1957* (New York: Oxford University Press, 1995), 158, note 79.
23 Thamsook Numnonda, "Pibulsongkram's Thai Nation-Building Programme during the Japanese Military Presence, 1941-1945," *Journal of Southeast Asian Studies* 9, 2 (September 1978): 237.
24 Darunee Tantiwiramanond and Shashi Ranjan Pandey, *By Women, For Women: A Study of Women's Organizations in Thailand* (Singapore: ISEAS, 1991), 43.
25 Cited in ibid., 44.
26 Ibid.
27 Kobkua, *Thailand's Durable Premier,* 139.
28 Darunee and Pandey, *By Women, For Women,* 46.
29 Ibid., 43.
30 The threat a minor wife poses to a primary wife, in terms of financial as well as emotional support, underlies the reason why many Thai wives tolerate their husbands' visiting prostitutes, who are considered to be much less of a threat. See the study by Mark Van Landingham et al., *Friends, Wives and Extramarital Sex in Thailand: A Qualitative Study of Peer and Spousal Influence on Thai Male Extramarital Sexual Behaviour and Attitudes* (Bangkok: Institute for Population Studies, Chulalongkorn University, 1995).
31 The recommendations addressed the concerns of married middle-class women, including the declaration that marriages registered after the first marriage are automatically void; the right of married women to choose their own career without their husband's approval; women's right to control property in their names without their husband's consent; women's right to sue for divorce on the grounds of a husband's adultery; after a divorce, the deduction of maintenance directly from a husband's wages. See Women Lawyers Association of Thailand, *Status of Women in Thailand* (Bangkok: Women Lawyers Association, 1972), 39-45; Darunee and Pandey, *By Women, For Women,* 77.
32 Of the temporary National Assembly appointed in 1973, 5.2 percent were women (122 out of 2,347). The smaller version of the assembly put in place later in 1973 included sixteen women out of a total of 299. In the 1974 elections, three women were elected out of a total of 269 members (1.1 percent). See Rangson Prasertsri, "Women in the Parliament of Thailand: Their Characteristics and Attitudes," (PhD diss., University of Mississippi, 1982), 8, note 25.

33 Women Lawyers Association of Thailand, *Status of Women in Thailand* (Bangkok: Women Lawyers Association, 1972), 31. See his 1962 article for a UN seminar entitled The Status of Women in Family Law, which argues that women should have equal rights but should remain in charge of the family. See Sanya Dharmasakti, "The Situation in Thailand," A Working Paper for the UN Seminar on the Status of Women in Family Law, Tokyo, Japan, 8-21 May 1962 (reprinted in Women Lawyers Association of Thailand, *Status of Women in Thailand.*
34 Srisurang Poolthupya, "The Changing Role of Thai Women." Seventh Conference of the International Association of Historians of Asia, Bangkok, August 1977, 15.
35 Abhinya Rathanamongkolmas, "Developmental Stances of Thai Women Elites: A Study of socialization, Social Roles and Social Policy Prescriptions" (PhD diss., Indiana University, 1983), 3.
36 Kattiya Karnasuta, "Education and Development Programs for Thai Women," in *Aspects of Thai Women Today* (Bangkok, Thailand National Commission on Women's Affairs, 1980), 43.
37 Caryl Rae Krannich and Ronald L. Krannich, "The Emerging Leadership Role of Women in Urban Thailand," *International Journal of Women's Studies* 3, 4 (1980): 358.
38 Ibid., 359.
39 As late as 1996 female politicians complained that one of the major barriers to women's entry into the political arena was the sexual innuendo cast their way while campaigning and in office. See Suwanna Asavaroengchai and Tanida Sirorattanakul, "Deadly Serious Soap Opera," *Bangkok Post*, 27 November 1996, Outlook, 1. See also, Juree Vichit-Vadakan, "Women in Politics in Thailand," in *Women in Politics: Australia, India, Malaysia, Philippines and Thailand,* ed. Latika Padgaankar (Bangkok: UNESCO, 1993), 198.
40 Women Lawyers Association, *Status of Women in Thailand,* 32.
41 Kukrit in *Siam Rath,* 20 March 1972. Cited in Mattani Rutnin, *Modern Thai Literature: The Process of Modernization and the Transformation of Values* (Bangkok: Thammasat University Press, 1988), 114.
42 Here, interestingly, Kukrit takes the modern/Western practice of monogamy (the husband politely declines Ploi's offer because of his love for her) and applies its positive connotations to his picture of the past. In this he reflects the elitist/royalist desire to construct the past both as traditional Thai and as equal to "civilized"/Western culture. See Mattani, *Modern Thai Literature,* 90.
43 Mattani, *Modern Thai Literature,* 82 and 79.
44 Darunee and Pandey, *By Women, For Women,* 51-2.
45 Rachel Harrison, "The 'Good,' the 'Bad' and the Pregnant: Why the Thai Prostitute as Literary Heroine Can't Be Seen to Give Birth," proceedings of the 6th International Conference on Thai Studies, Chiang Mai, Thailand, 14-17 October 1996, 40. Sukanya Hantrakul, "Prostitution in Thailand," in *Development and Displacement: Women in Southeast Asia,* ed. Glen Chandler, Norma Sullivan, and Jan Branson (Clayton, Australia: Centre of Southeast Asian Studies, Monash University, 1988), 117.
46 Rangson, *Women in the Parliament of Thailand,* 127. Both Rangson and Abhinya note the high socio-economic status of the women elites. Rangson found that the women came from a much higher socio-economic background than did the men in Parliament. See Rangson, *Women in the Parliament of Thailand,* 27. Abhinya notes that most of the Thai women elites were from the "comfortable classes." See Abhinya, *Developmental Stances of Thai Women Elites,* 64.
47 Abhinya, *Developmental Stances of Thai Women Elites,* app. 2, table 32.
48 Ibid., 43, 104. This same survey of women in government and business classified half of the women surveyed as "conservative" (i.e., as accepting the need for military intervention to preserve stability). The majority of those conservatives were top government officers, university professors, and volunteer social workers (the "khunyings"). See ibid., 32, 61.
49 Interview, Bangkok, 11 November 1996.
50 Ibid.
51 Vipa Chulachart, "Introduction," in *Aspects of Thai Women Today,* Thailand National Commission on Women's Affairs (Bangkok, Thailand National Commission on Women's Affairs, 1980), 5.
52 Interview, Bangkok, 11 November 1996.

53 Kukrit Pramoj, "Phanni," *Many Lives,* trans. Meredith Borthwick (Chiang Mai: Silkworm, 1995), 70.
54 Sukanya Hantrakul, "Prostitution in Thailand," Paper proposed to the Women in Asia Workshop, Monash University, Melbourne, 22-4 July, 1983, 9-11.
55 Darunee and Pandey, *By Women, For Women,* 124.
56 Interview, Bangkok, 1 November 1996.
57 Interview, Bangkok, 12 November 1996.
58 *Bangkok Post,* 30 May 1977. Cited in *ISIS International Bulletin* 13 (1979) 7; Darunee and Pandey, *By Women, For Women,* 125; Interview, Bangkok, 12 November 1996.
59 Interview, Bangkok, 12 November 1996.
60 Darunee and Pandey, *By Women, For Women,* 125.
61 Srisurang, "The Changing Role of Thai Women," 21-2. Emphasis added.
62 Ibid., 22. Emphasis added. The NCWT was teaching women new skills: "cooking, hair-dressing, manicurists, dress making, and making artificial flowers."
63 Committee for the Promotion of Welfare for Women. National Council on Social Welfare of Thailand (CPWW), *Women's Development through Non-formal Education: 1971-1989* (Bangkok: National Council on Social Welfare of Thailand, October 1989), 2.
64 Ibid., 4.
65 Philip Hirsch, "What Is *the* Thai Village?" *National Identity and Its Defenders,* ed. Craig J. Reynolds (Chiang Mai: Silkworm Books, 1991), 330.
66 Ibid., 328.
67 Ibid., 330.
68 Ibid., 331. These notions of rurality are sometimes part of a globalized discourse on the rural. As Hirsch points out, "Ironically, certain of the markers – such as white fences and wagon wheels - are reminiscent of 4-H clubs in the mid-western United states, quite probably reflecting the North American training of many Thai officials," See ibid., 331. They probably also reflect the global trade in images through film and television.
69 CPWW, *Women's Development,* 12-3.
70 Interview, Bangkok, 1 November 1996.
71 Abhinya, *Developmental Stances,* 39.
72 Ibid., 40.
73 Cited in Kevin Hewison, *Bankers and Bureaucrats: Capital and the Role of the State in Thailand* (New Haven: Yale Center for International and Area Studies, 1989), 125.
74 Srisurang, "The Changing Role of Thai Women," 24.
75 CPWW, *Women's Development,* 1, 9. Emphasis added.
76 Thus, for example, the committee did not object to women migrating to the cities; it only insisted that they should migrate for "honest work" (i.e., work that falls within the bounds of traditional values for women, such as domestic service). The CPWW report notes that some officials object to girls migrating and, therefore, refuse to collaborate in the program. "Ironically though, there are employment agencies who round up the girls by the truck loads and transport them out of the villages, with vague promises of good jobs and good pay." See ibid., 27-8.
77 Ibid. A 1978 survey showed that less than 4 percent of the rural women questioned wanted to work as housemaids. As the study points out, "Among this 4%, most are from the Northeast, the poorest region." See Department of Community Development, Ministry of Interior, *Report of the Survey on Problems and Needs of Rural Women,* conducted May 1978. Cited in Kanitta Meesook, "The Economic Role of Thai Women," in National Commission on Women's Affairs (NCWA), *Aspects of Thai Women Today,* presented by the delegation of Thailand as a background document to the World Conference of the United Nations Decade for Women, Copenhagen, 14-30 July 1980 (Bangkok, Thailand National Commission on Women's Affairs, 1980), 25.
78 Mary Beth Mills, "Rural Women Working in Bangkok: The Rocky Road of Social Change," final report to the National Research Council of Thailand, n.d., 8.
79 Indeed, servants in elite homes are expected to show respect to their employers by, for instance, maintaining a lower body position than their employers, kneeling to serve seated members of the family, and so on.

80 Pasuk and Baker, *Thailand*, 386; Ernst Gohlert, *Power and Culture: The Struggle against Poverty in Thailand* (Bangkok: White Lotus, 1991), 35.
81 Interview, Bangkok, 11 November 1996.
82 These included Dr. Saisuree Chutikul from the Education Board (later to become chair of the re-established NCWA); M.R. Dr. Chalermsuk Boonthai from the Department of Health (later secretary of the National Commission of Women of Thailand); and a number of academics, including leading economist Pasuk Pongpaichit (Chulalongkorn University), Naphat Sirisamphan (now head of women's studies at Chulalongkorn University), and Malee Pruekpongsawalee (now head of women's studies at Thammasat University).
83 NCWA, "Status of Thai Women," *Aspects of Thai Women Today*, 66-7.
84 Ibid., 64, 67.
85 Ibid., 59, 70, 71.
86 NCWA, *Summary of Long-term Women's Development Plan (1982-2001)*, prepared by the Task Force on Long-term Women's Development Plan, with the Cooperation of the US Agency for International Development (USAID). Thailand and the Department of Technical and Economic Cooperation, 1981, 25-6.
87 NCWA, "Status of Thai Women," 71, 62.
88 NCWA, *Summary*, 27, 24.

Chapter 4: Women's Groups and the Prostitution Question

1 Hong Lysa, "*Warasan Setthasat Kanmu'ang*: Critical Scholarship in Post-1976 Thailand," in *Thai Constructions of Knowledge*, ed. Manas Chitakasem and Andrew Turton (London: School of Oriental and African Studies, University of London, 1991), 107.
2 Kevin Hewison, *Bankers and Bureaucrats: Capital and the Role of the State in Thailand* (New Haven: Yale University Southeast Asia Studies, 1989), 110.
3 Pasuk Phongpaichit, "From Peasant Girls to Bangkok Masseuses," in *Tourism, Prostitution, Development*, ed. Ecumenical Coalition on Third World Tourism (hereafter ECTWT) (Bangkok: ECTWT, 1983), 76.
4 Hewison, *Bankers and Bureaucrats*, 110-1.
5 Ibid., 124.
6 Benedict Anderson, "Withdrawal Symptoms," *Bulletin of Concerned Asian Scholars* 9, 3 (July-September 1977): 18.
7 Pasuk Phongpaichit and Chris Baker, *Thailand: Economy and Politics* (New York: Oxford University Press, 1995), 202.
8 "The Labour Situation," *Bangkok Post* (supplement), 21, reprinted in *Tourism, Prostitution, Development: Documentation*, ed. ECTWT (Bangkok, Ecumenical Coalition on Third World Tourism, n.d.), 77.
9 Hewison, *Bankers and Bureaucrats*, 125.
10 Water F. Meyer, "Beyond the Mask: Toward a Transdisciplinary Approach of Selected Social Problems Related to the Evolution and Context of International Tourism in Thailand" (PhD diss., University of Geneva, 1987), 306.
11 Thongbai Thongpao, "The State of Human Rights in Thailand in 1985," *Thai Development Newsletter* 3, 4 (1986): 13.
12 Pasuk and Baker, *Thailand*, 198-9.
13 Sukanya Hantrakul, "The Spirit of a Fighter – Women and Prostitution in Thailand," *Manushi* 18 (October-November 1983): 34.
14 Thahn-dam Truong, *Sex, Money and Morality: Prostitution and Tourism in Southeast Asia* (London: Zed, 1990), 160-1, 163.
15 Chris Dixon, "Thailand's Rapid Economic Growth: Causes, Sustainability and Lessons," *Uneven Development in Thailand*, ed. Michael J.G. Parnwell (Brookfield: Avebury, 1996), 42.
16 Truong, *Sex, Money and Morality*, 170.
17 See the advertising collected in ECTWT, *Tourism, Prostitution, Development*.
18 Cited in Truong, *Sex, Money and Morality*, 179; see also the discussion in chap. 4, 202.
19 Ibid., 167.
20 Wathinee Boonchalaksi and Philip Guest, *Prostitution in Thailand* (Bangkok: Institute for Population and Social Research, Madihol University, 1994), 31. The "numbers debate"

continues in research on prostitution in Thailand. Because of the difficulty in attaining accuracy with regard to such an underground, and often temporary, activity, estimates have varied wildly from the conservative numbers of the Department of Public Health (approximately 75,000 in 1992) to 2.8 million. A number of researchers agree on an approximate number of 700,000, while still others argue that rigorous methods produce a much lower number of 200,000 to 300,000 working in the industry in any given year. See Wathinee and Guest, *Prostitution,* 31-3.

21 Skrobanek Siriporn, "The Transnational Sex-exploitation of Thai Women," master's research paper, Institute of Social Studies, The Hague, March 1993, 26.
22 Meyer, *Beyond the Mask,* 327.
23 Sukanya Hantrakul, "The Spirit of a Fighter," *Manushi* 18 (October/November 1983): 31.
24 Gail Omvedt, *Women in Popular Movements: India and Thailand during the Decade of Women* (Geneva: UNRISD, 1986), 49. See also Gail Pheterson, *A Vindication of the Rights of Whores* (Seattle: Seal Press, 1989), 67.
25 Darunee Tantiwiramanond and Shashi Ranjan Pandey, *By Women, For Women: A Study of Women's Organizations in Thailand* (Singapore: ISEAS, 1991), 93.
26 My distinction between "elite" and "middle-class" women is loosely drawn and permeable, but it rests upon a distinction between women with university educations who work in professional jobs and the elite class that is closely connected to the inner circle of power, particularly the royal family.
27 This became a problem within the women's organizations themselves, and it led to some women leaving Friends of Women when it opened a "women's café" that excluded men. Some members of Friends of Women were uncomfortable with the exclusion, fearing they would be labelled as "radicals" or "lesbians" and as "foreign" to Thai culture. See Darunee and Pandey, *By Women, For Women,* 110. See also "NGOs Working on Women's Issues," *Thai Development Newsletter* 21 (1992), 54. The women's groups have never fit comfortably with the rest of the NGO movement, which sees itself as addressing broader issues of poverty rather than "women's issues."
28 Darunee and Pandey, *By Women, For Women,* 94.
29 Ibid., 107, note 3.
30 "An Open Letter to the Japanese Prime Minister from Thai Women," 19 January 1981, reproduced in Darunee and Pandey, *By Women, For Women,* appendix D, 176.
31 Darunee and Pandey, *By Women, For Women,* 103.
32 Siriporn, "The Transnational," 37-40.
33 Ibid., 26.
34 Darunee and Pandey, *By Women, For Women,* 110; *Thai Development Newsletter* 2, 3: 21-22.
35 Interview with Rangsima Limpisawas, Bangkok, 26 November 1996.
36 Sukanya Hantrakul, "Prostitution in Thailand." Paper proposed to the Women in Asia Workshop, Monash University, Melbourne, 22-4 July 1983, 13.
37 Sukanya Hantrakul, "Prostitutes and Human Rights in Thailand." Unpublished paper (1982), 9-11.
38 "Tourism Promotion and Its Effects on Thai Women," *Thai Development Newsletter* 4, 1 (1986): 10-14.
39 See the regular reports in the *Thai Development Newsletter,* 1985-9.
40 Saowarop Panyacheewin, "Child Prostitution" *Bangkok Post,* 7 December 1983, reprinted in ECTWT, *Tourism, Prostitution, Development,* 30.
41 Malee Pluksponsawalee, "Women and the Law," *Women in Development: Implications for Population Dynamics,* ed. Suchart Prasith-rathsint and Suwanlee Piampiti (Bangkok: National Institute of Development Administration, 1982), 157.
42 See Sucheela Tuanchainan, "Sexual Violence against Women and the Women's Movement in Thailand," *Thai Development Newsletter* 3, 4 (1986): 5-6.
43 Siriporn herself noted instances during her research when she was assumed to be a prostitute. Almost all of the women I interviewed in 1996 reported similar instances of sexual harassment overseas due to the assumed sexual availability of Thai women.
44 See Nerida Cook, "Thailand: "Dutiful Daughters," Estranged Sisters," in *Gender and Power in Affluent Asia,* ed. Krishna Sen and Maila Stivens (New York: Routledge, 1998), 265.

45 Pasuk Phongpaichit, *From Peasant Girls to Bangkok Masseuses* (Geneva: International Labour Office, 1982), 74-5.
46 Interview with Pasuk Phongpaichit, Bangkok, 8 November 1996.
47 Ibid.
48 Sukanya, "Prostitution," (1983), 35-6.
49 Ibid.
50 Ibid., 34-5.
51 Siriporn Skrobanek, "Strategies against Prostitution: The Case of Thailand," *Thai Development Newsletter* 4, 1 (1986): 23.
52 Arun, *Nation*, 1981, reprinted in ECTWT, *Tourism, Prostitution, Development*, 15.
53 "Tourism Promotion and Its Effects on Thai Women," *Thai Development Newsletter* 4, 1 (1986): 13; see also "Promoting Tourism May Encourage Prostitution" *Nation Review*, 4 February 1986, reprinted in *Thai Development Newsletter* 4, 1 (1986): 14.
54 "Promoting Tourism May Encourage Prostitution," *Nation Review*, 4 February 1986, reprinted in *Thai Development Newsletter* 4, 1 (1986): 14.
55 Kobkul Rayanakorn, *Special Study on Laws Relating to Prostitution and Traffic in Women* (Bangkok: Foundation for Women, 1995), 29-30; "Sex Tourism to Thailand," *ISIS International Bulletin* 13 (1979): 10-1.
56 Ilse Lenze, "Tourism Prostitution in Asia," *ISIS International Bulletin* 13 (1979): 6.
57 Sukanya, "Prostitution," (1983), 32.
58 Meyer, *Beyond the Mask,* 354-61.
59 Truong, *Sex, Money and Morality,* 182.
60 "Working on White Slavery," *Thai Development Newsletter* 2, 3 (1985): 22.
61 Kobkul, *Special Study,* 29.
62 Meyer, *Beyond the Mask,* 354-6.
63 See Satako Watenabe's discussions with migrant Thai sex workers in Japan: "From Thailand to Japan: Migrant Sex Workers as Autonomous Subjects," in *Global Sex Workers: Rights, Resistance and Redefinition,* ed. Kamala Kempadoo and Jo Doezema (New York: Routledge, 1998), 114-23.
64 One large-scale survey taken during the mid-1980s showed that 32.2 percent of respondents favoured revising the law to increase penalties on procurers and that 23.9 percent favoured legalization, with women more likely to favour increased penalties and men more likely to prefer legalization. See UN Educational Scientific and Cultural Organization (UNESCO), "Thailand," in *Identification of Issues Concerning Women and Their Consideration in Development Planning* (Bangkok: UNESCO, 1987), 61.
65 "Cabinet Okays Stiff Anti-Prostitution Bill," *Human Rights in Thailand Report* 10, 1 (1986): 19.
66 "Tourism Promotion," 10.
67 National Commission on Women's Affairs (NCWA), *Women's Development in Thailand* (Bangkok: National Committee for International Cooperation, National Commission on Women's Affairs, 1985), 148-9.
68 "Working on White Slavery," 21. The issue of punishing clients was also raised in meetings with police, public welfare officials, and prosecutors; however, resistance to the idea led to an agreement to "drop the issue." See "New Vice Control Bill Completed," *Bangkok Post* 29 August 1984, reprinted in ECTWT, *Tourism, Prostitution, Development,* 108.
69 "Tourism Promotion," 12.
70 "Flesh Traders in for Stiff Penalties," reprinted in ECTWT, *Tourism, Prostitution, Development,* 110.
71 "Working on White Slavery," 20.
72 Sukanya, "Prostitution," (1983), 29.
73 "The Interview with Phuket Chief Inspector" *Thai Rath*, 30 January 1984. Cited in "An Open Letter on the Case of Prostitutes Killed in a Fire at Phuket," *Thai Development Newsletter* 2, 3 (1984): 22.
74 Truong, *Sex, Money and Morality,* 182.
75 Meyer, *Beyond the Mask,* 361.
76 Sukanya, "Prostitution," (1983), 28.

77 Ibid., 15.
78 Wiboon Nakornjarupong "Patronage and the Night Queens," *Business in Thailand* (November 1981) 48. Cited in Sukanya, "Prostitution," (1983), 15.
79 Cited in Malee, "Women and the Law," 160.
80 *Bangkok Post,* 14 June 1984 reprinted in ECTWT, *Tourism, Prostitution, Development,* 110.
81 "An Open Letter on the Case of Prostitutes Killed in a Fire at Phuket," *Thai Development Newsletter* 2, 3 (1984): 23.
82 Pasuk and Baker, *Thailand,* 346.
83 "Working on White Slavery," 21.
84 "Cabinet Okays Stiff Anti-Prostitution Bill," 19.
85 Ibid., 19; "Women's Rights Groups voice Support for Anti-prostitution Bill," *Thai Development Newsletter* 4, 2 (1986): 5.

Chapter 5: The Politics of Prostitution and the "New Man"

1 Sukhumbhand Paribatra, "State and Society in Thailand: How Fragile the Democracy?" *Asian Survey* 33, 9 (September 1993): 884.
2 Pasuk Phongpaichit, "The Thai Middle Class and the Military: Social Perspectives in the Aftermath of May 1992," in *The May 1992 Crisis in Thailand: Background and Aftermath,* ed. Peter A. Jackson (Canberra: Australia National University, 1993), 30.
3 Cited in Thomas L. Friedman, "Is Thailand Singing a New Song?" *Globe and Mail,* 16 December 1997, A27.
4 Renate Wilke, "Protest Is Not Ineffective," *Der Uberblick,* April 1981, reprinted in Ecumenical Coalition On Third-World Tourism (hereafter ECTWT), *Tourism, Prostitution, Development: Documentation* (Bangkok, Ecumenical Coalition on Third World Tourism, n.d.), 105.
5 "Working on White Slavery," *Thai Development Newsletter* 2, 3 (1985): 21.
6 "Penalties Urged for Sex Tour Agencies," *Bangkok Post,* August 1984, reprinted in ECTWT, *Tourism, Prostitution, Development,* 109.
7 See "Official Blessings for the 'Brothel of Asia,'" *Southeast Asia Chronicle,* 78, reprinted in ECTWT, *Tourism, Prostitution, Development,* 41-2.
8 "Penalties Urged for Sex Tour Agencies," *Bangkok Post,* August 1984, reprinted in ECTWT, *Tourism, Prostitution, Development,* 109-10.
9 Wathinee Boonchalaksi and Philip Guest, *Prostitution in Thailand* (Bangkok: Institute for Population and Social Research, Mahidol University, 1994), 17.
10 *Thai Development Newsletter,* 27-8 (1995): 15.
11 Wathinee and Guest, *Prostitution,* 17.
12 Richard Rhodes, "Death in the Candy Store," *Rolling Stone Magazine,* 28 November 1991, 70. Emphasis added. This article appeared in a magazine that, less than ten years previously, had celebrated Western male sexual abandon in Thailand. Consider, for example, the following: "Used to be man could get a blow job while taking a dump in any barn in Bangkok, or so they say ... Here is where you drink till your face goes numb, here is where you find your dark-eyed orb for the evening, here is your frat house, your locker room, and your Elks club." Cited in Catherine Hill, "Planning for Prostitution: An Analysis of Thailand's Sex Industry," *Women's Lives and Public Policy,* ed. Meredeth Turshen and Braivel Holcomb (Westport: Praeger, 1993), 132.
13 Ryan Bishop and Lillian S. Robinson, *Night Market: Sexual Cultures and the Thai Economic Miracle* (New York: Routledge, 1998), 52.
14 Steve Kendrick, "Sex Trafficking in Kids: When Will Thailand get Angry?" *Business in Thailand* 25, 5 (15 May 1994): 41-2.
15 Such contradictory images of colonized men as being both "feminized" and "hypermasculine" are, in fact, key to the sustainability of the stereotype. As Jan Pettman points out, in the colonial era "a contradictory bundle of images could be activated simultaneously or in different situations. Colonised/black men were seen to have too little of some masculine characteristics, such as responsibility and stability, and too much of others, especially in terms of a sexualised hypermasculinity, which was a threat to white women, and to the black/colonised women too." See Jan Pettman, *Worlding Women* (New York: Routledge, 1996), 33.

16 Rhodes, "Death in the Candy Store," 65.
17 Chris Lyttleton, "The Good People of Isan: Commercial Sex in Northeast Thailand," *Australian Journal of Anthropology*, 5, 3 (1994): 265. As Lyttleton points out, such studies underrepresent rural men but are considered to cover the entire population. Lyttleton argues that "attitudes to commercial sex and frequency of patronage vary both individually and regionally."
18 The elision of Western culpability is also reinforced here as it is Thai male sexuality in general that is considered to be problematic rather than the "deviant individuals" involved in Western sex tourism. As Julia O'Connell Davidson has revealed in her interviews with Western sex tourists in Thailand, they share a sense of moral superiority, seeing themselves as more refined and proper in their sexual behaviour than racial others (specifically, Arab sex tourists), who are pictured as rapists, cheaters, and homosexuals. See Julia O'Connell Davidson and Jacqueline Sanchez Taylor, *Sex Tourism: Thailand* (Bangkok: ECPAT, 1996), 12-3.
19 Andrew Vachss, "D!B!T! Mission Statement," D!B!T! homepage, available on-line at http://users.aol.com/bdtlori/dbt1.html.
20 "The Don't!Buy!Thai! Campaign," *Nation*, 21 February 1996, A6.
21 "Support for D!B!T! from Mr. Sompop Jantraka, A True Warrior against the Enslavement of Children." Received via e-mail 16 January 1997, available on D!B!T! website. Written by Lou Bank, Dark Horse Comics.
22 Letter from Akrasid Amatayakul, Charge d'Affaires, reproduced on D!B!T! website, available on-line at http://users.aol.com/bdtlori/dbt1.html.
23 Royal Thai Government, Foreign Affairs, "Question of Child Prostitution in Thailand." Public Official Response. n.d. Emphasis added.
24 "Note from Human Rights Watch/Asia," *Women's Studies News* 7, 15 (November 1995): 38.
25 Human Rights Watch noted increasing surveillance of groups working on these issues and described an incident in which a relief centre for HIV/AIDS was harassed by local authorities and police, who wanted them to move out of the area. The centre was closed after the staff had received death threats and it was bombed. No official inquiry was held into the incident. Ibid., 38.
26 "Foreign Media Report Raises Ire of PM's Secretary," *Nation*, 17 April 1997, available on-line at www.nationmultimedia.com.
27 Samak Sundaravej, cited in *Bangkok Post*, 11 September 1996, A1.
28 See reports in the *Nation*, June 1997; *Bangkok Post* 11 June 1997, available on-line at www.bangkokpost.com.
29 "Media Blitz to Prop up Govt Image," *Bangkok Post*, 3 November 1997, available on-line at www.bangkokpost.com.
30 See "Sex Tourist Information Goes Out on Global Computer Link," *Thai Development Newsletter* 27-8 (1995): 16.
31 Ibid.
32 Ibid.
33 Although, as Pasuk points out, the larger structure of military power remained intact despite Anand's highly publicized moves. See Pasuk Phongpaichit, "The Thai Middle Class and the Military: Social Perspectives in the Aftermath of May 1992," in *The May 1992 Crisis in Thailand: Background and Aftermath*, ed. Peter A. Jackson (Canberra: National Thai Studies Centre, Australia National University, 1993), 32.
34 Given Boonchu's close connections with well known provincial "godfathers" Sia Jiew (who made his money in hotels) and the infamous Kamnan Pho, his support for tourism prostitution is not surprising. See Pasuk and Baker, *Thailand*, 337.
35 Ibid., 344.
36 Organized crime's involvement in the prostitution industry is a dangerous area of research. Consequently, while it has always been assumed, it has only recently come under academic scrutiny. See Pasuk Phongpaichit, *Guns, Girls, Gambling, Ganja: Thailand's Illegal Economy and Public Policy* (Chiang Mai: Silkworm, 1998).
37 Pasuk and Baker, *Thailand*, 335.
38 Cited in ibid., 335.

39 Ibid., 335-6. See also Benedict Anderson, "Murder and Progress in Modern Siam," *New Left Review* 181 (May-June 1990): 33-48.
40 Pasuk and Baker, *Thailand,* 336-7.
41 Ibid., 344-5.
42 "Summary of Political Events in Thailand 1991 and 1992," in *The May 1992 Crisis in Thailand: Background and Aftermath,* ed. Peter A. Jackson (Canberra: National Thai Studies Centre, Australia National University, 1993), 4-6.
43 Kevin Hewison, "Emerging Social Forces in Thailand: New Political and Economic Roles," in *The New Rich in Asia: Mobile Phones, McDonald's and Middle-Class Revolution,* ed. Richard Robinson and David S.G. Goodman (New York: Routledge, 1996), 155.
44 See Richard Basham's discussion in "Democracy Means Never Having to Say You're Sorry: Notions of Freedom and Fairness in Thai Attitudes Towards Democracy," in *The May 1992 Crisis in Thailand: Background and Aftermath,* ed. Peter A. Jackson (Canberra: National Thai Studies Centre, Australia National University, 1993), 15-7.
45 Cited in Basham "Democracy Means Never Having to Say You're Sorry," 16-7.
46 "Sex Tourist Information," *Thai Development Newsletter* 27-8 (1995): 16.
47 "We Must Tackle Our Problem First," *Bangkok Post,* 1 September 1996, 6. Emphasis in original.
48 *Nation,* 8 October 1996, A4.
49 "Enough Shame, End the Farce," *Bangkok Post,* 27 September 1996, 12.
50 Nok, cartoon, *Bangkok Post,* 25 October 1996, 10.
51 See, for example, "PM's Second Wife Recalls Her First Love," *The Nation,* 28 March 1997, available on-line at www.nationmultimedia.com; "PM Admits to Womanising during Youth," *Nation,* 30 March 1997, available on-line at www.nationmultimedia.com.
52 "Snoh's 'Other Wife' Mounts Vigil at Government House," *Nation,* 2 February 1997, available on-line at www.nationmultimedia.com.
53 "Anonymous Ministers Accused of Adultery," *Nation,* 13 September 1996, A6.
54 This is not to say that Thai women passively accepted their husbands' behaviour. While many remain convinced that the "nature" of male behaviour was promiscuous, women also assumed some strategic control over their husbands' behaviour by accepting visits to prostitutes but not the taking of minor wives, who would pose more of a threat to the family and family resources. See Mark VanLandingham et al., *Friends, Wives and Extramarital Sex in Thailand* (Bangkok, Institute of Population Studies, Chulalongkorn University: 1995); and Kanchana Tangchonlatip and Nicholas Ford, "Husbands' and Wives' Attitudes towards Husbands' Use of Prostitutes in Thailand," in *UK/Thai Collaborative Research Development in Reproductive and Sexual Health: Proceedings of the Symposium on the Mahidol-Exeter British Council Link* (Bangkok, Institute of Population and Social Research, Mahidol University, November 1993). The stories of open female anger are also rife, with Thailand's medical community claiming the greatest proficiency in penile reattachment surgery. Stories of women cutting off their husbands' penises in a fit of rage appear frequently in the newspapers.
55 Mary Packard Winkler, "Construction of Knowledge in Discourse in Middle-Class Marriage: Implications of Coping with Sexual Risk among Urban Thais," paper presented at the 6th International Conference on Thai Studies, Chiang Mai, Thailand, October 1996, 13.
56 National Commission on Women's Affairs (NCWA), *Thailand's Combined Second and Third Report to the Committee on the Elimination of Discrimination against Women* (Bangkok: NCWA, July 1996), 21-2.
57 "Apocalypse Soon," *Nation, Mid-Year Report,* 1993, reprinted in Thai Development Newsletter 31 (1996): 24.
58 "Justice in Action," *Nation,* 15 February 1998, C3.
59 Results of the Foundation for Women/Assumption University Poll Research Centre's poll in *Voices of Thai Women* 26 (October 1997): 13-5.
60 Radda Larpnun, "Academic's Education a Child's Affair," *Nation,* 17 November 1996, B2.
61 Marissa Chantamas, "'House-husbands Now Targeted by Advertisers," *Nation,* 17 November 1996, B2.
62 Cited in Kulcharee Tansubhapol, "Champion of Children's Rights," *Bangkok Post,* 21 September 1996, Outlook, 1, 8.

63 Kasem Adchesai, "Of Love, Lust and Human Nature," *Nation*, 21 March 1997, available online at www.nationmultimedia.com.
64 Cited in Wathinee and Guest, *Prostitution*, 17.
65 See Katherine Moon, "East Meets West: Sex Industries in East Asia," paper presented at the International Studies Association, Toronto, 1997, 6-8, for a discussion of the re-assertion of masculinity in Asia.
66 Chatsumarn Kabilsingh, *Thai Women in Buddhism* (Berkeley: Parallax Press, 1991), 74.
67 Penny van Esterik, "Thai Prostitution and the Medical Gaze," in *Gender and Development in Southeast Asia*, ed. Penny van Esterik and John van Esterik, CCSEAS (Canadian Council for Southeast Asian Studies) 20, vol. 2 (Montreal: Canadian Asian Studies Association, 1991), 143. In a letter to the *Nation*, Meechai argued that the number infected in 1990 might be closer to 800,000. See S.D. Bamber, K.J. Hewison, and P.J. Underwood, "A History of Sexually Transmitted Diseases in Thailand: Policy and Politics" *Genitourinary Medicine* 69 (1993): 153.
68 Bamber et al., "A History of Sexually Transmitted Diseases in Thailand," 154; van Esterik, "Thai Prostitution and the Medical Gaze," 145.
69 van Esterik, "Thai Prostitution and the Medical Gaze," 145; Ji Ungphakorn, "Politics and 'Morality' of Aids in Thailand," *Nation* 13 and 21 March 1994, reprinted in *Thai Development Newsletter* 31 (1996): 27.
70 van Esterik, "Thai Prostitution and the Medical Gaze," 145.
71 Cited in Bamber et al., "A History of Sexually Transmitted Diseases in Thailand," 154.
72 Ibid., 154-5.
73 Ibid., 154
74 Darunee and Pandey, *By Women, For Women*, 33.
75 National Commission on Women's Affairs, "Women and the Law," in *Perspective Policies and Planning for the Development of Women (1992-2011)* (Bangkok: National Committee on the Perspective Plan and Policies for Women's Development, National Commission on Women's Affairs, Office of the Prime Minister, 1995), s. 12-12.
76 "60-day Maternity Leave Approved" *Friends of Women Newsletter* 2, 2 (December 1991): 11-2.
77 Chaiyaporn Chaicharoen, "Maternity Leave for Men: Some Revelations," *Nation*, 15 June 1991, reprinted in *Voices of Thai Women* 5 (July 1991): 18-20.
78 There is a sense of resignation in the expression "pachot"; it may be compared to "fine, I give in." Interview, Bangkok, 27 November 1996.
79 Asia Watch and the Women's Rights Project, *A Modern Form of Slavery: Trafficking of Burmese Women and Girls into Brothels in Thailand* (New York: Human Rights Watch, 1993), 30.
80 Centre for the Protection of Children's Rights (CPCR), "Case Study Report on Commercial Sexual Exploitation of Children in Thailand," (Bangkok: Centre for the Protection of Children's Rights, October 1996), 29-30; Saisuree Chutikul, "Women and Commercial Sex in Thailand," *Canadian Women Studies* 15, 2 and 3 (1995): 118-9
81 Children and Youth Development Plan during the Seventh National Economic and Social Development Plan, 1992-6, National Youth Bureau, Office of the Prime Minister. Cited in CPCR "Case Study Report on Commercial Sexual Exploitation of Children in Thailand."
82 NCWA, *Perspective Policies and Planning*, s. 1-33.
83 Saisuree Chutikul, "Who are the Clients – the Exploiters?" *Child Workers in Asia* 12 (1996): 9.
84 Saisuree, "Women and Commercial Sex in Thailand," 118-9.
85 NCWA, *Perspective Policies and Planning*, s. 11-10.
86 NCWA, *National Policy and Plan of Action*, 2.
87 Vitit Muntarbhorn, "The Undoing of Thailand's Image," *Nation*, 25 October 1996, A5.
88 NCWA, *National Policy and Plan of Action*, 2.
89 Wathinee and Guest, *Prostitution* (Bangkok: Institute for Population and Social Research, Mahidol University, 1994), 24.
90 Two provincial officers, two police officers, the son-in-law of the brothel owners, and a pimp were eventually charged. This was one of the very rare occasions on which a police officer was actually charged. See Asia Watch, 80-1; CPCR, "Case Study Report," 17.

91 Asia Watch, *A Modern Form of Slavery*, 33-34.
92 Suchit Bunbongkarn, *Thailand: State of the Nation*, (Singapore: Institute of Southeast Asian Studies, 1996), 33.
93 Suchit, *Thailand*, 103.
94 "Statement on the Call Girl Scandal," *Friends of Women Newsletter* 4,2 (1993): 4-5.
95 Asia Watch, *A Modern Form of Slavery*, 76.
96 Suchit, *Thailand*, 37.
97 Teena Gill, "Prostitution Law Misses the Target say Activists," Gemini News Service, News-Scan International Limited, 1995 (World Sex Guide). Indeed, the Banharn government was brought down shortly after passing the new bill, which was followed by several scandals, including the involvement of Cabinet members in bilking the Bangkok Bank of millions of baht (which eventually led to the 1997 financial meltdown).
98 "Marriage Bills Aim to Provide Women with Equal Rights," *Nation*, 10 April 1996.
99 Interview, Bangkok, 12 November 1996.
100 Interview, Bangkok, 27 November 1996.
101 The penalties were set for two to twenty years and a fine of 40,000 to 400,000 baht for visiting prostitutes under the age of fifteen, with lesser penalties for using prostitutes between the ages of fifteen and eighteen. See Thongbai Thongpao, "Anti-Prostitution Bill Must Be Passed," *Bangkok Post*, 7 April 1996, 5.
102 Danairit Watcharaporn, executive member of the Parliamentary Committee. Quoted in *Bangkok Post*, 29 January 1996. In the original version of the bill proposed under Chuan the fine was raised from 1,000 to 10,000 baht. See Victoria Combe, "Child Sex Trade Forced Underground," *Nation*, 30 January 1993, C1.
103 Thongbai Thongpao, "Anti-prostitution Bill Must be Passed," *Bangkok Post*, 7 April 1996.
104 CPCR, "Case Study Report"; Interview, Bangkok, 12 November 1996, 5.
105 Supawadee Susanpoolthong, "Key Hurdle for Tough Bill on Child Prostitution," *Bangkok Post*, 29 January 1996.
106 Interview, Bangkok, 12 November 1996.
107 Section 8, *The Prostitution Prevention and Suppression Act B.E. 2539*, draft, November 1996; "Prostitution Bill Seen Clearing Second Reading," *Bangkok Post*, 29 March 1996.
108 Under the penal code the penalty for statutory rape is four to twenty years and a fine of 8,000 to 40,000 baht if the girl is under fifteen, and it is life imprisonment or seven to twenty years with a fine of 14,000 to 40,000 baht if the girl is under thirteen. See Section 277, Penal Code Amendment Act No. 8, BE 2530. The lower age of marriageability and the lack of a marital rape provision in Thai law led to the inclusion of the following rider to Section 8 of the new act: "if the commission of the offence as specified in the first paragraph is against the marriage partner of the offender, and is not committed for sexual gratification of the third person, the offender is not guilty."

Chapter 6: The Middle Class and the Material Girl

1 Interview with Rangsima Limpisawas, Bangkok, 26 November 1996.
2 Sukanya Hantrkul, "The Spirit of a Fighter: Women and Prostitution in Thailand." *Manushi* 18 (October-November 1983): 34.
3 Sukanya, "Spirit," 32.
4 Ibid., 31.
5 Sukanya Hantrakul, "Prostitutes and Human Rights in Thailand," (N.p. 1982), 25.
6 Interview with EMPOWER staff, Bangkok, 21 November 1996.
7 Darunee Tantiwiramanond and Shashi Ranjan Pandey, *By Women, For Women: A Study of Women's Organizations in Thailand* (Singapore: ISEAS, 1991), 131.
8 Interview with EMPOWER staff, Bangkok, 21 November 1996.
9 Ibid.
10 Interview with Siriporn Skrobanek, Bangkok, 4 November 1996.
11 Siriporn Skrobanek, "In Pursuit of an Illusion: Thai Women in Europe," *Southeast Asia Chronicle* 96 (1985): 11.
12 See Barry's 1979 and 1995 books, *Female Sexual Slavery* (New York: New York University Press, 1979) and *The Prostitution of Sexuality* (New York: New York University Press, 1995).

For an account of the beginnings of Barry's international campaign (of which Siriporn was a part before breaking away to form the Global Alliance against Trafficking in Women, which respects the right of women to choose to enter prostitution) see Kathleen Barry, Charlotte Bunch, and Shirley Castley, ed., *International Feminism: Networking against Female Sexual Slavery,* Report of the Global Feminist Workshop to Organize against Traffic in Women, Rotterdam, The Netherlands, 6-16 April 1983 (New York: International Women's Tribune Centre, 1984).

13 Interview with Siriporn Skrobanek, Bangkok, 4 November 1996.

14 Siriporn, "In Pursuit of an Illusion," 12.

15 See Jo Doezma, "Forced to Choose: Beyond the Voluntary v. Forced Prostitution Distinction." in *Global Sex Workers: Rights, Resistance, Redefinition,* ed. Kamala Kempadoo and Jo Doezema (New York: Routledge, 1998), 34-50.

16 Nerida Cook, "Thailand: 'Dutiful Daughters,' Estranged Sisters," in *Gender and Power in Affluent Asia,* ed. Krishna Sen and Maila Stivens (New York: Routledge, 1998), 278.

17 Chatsumarn Kabilsingh, *Thai Women in Buddhism* (Berkeley: Parallax Press, 1991), 80-1.

18 Sukhumbhand Paribatra, "State and Society in Thailand: How Fragile the Democracy?" *Asian Survey* 33, 9 (September 1993): 885.

19 Kevin Hewison, "Emerging Social Forces in Thailand: New Political and Economic Roles," in *The New Rich in Asia: Mobile Phones, McDonald's and Middle-Class Revolution,* ed. Richard Robison and David S.G. Goodman (New York: Routledge, 1996), 151.

20 Ibid.

21 Nation Publishing, "A Year of Drama and Disaster," 1989. Cited in Hewison, "Emerging Social Forces in Thailand," 149.

22 Kasian Tejapira, "The Postmodernization of Thainess," in *House of Glass: Culture, Modernity and the State in Southeast Asia,* ed. Yao Souchou (Singapore: Institute of Southeast Asian Studies, 2000), 153.

23 Ibid.

24 Christine Szanton-Blanc, "The Thoroughly Modern 'Asian,'" in *Ungrounded Empires,* ed. Aihwa Ong and Donald Nonini (New York: Routledge, 1997), 271.

25 Ibid., 270-1.

26 Ibid., 280.

27 Peter Vandergeest, "Real Villages: National Narratives of Rural Development," in *Creating the Countryside: The Politics of Rural and Environmental Discourse,* ed. E. Melanie DuPuis and Peter Vandergeest (Philadelphia: Temple University Press, 1996), 279-302.

28 Heather Montgomery, "Pattaya and Child Prostitution as a Form of Cultural Crisis," paper presented at the Sixth International Thai Studies Conference, Chiang Mai, Thailand, 1996, CD-ROM.

29 Pasuk Phongpaichit and Chris Baker, *Thailand: Economy and Politics* (New York: Oxford University Press, 1995), 386-9.

30 Kevin Hewison, "Thailand: Capitalist Development and the State," in *The Political Economy of South-East Asia: An Introduction,* ed. Garry Rodan, Kevin Hewison, and Richard Robison (New York: Oxford University Press, 1997), 111-2.

31 "Brokerage High-flyer Finds Relaxation in Merit-making," *Bangkok Post,* Business, 7 December 1996, 10.

32 *Sunday Post,* 3 October 1993. Cited in Montgomery, "Pattaya and Child Prostitution."

33 In recent years, after the emergence of reports of university students' involvement in prostitution-related activities, concern over rising consumerism has also attached itself to middle-class youth.

34 See, for example, "Voice of the Press: Flown to Japan," *Nation Review,* 21 September 1983, reprinted in Ecumenical Coalition On Third-World Tourism (hereafter ECTWT), *Tourism, Prostitution, Development: Documentation* (Bangkok, ECTWT, n.d.), 72; Pichai Chuensuksawadi, "Thai Girls in Hong Kong: A Case of Paradise Lost," *Bangkok Sunday,* 17 July 1983, reprinted in ECTWT, *Tourism, Prostitution, Development,* 48.

35 "Flown to Japan" *Nation Review,* 21 September 1983, reprinted in ECTWT, *Tourism, Prostitution, Development,* 72.

36 Chitraporn Vanaspong, "A multi-million baht business," *Bangkok Post*, Perspective, 18 August 1996, 4. Chitraporn points out, however, that only one-third of the money made goes to the woman herself, the rest goes to the agents and mamasan.

37 Marjorie Muecke, "Mother Sells Food, Daughter Sells Her Body: The Cultural Continuity of Prostitution," *Social Science and Medicine* 35, 7 (1992): 895.

38 "Migration and Prostitution," *Nation*, 5 February 1984, reprinted in ECTWT, *Tourism, Prostitution, Development*, 84.

39 Ibid., 83.

40 "Flesh Trade Seminar," *Thai Development Newsletter* 2, 3 (1984): 25.

41 Mayuree Rattanawannatip, "Prostitution: Necessity or Naked Greed?" *Nation*, 29 June 1990, 25.

42 Cited in ibid., 25. Emphasis added.

43 NCWA, *National Policy and Plan of Action*, s. 11-1.

44 "Flesh Trade Seminar," *Thai Development Newsletter* 2, 3 (1984): 25.

45 Mattani Rutnin, "The Role of Thai Women in Dramatic Arts and Social Development, Problems Concerning Child Prostitution in Thailand: A Case Study Accompanied by a Video-tape on the Lives of Child Prostitutes," *Customs and Tradition, The Role of Thai Women*, International Conference on Thai Studies, 22-4 August 1984, Thai Studies Program, Chulalongkorn University, Bangkok, 3-4, 11-2.

46 Mattani Rutnin, cited in Ernst Gohlert, *Power and Culture: The Struggle against Poverty in Thailand* (Bangkok: White Lotus, 1991), 48. Emphasis added.

47 Ibid., 49.

48 Walter F. Meyer, "Beyond the Mask: Toward a Transdisciplinary Approach to Selected Social Problems Related to the Evolution and Context of International Tourism in Thailand" (PhD diss., University of Geneva, 1987), 318; Pasuk Phongpaichit, *From Peasant Girls to Bangkok Masseuses* (Geneva: ILO, 1982), 69.

49 Pasuk Phongpaichit, "The Middle Class and the Military," in *The May 1992 Crisis in Thailand: Background and AFtermath*, ed. Peter A. Jackson (Canberra: National Thai Studies Centre, Australia National University, 1993), 33.

50 Hewison, "Emerging Social Forces in Thailand," 148.

51 See Pasuk and Baker, *Thailand*, chap. 2, for a discussion of the changing economy of the rural areas.

52 Meyer, *Beyond the Mask*, 318; Foundation for Women, *Final Report on the Research and Action Project on Traffic in Women (Thailand)* (Bangkok: Foundation for Women, 1996), 58.

53 Foundation for Women, *Final Report*, 34.

54 See, for example, ibid., 22-3.

55 Kanchana Tangchonlatip and Nicholas Ford, "Husbands' and Wives' Attitudes towards Husbands' Use of Prostitutes in Thailand," in *UK/Thai Collaborative Research Development in Reproductive and Sexual Health*, Proceedings of the Symposium on the Mahidol-Exeter British Council Link, Institute of Population Studies Research, Mahidol University, Bangkok, November 1993, 125.

56 Foundation for Women, *Final Report*, 58. However, this should not be taken as an argument that prostitution work is "raising the status" of rural women overall; rather it indicates that some women can and do use their financial gain (and modern ways) to create some negotiating room for themselves within the family and village structure.

57 Ibid., 61.

58 See Mary Beth Mills, "Rural Women Working in Bangkok: The Rocky Road of Social Change," Final report to the Research Council of Thailand, n.d., 8.

59 Aiwha Ong, *Spirits of Resistance and Capitalist Discipline: Factory Women in Malaysia* (New York: State University of New York, 1987), 181. Mary Beth Mills' work on female factory workers in Thailand points to a similar process as factory workers, like prostitutes, negotiate rural/urban and modern/traditional identities while experiencing the exploitation of waged labour. See Mary Beth Mills, *Thai Women in the Global Labour Force: Consuming Desires, Contested Selves* (New Brunswick, NJ: Rutgers University Press, 1999).

60 Ong, *Spirits of Resistance*, 199.

61 National Commission on Women's Affairs, *Thailand's Combined Second and Third Report to the Committee for the Elimination of Discrimination against Women* (Bangkok: Office of the Prime Minister, 1996), 6-7.
62 Cited in Pam Simmons, "Facing the Truth about Teenage Sex," *Nation*, 19 August 1997, reprinted in *Voices of Thai Women* 16 (October 1997), 11.
63 "Chula Women Skirt Disaster," *Bangkok Post Week in Review*, 25-31 January 1998, available on-line at www.geocities.com/newsthai.
64 See, for example, the complaints made by female politicians in the wake of the 1996 election regarding the limitations they face because of the concern about their sexual propriety. These women face constant accusations of infidelity and sexual misconduct while on the campaign trail and outside the protective confines of their home territory. As one female politician pointed out, this greatly limits not only their ability to campaign effectively, but also their ability to investigate the conditions of, for example, sex workers since entering a sex-entertainment place would indelibly mar a female politician's image. See "Deadly Serious Soap Opera," *Bangkok Post,* Outlook, 27 November 1996, 1.
65 Thongbai Thongpao, "Anti-prostitution Bill Must be Passed," *Bangkok Post*, 7 April 1996, 5.
66 Victoria Coombe, "Child Sex Trade Forced Underground," *Nation*, 30 January 1993, C1.
67 Cited in ibid., C1.
68 See for example, Marissa Chatamas, "Old Attitudes Still Difficult to Eradicate," *Nation*, 17 November 1996, B3.
69 "Thais' Woes on AIDS: Ignorance, Old Habits, and Sex Taboo," *Thai Development News-letter* 27-8 (1995): 17. However, it is not simply "uneducated" men who continue to take risks vis-à-vis HIV. Bamber et al. relate a 1992 social meeting with officials from the Ministry of Public Health to discuss AIDS, after which "three young women were brought for the selection and use of the senior official." See Kevin Bamber et al., "A History of Sexually Transmitted Diseases in Thailand: Policy and Politics," *Genitourinary Medicine* 69 (1993): 154.
70 Cited in Saisuree Chutikul, *Children in Especially Difficult Situations*, vol. 1, *Thailand,* report to UNICEF (National Youth Bureau, Office of the Prime Minister, June 1986), 43.
71 National Commission on Women's Affairs (NCWA) *Perspective Policies and Planning for the Development of Women* (1992-2011) (Bangkok: National Commission on Women's Affairs, Office of the Prime Minister, 1995), s. 11-8.
72 Teena Gill, "Prostitution Law Misses the Target Say Activists," Gemini News Service, News-Scan International Ltd., 1995. World Sex Guide, Prostitution by Country, Thailand.
73 Jasmine Caye, *Preliminary Survey on Regional Child Trafficking for Prostitution in Thailand* (Bangkok: Centre for the Protection of Children's Rights, 1995), 10.
74 "Sex Trade Agents Face Tough Action," *Nation*, 23 March 1994, reprinted in *Voices of Thai Women* 11 (1994): 3.
75 Thongbai Thongpao, "Anti-Prostitution Bill Must Be Passed," 5
76 Section 12, Prostitution Prevention and Suppression Act, BE 2539.
77 Section 13, Prostitution Prevention and Suppression Act, BE 2539.
78 Interview with CPCR staff, Bangkok, 12 December 1996.
79 Ibid.
80 Interview with Rangsima Limpisawas, Bangkok, 26 November 1996.
81 Ibid.
82 Section 7, Prostitution Prevention and Suppression Act, BE 2539.
83 Brothel owners appeared to be singularly unconcerned with the new provisions, however, citing "loopholes," "needy parents," and the fact that many young children are coming in from Burma and China rather than from Thailand. See "Brothel Owners Indifferent to Prostitution Bill," *Bangkok Post*, 1 April 1996, 6.
84 Section 12, para. 2, Prostitution Prevention and Suppression Act, BE 2539.
85 "Bill on Child Prostitution Stalls Again," *Nation*, 11 April 1996, A3.
86 Section 39, Prostitution Prevention and Suppression Act, BE 2539.
87 Centre for the Protection of Children's Rights (hereafter CPCR), *Case Study Report on Commercial Sexual Exploitation of Children in Thailand* (Bangkok: Centre for the Protection of Children's Rights, October 1996) 20.

88 CPCR, *Case Study Report*, 21. Police powers were expanded in response to complaints that their hands were legally tied, particularly because women often travel alone for prostitution purposes and they (the police) are unable to stop them at the border. See Kobkul Rayanakorn, *Special Study on Laws Relating to Prostitution and Traffic in Women* (Bangkok: Foundation for Women, 1995), 19. The new anti-trafficking act was passed on 17 November 1997, and it reduced custody time to no longer than half an hour (although it could be extended to ten days). See *Friends of Women Newsletter* 8 (January-December 1997): 9.
89 CPCR, *Case Study Report*, 23.
90 NCWA, *Perspective Policies and Planning*, s. 11-1.
91 Interview, Bangkok, 12 November 1996.
92 "Prostitution Bill seen Clearing Second Reading," *Bangkok Post*, 29 March 1996, 3.
93 Interview, Bangkok, 25 October 1996.
94 Drafters in the NCWA and the Department of Public Welfare had originally tried to reduce the fine for solicitation to 500 baht, but the Senate dropped this section (derived from the original act), which would have made it an offence to loiter in a public place "overtly inducing prostitution." The Senate believed that the clause would pose a danger to the liberty of women waiting for buses or other "legitimate" reasons. See "Cracking Down on Prostitution," *Bangkok Post*, 3 February 1993, Marut Bunnag, "New Laws Planned to Govern Sex Trade," *Bangkok Post*, 10 August 1996, 11.
95 Section 9, Prostitution Prevention and Suppression Act, BE 2539.
96 CPCR, *Case Study Report*, 20.
97 Section 38, Prostitution Prevention and Suppression Act, BE 2539.
98 Mukdawan Sakboon, "Prostitution Bill Is Not the Answer to the Problem," *Nation*, 9 April 1996, A5.
99 "Anti-prostitution Bill Slammed by Women's Groups," *Voices of Thai Women* 13 (April 1996): 6.
100 Vitit Muntahbhorn, "The Undoing of Thailand's Image," *Nation*, 25 October 1996, A5.
101 Interview with CPCR staff, Bangkok, December 1996; "Anti-Prostitution Bill Slammed," 6.
102 Cited in Coombe, "Child Sex Trade," C1.
103 Sukanya Hantrakul, "New Law No Deterrent to Child Prostitution," *Nation*, 3 November 1999 <www.nationmultimedia.com>.
104 Interview with EMPOWER staff, Bangkok, 21 November 1996.
105 Ibid.
106 Interview with Rangsima Limpisawas, Bangkok, 26 November 1996.
107 Sukanya, "New Law No Deterrent," <www.nationmultimedia.com>.

Chapter 7: The Politics of Prostitution: Gender, Class, and Nation
1 Interview with Sanitsuda Ekachai, Bangkok, 15 November 1996.
2 Interview at Friends of Women, Bangkok, 29 November 1996.
3 Partha Chaterjee, *The National and Its Fragments: Colonial and Postcolonial Histories* (Princeton: Princeton University Press, 1993), 6.
4 Ibid.
5 Aihwa Ong and Michael G. Peletz, "Introduction," in *Bewitching Women and Pious Men: Gender and Body Politics in Southeast Asia*, ed. Aihwa Ong and Michael G. Peletz (Berkeley, University of California Press, 1995), 5-6.
6 See Suzanne Brenner "Why Women Rule the Roost: Rethinking Javanese Ideologies of Gender and Self-Control" and Evelyn Blackwood, "Senior Women, Model Mothers, and Dutiful Wives: Managing Gender Contradictions in a Minangkabau Village" in *Bewitching Women and Pious Men: Gender and Body Politics in Southeast Asia*, ed. Aihwa Ong and Michael G. Peletz, (Berkeley, University of California Press, 1995), 19-50.
7 Brenner, "Why Women Rule the Roost," 40.
8 Geraldine Heng and Janadas Devan, "State Fatherhood: The Politics of Nationalism, Sexuality, and Race in Singapore" in *Bewitching Women and Pious Men: Gender and Body Politics in Southeast Asia*, ed. Aihwa Ong and Michael G. Peletz, (Berkeley, University of California Press, 1995), 203-9.

9 See, for example, Ashis Nandy, *The Intimate Enemy, Loss and Recovery of Self under Colonialism* (Delhi: Oxford University Press, 1983).

10 L.H.M. Ling, "The Other Side of Globalization: Hypermasculine Developmentalism in East Asia," paper presented at the International Studies Association, 18-22 March 1997, Toronto, 10.

11 Thanks to Steve Niva for pointing this out.

Bibliography

Note: Thai names appear under given names first, according to Thai usage.

Abhinya Rathanamongkolmas. "Developmental Stances of Thai Women Elites: A Study of Socialization, Social Roles and Social Policy Prescriptions." PhD diss., Indiana University, 1983.

Amara Pongsapich. "Women's Social Protest in Thailand." *Journal of Social Research* (Chulalongkorn University Social Research Institute, Bangkok) 10 (1987): 1-12.

Andaya, Barbara Watson. "From Temporary Wife to Prostitute: Sexuality and Economic Change in Early Modern Southeast Asia." *Journal of Women's History* 9, 4 (Winter 1998): 11-34.

Anderson, Benedict. "Withdrawal Symptoms: Social and Cultural Aspects of the October 6 Coup." *Bulletin of Concerned Asian Scholars* 9, 3 (July-September, 1977): 13-8.

–. "Murder and Progress in Modern Siam." *New Left Review* 181 (May-June 1990): 33-48.

–. *Imagined Communities*. Rev. ed. New York: Verso, 1991.

Anderson, Benedict, and Ruchira Mendiones, eds. *In the Mirror: Literature and Politics in Siam in the American Era*. Bangkok: Duang Kamol, 1985.

Anthias, Floya, and Nira Yuval-Davis. *Woman-Nation-State*. New York: St. Martin's Press, 1989.

Asia Watch and the Women's Rights Project. *A Modern Form of Slavery: Trafficking of Burmese Women and Girls into Brothels in Thailand*. New York: Human Rights Watch, 1993.

Bamber, S.D., K.J. Hewison, and P.J. Underwood. "A History of Sexually Transmitted Diseases in Thailand: Policy and Politics." *Genitourinary Medicine* 69 (1993): 148-57.

Barmé, Scot. *Luang Wichit Wathakan and the Creation of Thai Identity*. Singapore: Institute of Southeast Asian Studies, 1996.

Barry, Kathleen. *Female Sexual Slavery*. New York: New York University, 1979.

–. *The Prostitution of Sexuality: The Global Exploitation of Women*. New York: New York University Press, 1995.

Barry, Kathleen, Charlotte Bunch, and Shirley Castley, eds. *International Feminism: Networking against Female Sexual Slavery*. Report of the Global Feminist Workshop to Organize against Traffic in Women, Rotterdam, The Netherlands, 6-15 April 1983. New York: International Women's Tribune Centre, 1984.

Basham, Richard. "Democracy Means Never Having to Say You're Sorry: Notions of Freedom and Fairness in Thai Attitudes Towards Democracy." In *The May 1992 Crisis in Thailand: Background and Aftermath*, ed. Peter A. Jackson, 11-20. Canberra: National Thai Studies Centre, Australia National University, 1993.

Bhassorn Limanonda. "Female Commercial Sex Workers and AIDS: Perspectives from Thai Rural Communities." Paper presented at the 5th International Conference on Thai Studies, Centre of South East Asian Studies, School of Oriental and African Studies, University of London, 5-10 July 1993.

–. *The Demographic and Behavioural Study of Female Commercial Sex Workers in Thailand.* Bangkok: Institute for Population Studies, Chulalongkorn University, October 1993. IPS Publication #210/93.

Bishop, Ryan, and Lillian Robinson. *Night Market: Thai Sexual Cultures and the Economic Miracle.* New York: Routledge, 1998.

Bowie, Katherine A. *Rituals of National Loyalty: An Anthropology of the State and the Village Scout Movement in Thailand.* New York: Columbia University Press, 1997.

Bowring, Sir John. *The Kingdom and People of Siam.* 2 vols. London: John W. Parker and Son, 1857.

Bradley, William L. *Siam Then: The Foreign Colony in Bangkok Before and After Anna.* Pasadena, CA: William Carey Library, 1981.

Brailey, Nigel J. *Thailand and the Fall of Singapore.* Boulder, CO: Westview Press, 1986.

–. *Two Views of Siam on the Eve of the Chakri Reformation.* Whiting Bay, Scotland: Kiscadale Publications, 1989.

Brock, Rita Nakashima, and Susan Brooks Thistlethwaite. *Casting Stones: Prostitution and Liberation in Asia and the United States.* Minneapolis: Fortress Press, 1996.

Caye, Jasmine. "Preliminary Survey on Regional Child Trafficking for Prostitution in Thailand." Commissioned by UNICEF EAPRO. Bangkok: Centre for the Protection of Children's Rights, August-November 1995.

Centre for the Protection of Children's Rights. "Case Study Report on Commercial Sexual Exploitation of Children in Thailand." Bangkok: Centre for the Protection of Children's Rights, October 1996.

Chai-anan Samudavanija. "Thailand: A Stable Semi-democracy." In *Politics in Developing Countries*, ed. Larry Diamond, Juan J. Linz, and Seymour Martin Lipset, 271-312. Boulder, CO: Lynne Rienner, 1990.

–. "Economic Development and Democracy." In *Thailand's Industrialization and Its Consequences*, ed. Medhi Krongkaew. New York: St Martin's Press, 1995.

Chaiyan Rajchagool. *The Rise and Fall of the Thai Absolute Monarchy.* Bangkok: White Lotus Press, 1994.

Chapkis, Wendy. *Live Sex Acts.* New York: Routledge, 1997.

Chaterjee, Partha. *The National and Its Fragments: Colonial and Postcolonial Histories.* Princeton: Princeton University Press, 1993.

Chatsumarn Kabilsingh. *Thai Women in Buddhism.* Berkeley: Parallax Press, 1991.

Chatthip Nartsupha. "The Community Culture School of Thought." In *Thai Constructions of Knowledge*, ed. Manas Chitakasem and Andrew Turton, 118-41. London: School of Oriental and African Studies, University of London, 1991.

Cohen, Eric. "Thai Girls and Farang Men: The Edge of Ambiguity." *Annals of Tourism Research* 9 (1982): 403-28.

Committee for the Promotion of Welfare for Women. National Council on Social Welfare of Thailand. *Women's Development through Non-formal Education: 1971-1989.* Reported by Khunying Dithakar Bhakdi. Bangkok: National Council on Social Welfare of Thailand, October 1989.

Connell, Robert. *Masculinities.* Berkeley: University of California Press, 1995.

Cook, Nerida. "Thailand: 'Dutiful Daughters,' Estranged Sisters." In *Gender and Power in Affluent Asia*, ed. Krishna Sen and Maila Stivens. New York: Routledge, 1998.

Darling, Frank C. *Thailand and the United States.* Washington, DC: Public Affairs Press, 1965.

Darunee Tantiwiramanond and Shashi Ranjan Pandey. *By Women, For Women: A Study of Women's Organizations in Thailand.* Singapore: ISEAS, 1991.

–. "The Status and Role of Thai Women in the Pre-Modern Period: A Historical and Cultural Perspective." *Sojourn* 2, 1 (1987): 125-49.

Dixon, Chris. "Thailand's Rapid Economic Growth: Causes, Sustainability and Lessons." In *Uneven Development in Thailand*, ed. Michael J.G. Parnwell, 28-48. Brookfield: Avebury, 1996.

Ecumenical Coalition on Third World Tourism. *Tourism, Prostitution, Development: Documentation.* Bangkok: Ecumenical Coalition on Third World Tourism, n.d.

Embree, J.F. "Thailand: A Loosely Structured Social System." *American Anthropologist* 52, 2 (1950): 181-93.

Enloe, Cynthia. *Bananas, Beaches and Bases: Making Feminist Sense of International Politics.* Berkeley: University of California Press, 1990.

Fane, Carole, Françoise Joaquin, and Wendy Madrigal. "Mixed Fortunes." *Asia Magazine,* 2-4 August 1996, 10-4.

Foundation for Women. *Final Report of the Research and Action Project on Traffic in Women (Thailand).* Bangkok: Foundation for Women, 1996.

Fox, Morris G. "Problem of Prostitution in Thailand." In *Social Service in Thailand,* 139-65. Bangkok: Department of Public Welfare, Ministry of the Interior, 1960.

Gawin Chutima. "Thai NGOs and Civil Society." In *Thai NGOs: The Continuing Struggle for Democracy,* 135-44. Bangkok: Thai NGO Support Project, 1995.

Girling, John L.S. *Thailand: Society and Politics.* Ithaca: Cornell University Press, 1981.

–. "Thailand in Gramscian Perspective." *Pacific Affairs* 5, 3 (Fall 1984): 385-403.

Glasser, Jeffrey D. *The Secret Vietnam War: The United States Air Force in Thailand, 1961-1975.* Jefferson, NC: McFarland, 1995.

Gohlert, Ernst. *Power and Culture: The Struggle against Poverty in Thailand.* Bangkok: White Lotus Press, 1991.

Gong, Gerrit W. *The Standard of "Civilization" in International Society.* Oxford: Clarendon Press, 1984.

Gorham, Deborah. "The 'Maiden Tribute of Modern Babylon' Re-Examined: Child Prostitution and the Idea of Childhood in Late-Victorian England." *Victorian Studies* 2, 3 (Spring 1978): 353-80.

Harrison, Rachel. "The 'Good' the 'Bad' and the Pregnant: Why the Thai Prostitute as Literary Heroine Can't Be Seen to Give Birth." In *Proceedings of the 6th International Conference on Thai Studies.* Theme 5: *Women, Gender Relations and Development in Thai Society,* 31-48. Chiang Mai, Thailand, 14-17 October 1996.

–. "The Writer, the Horseshoe Crab, his "Golden Blossom" and her Clients: Tales of Prostitution in Contemporary Thai Short Stories." *Southeast Asia Research* 3 (Sept. 1995): 125-52.

Hekman, Susan. *Gender and Knowledge: Elements of a Postmodern Feminism.* Boston: Northeastern University Press, 1990.

Hershatter, Gail. "Courtesans and Streetwalkers: The Changing Discourses on Shanghai Prostitution, 1890-1949." *Journal of the History of Sexuality* 3, 2 (1992): 245-69.

Hewison, Kevin. *Bankers and Bureaucrats: Capital and the Role of the State in Thailand.* Monograph Series 34. Yale University Southeast Asia Studies. New Haven: Yale Center for International and Area Studies, 1989.

–. "Of Regimes, State and Pluralities: Thai Politics Enters the 1990s." In *Southeast Asia in the 1990s: Authoritarianism, Democracy and Capitalism,* ed. Kevin Hewison, Richard Robinson, and Garry Rodan, 161-89. Sydney: Allen and Unwin, 1993.

–. "Emerging Social Forces in Thailand: New Political and Economic Roles." In *The New Rich in Asia: Mobile Phones, McDonald's and Middle-Class Revolution,* ed. Richard Robinson and David S.G. Goodman, 137-60. New York: Routledge, 1996.

–. "Thailand: Capitalist Development and the State." In *The Political Economy of South-East Asia: An Introduction,* ed. Garry Rodan, Kevin Hewison, and Richard Robison, 93-120. New York: Oxford University Press, 1997.

Hicks, George. *The Comfort Women: Sex Slaves of the Japanese Imperial Forces.* Chiang Mai: Silkworm, 1995.

Hill, Catherine. "Planning for Prostitution: An Analysis of Thailand's Sex Industry." In *Women's Lives and Public Policy: The International Experience,* ed. Meredeth Turshen and Braivel Holcomb, 133-44. Westport: Praeger, 1993.

Hirsch, Philip. "What Is *the* Thai Village?" In *National Identity and Its Defenders,* ed. Craig J. Reynolds, 323-40. Chiang Mai: Silkworm, 1991.

Hong, Lysa. "*Warasan Setthasat Kanmu'ang*: Critical Scholarhsip in Post-1976 Thailand." In *Thai Constructions of Knowledge,* ed. Manas Chitakasem and Andrew Turton, 99-117. London: School of Oriental and African Studies, University of London, 1991.

Human Rights in Thailand Report 9.2 (April/July 1985) to 10.1 (January/March 1986).

ISIS International Bulletin 13 (1979).

Jackson, Peter, ed. *The May 1992 Crisis in Thailand: Background and Aftermath*. Selected Papers from the Thailand Update Conference. University of Sydney, 16 October 1992. Canberra: National Thai Studies Centre, Australia National University, 1993.

Jayawardena, Kumari. *Feminism and Nationalism in the Third World*. London: Zed, 1986.

Kammerer, Cornelia Ann, Otome Klein Hutheesing, Ralana Maneeprasert, and Patricia V. Symonds. "HIV Infection among Hilltribes in Northern Thailand." In *Culture and Sexual Risk: Anthropological Perspectives on AIDS*, ed. Han ten Brummelhuis and Gilbert Herdt, 53-75. Amsterdam: Gordon and Beach, 1995.

Kanchana Tangchonlatip, and Nicholas Ford. "Husbands' and Wives' Attitudes towards Husbands' Use of Prostitutes in Thailand." In *UK/Thai Collaborative Research Development in Reproductive and Sexual Health*. Proceedings of the Symposium on the Mahidol-Exeter British Council Link, 117-34. Bangkok: IPSR, Mahidol University, November 1993.

Kandiyoti, Deniz. "Identity and Its Discontents: Women and the Nation." In *Colonial Discourse and Post-Colonial Theory: A Reader*, ed. Patrick Williams and Laura Chrisman, 376-91. New York: Columbia University Press, 1994.

Kanitta Meesook. "The Economic Role of Thai Women." In *Aspects of Thai Women Today*. Presented by the Delegation of Thailand as a background document to the World Conference of The United Nations Decade for Women, Copenhagen, 14-30 July 1980, 7-28. Bangkok: Thailand National Commission on Women's Affairs, 1980.

Kasian Tejapira. "The Postmodernization of Thai-ness." In *House of Glass: Culture, Modernity, and the State in Southeast Asia*, ed. Yao Souchou, 150-72. Singapore: Institute of Southeast Asian Studies, 2000.

Kattiya Karnasuta. "Education and Development Programs for Thai Women." In *Aspects of Thai Women Today*. Presented by the Delegation of Thailand as a background document to the World Conference of the United Nations Decade for Women, Copenhagen, 14-30 July 1980, 29-46. Bangkok: Thailand National Commission on Women's Affairs, 1980.

Kempadoo, Kamala, and Jo Doezema, eds. *Global Sex Workers: Rights, Resistance and Redefinition*. New York: Routledge, 1998.

Keyes, Charles F. "Mother or Mistress But Never a Monk, Buddhist Notions of Female Gender in Rural Thailand." *American Ethnologist* 11, 2 (1984): 223-41.

–. *Thailand: Buddhist Kingdom as Modern Nation State*. London: Westview Press, 1987.

–. "Hegemony and Resistance in Northeastern Thailand." In *Regions and National Integration in Thailand: 1892-1992*, ed. Volker Grabowsky, 154-82. Wiesbaden: Harrossowitz Verlag, 1995.

Kirk, Donald. *Wider War: The Struggle for Cambodia, Thailand and Laos*. New York: Praeger, 1971.

Kirsch, Thomas. "Text and Context: Buddhist Sex Roles/Culture of Gender Revisited" *American Ethnologist* 12, 2 (1985): 302-20.

Kobkua Suwannatha-Piat. *Thailand's Durable Premier: Phibun through Three Decades, 1932-1957*. New York: Oxford University Press, 1995.

Kobkul Rayanakorn. "Women and the Law in Thailand and Canada." Paper Number 6, Working Paper Series, Thai Studies Project, Women in Development Consortium in Thailand. Toronto: York University, 1990.

–. *Special Study on Laws Relating to Prostitution and Traffic in Women*. Bangkok: Foundation for Women, 1995.

Krannich, Caryl Rae, and Ronald L. Krannich. "The Emerging Leadership Role of Women in Urban Thailand." *International Journal of Women's Studies* 3, 4 (1980): 358-72.

Kukrit Pramoj. *Many Lives*. 1954. Trans. Meredith Borthwick. Chiang Mai: Silkworm, 1995.

la Loubère, Simon de. *The Kingdom of Siam*. 1697. Oxford in Asia Historical Reprints. New York: Oxford University Press, 1969.

Laiad Pibulsonggram. "Thai Women." In *Aspects and Facets of Thailand*, ed. Witt Siwasariyanon, 45-7. Bangkok: Public Relations Department, 1958.

Landon, Kenneth Perry. *The Chinese in Thailand*. New York: Russell and Russell, 1977.

League of Nations. Commission of Enquiry into Traffic in Women and Children in the Far East. "Siam: Internal Conditions Relating to Traffic." *Report to the Council*, 1933.

Lenze, Ilse. "Tourism Prostitution in Asia." *ISIS International Bulletin* 13 (1979): 6-8.

Leonowens, Anna. *The Romance of the Harem*. Charlottesville: University Press of Virginia, 1991.

Likhit Dhiravegin. *Political Attitudes of the Bureaucratic Elite and Modernization in Thailand*. Bangkok: Thai Watana Panich, 1973.

Lim, Lin Lean, ed. *The Sex Sector: The Economic and Social Bases of Prostitution in Southeast Asia*. Geneva: International Labour Office, 1998.

Ling, L.H.M. "The Other Side of Globalization: Hypermasculine Developmentalism in East Asia." Paper presented at the International Studies Association Meeting, Toronto, 18-22 March 1997.

Lingat, Robert. *Le statut de la femme au Siam*. N.p., 1959.

London, Bruce. *Metropolis and Nation in Thailand: The Political Economy of Uneven Development*. Boulder, CO: Westview Press, 1980.

Lomax, Louis E. *Thailand: The War That Is the War That Will Be*. New York: Random House, 1967.

Lyttleton, Chris. "The Good People of Isan: Commercial Sex in Northeast Thailand." *Australian Journal of Anthropology* 5, 3 (1994): 257-79.

–. "Knowledge and Meaning: The AIDS Education Campaign in Rural Northeast Thailand." *Social Science and Medicine* 38, 1 (1994): 135-46.

McClintock, Ann. "Family Feuds: Gender, Nationalism and the Family." *Feminist Review* 44 (1993): 61-80.

Malee Pluksponsawalee. "Women and the Law." In *Women in Development: Implications for Population Dynamics*, ed. Suchart Prasith-rathsint and Suwanlee Piampiti, 144-76. Bangkok: National Institute of Development Administration, 1982.

Manderson, Lenore. "Public Sex Performances in Patpong and Exploration of the Edges of Imagination." *Journal of Sex Research* 29, 4 (1992): 451-75.

–. "The Pursuit of Pleasure and the Sale of Sex." In *Sexual Nature, Sexual Culture*, ed. Paul R. Abramson and Steven D. Pinkerton, 305-29. Chicago: University of Chicago Press, 1995.

–. "Parables of Imperialism and Fantasies of the Exotic: Western Representations of Thailand – Place and Sex." In *Sites of Desire/Economies of Pleasure in Asia and the Pacific*, ed. Lenore Manderson and Margaret Jolly, 123-44. Chicago: Chicago University Press, 1997.

Mattani Mojdara Rutnin. "The Role of Thai Women in Dramatic Arts and Social Development, Problems Concerning Child Prostitution in Thailand: A Case Study Accompanied by a Video-tape on the Lives of Child Prostitutes." In *Customs and Tradition: The Role of Thai Women*, 1-15. International Conference on Thai Studies, Bangkok, Thai Studies Program, Chulalongkorn University, 22-4 August 1984.

–. *Modern Thai Literature: The Process of Modernization and the Transformation of Values*. Bangkok: Thammasat University Press, 1988.

Merrick, Jeffrey. "Sexual Politics and Public Order in Late Eighteenth-Century France: The *Memoires secretes* and the *Correspondance secrete*." In *Forbidden History: The State, Society and the Regulation of Sexuality in Modern History*, ed. John C. Fout, 171-87. Chicago: University of Chicago Press, 1992.

Meyer, Walter F. "Beyond the Mask: Toward a Transdisciplinary Approach to Selected Social Problems Related to the Evolution and Context of International Tourism in Thailand." PhD diss. Geneva: University of Geneva, 1987.

Mills, Mary Beth. *Thai Women in the Global Labour Force: Consuming Desires, Contested Selves*. New Brunswick, NJ: Rutgers University Press, 1999.

–. "Rural Women Working in Bangkok: The Rocky Road of Social Change." Final Report to the National Research Council of Thailand, N.d.

Ministry of Foreign Affairs. *Statements by Chairmen of the Delegations of Thailand at the Second to Fortieth Sessions of the UNGA (1947-1985)*. Bangkok: Ministry of Foreign Affairs, International Organizations Department, 1986.

Moffat, Abbot Low. *Mongkut, The King of Siam*. Ithaca: Cornell University Press, 1961.

Mohanty, Chandra. "Under Western Eyes: Feminist Scholarship and Colonial Discourses." In *Third World Women and the Politics of Feminism,* ed. Chandra Mohanty, Ann Russo, and Lourdes Torres, 51-80. Bloomington: Indiana University Press, 1991.

Montgomery, Heather. "Pattaya and Child Prostitution as a Form of Cultural Crisis." Paper presented at the Sixth International Thai Studies Conference. Chiang Mai, Thailand, 1996. CD-ROM.

Moon, Katherine H.S. "East Meets West: Sex Industries in East Asia." Paper presented at the Annual Meeting of the International Studies Association, Toronto, 18-22 March 1997.

–. *Sex among Allies: Military Prostitution in U.S.-Korea Relations.* New York: Columbia University Press, 1997.

Morell, David, and Chai-anan Samudavinjia. *Political Conflict in Thailand: Reform, Reaction, Revolution.* Cambridge, MA: Oelgeschlager, Gunn, and Hain, 1981.

Mosse, George. *Nationalism and Sexuality.* New York: Howard Ferrig, 1985.

Muecke, Majorie. "Mother Sells Food, Daughter Sells Her Body: The Cultural Continuity of Prostitution." *Social Science and Medicine* 35, 7 (1992): 891-901.

Muscat, Robert J. *Thailand and the United States: Development, Security and Foreign Aid.* New York: Columbia University Press, 1990.

Nandy, Ashis. *The Intimate Enemy: Loss and Recovery of Self under Colonialism.* Delhi: Oxford University Press, 1983.

National Commission on Women's Affairs. *Summary of Long-term Women's Development Plan (1982-2001).* Prepared by the Task Force on Long-term Women's Development Plan, with the Cooperation of USAID Thailand and the Department of Technical and Economic Cooperation, 1981.

–. *Women's Development in Thailand.* Bangkok: National Committee for International Cooperation, National Commission on Women's Affairs, 1985.

–. *Thailand's Report on the Status of Women and Platform for Action 1994.* For the Fourth World Conference on Women, Beijing, the People's Republic of China, 4-15 September 1995. National Commission on Women's Affairs, Office of the Prime Minister, 1994.

–. *Perspective Policies and Planning for the Development of Women (1992-2011).* National Committee on the Perspective Plan and Policies for Women's Development, National Commission on Women's Affairs, Office of the Prime Minister, 1995.

–. *National Policy and Plan of Action for the Prevention and Eradication of the Commercial Sexual Exploitation of Children.* National Committee for the Eradication of Commercial Sex, National Commission on Women's Affairs, Office of the Prime Minister, 1996.

–. *Thailand's Combined Second and Third Report to the Committee for the Elimination of Discrimination against Women.* Bangkok: Committee for Thailand's Second Report on the Implementation of the Convention on the Elimination of Discrimination against Women, NCWA, Office of the Prime Minister, 1996.

National Identity Board. *Thai Life: Thai Women.* Bangkok: National Identity Board, Prime Minister's Office, 1983.

"Note from Human Rights Watch/Asia." *Women's Studies News* 7, 15 (November 1995): 38.

O'Connell Davidson, Julia, and Jacqueline Sanchez Taylor. *Sex Tourism: Thailand.* Bangkok: ECPAT, 1996.

Odzer, Cleo. "Patpong Prostitution: Its Relationship to, and Effect on, the Position of Women in Thai Society." PhD diss. New School for Social Research, 1990.

Omvedt, Gail. *Women in Popular Movements: India and Thailand during the Decade of Women.* Geneva: UNRISD, 1986.

Ong, Aiwha. *Spirits of Resistance and Capitalist Discipline: Factory Women in Malaysia.* Albany: State University of New York Press, 1987.

Ong, Aiwha, and Michael Peletz. "Introduction." In *Bewitching Women, Pious Men: Gender and Body Politics in Southeast Asia,* ed. Aiwha Ong and Michael G. Peletz, 1-18. Berkeley: University of California Press, 1995.

Pasuk Phongpaichit. *From Peasant Girls to Bangkok Masseuses.* Geneva: International Labour Office, 1982.

–. "From Peasant Girls to Bangkok Masseuses." In *Tourism, Prostitution, Development.* Ecumenical Coalition on Third World Tourism. Bangkok: ECTWT, 1983.

–. *Guns, Girls, Gambling, Ganja: Thailand's Illegal Economy and Public Policy.* Chiang Mai: Silkworm, 1998.

–. "The Thai Middle Class and the Military: Social Perspectives in the Aftermath of May 1992." In *The May 1992 Crisis in Thailand: Background and Aftermath* (Selected Papers from the Thailand Update Conference), ed. Peter A. Jackson, 29-35. University of Sydney, 16 October 1992, Canberra: National Thai Studies Centre, Australia National University, 1993.

Pasuk Phongpaichit and Chris Baker. *Thailand: Economy and Politics.* New York: Oxford University Press, 1995.

Pawadee Tongudai. "Women, Migration and Employment: A Study of Migrant Workers in Bangkok." PhD diss. New York University, 1982.

–. "Women and Work in Thailand and the Philippines." In *Women's Economic Participation in Asia and the Pacific*, 191-219. Bangkok: United Nations Economic and Social Committee for Asia Pacific, 1987. ST/ESCAP/510.

Perry, Ruth. "Colonizing the Breast: Sexuality and Maternity in Eighteenth-century England." In *Forbidden History: The State, Society, and the Regulation of Sexuality in Modern Europe,* ed. John C. Fout, 107-38. Chicago: University of Chicago Press, 1992.

Pettman, Jan. *Worlding Women.* New York: Routledge, 1996.

Pheterson, Gail. *A Vindication of the Rights of Whores.* Seattle: Seal Press, 1989.

–. "The Whore Stigma: Female Dishonour and Male Unworthiness." *Social Text* 37 (Winter 1993): 39-64.

Prizzia, Ross. *Thailand in Transition.* Honolulu: University of Hawaii Press, 1985.

"Prostitution in Selected Countries of Asia and the Far East." *International Review of Criminal Policy* 13 (October 1958): 44-55.

Purcell, Victor. *The Chinese in Southeast Asia.* 2nd ed. Kuala Lampur: Oxford University Press, 1965.

Rangson Prasertsri. "Women in the Parliament of Thailand: Their Characteristics and Attitudes." PhD diss. University of Mississippi, 1982.

Reid, Anthony. *Southeast Asia in the Age of Commerce.* Vol. 1: *The Land below the Winds.* New Haven: Yale University Press, 1988.

–. *Southeast Asia in the Age of Commerce.* Vol. 2: *Expansion and Crisis.* New Haven: Yale University Press, 1993.

Reynolds, Craig. "A Nineteenth Century Thai Buddhist Defense of Polygamy and Some Remarks on the Social History of Women in Thailand." A Paper Prepared for the Seventh Conference of the International Association of Historians of Asia, Bangkok, 22-6 August 1977.

–. *Thai Radical Discourse: The Real Face of Thai Feudalism Today.* Ithaca: Cornell University Press, 1987.

–. "Introduction: National Identity and Its Defenders." In *National Identity and Its Defenders,* ed. Craig J. Reynolds, 1-34. Chiang Mai: Silkworm, 1991.

Rhodes, Richard. "Death in the Candy Store." *Rolling Stone.* 28 November 1991: 62-70, 105, 113-14.

Riley, Denise. *"Am I That Name?" Feminism and the Category of "Woman" in History.* Minneapolis: University of Minnesota, 1988.

Royal Thai Government. "Act for the Abatement of Prostitution, B.E. 2503 (1960)." *Royal Thai Government Gazette* 2, 212 (28 November 1960).

Said, Edward. *Culture and Imperialism.* New York: Alfred A. Knopf, 1993.

Saisuree Chutikul. "Who are the Clients – the Exploiters?" *Child Workers in Asia* 12 (1996): 9.

–. *Children in Especially Difficult Situations.* Vol. 1, *Thailand* (Report to UNICEF). National Youth Bureau, Office of the Prime Minister, June 1986.

–. "Women and Commercial Sex in Thailand." *Canadian Women Studies* 15, 2 and 3 (1995): 118-19.

Scott, Joan W. "'Experience.'" In *Feminists Theorize the Political,* ed. Judith Butler and Joan W. Scott. New York: Routledge, 1992.

Sedghi, Hamideh. "Third World Feminist Perspectives on World Politics." In *Women,*

Gender and World Politics, ed. Peter R. Beckman and Francine D'Amico, 89-105. Westport, CT: Bergin and Garvey, 1994.

"Sex Tourism to Thailand." *ISIS International Bulletin* 13 (1979): 9-12.

Sharpe, Joanne P. "A Feminist Engagement with National Identity." In *Body Space,* ed.
Nancy Duncan. New York: Routledge, 1996.

Siriporn Skrobanek. "The Transnational Sex-Exploitation of Thai Women." Master's research paper. The Hague: Institute of Social Studies, 1983.

Spector, Ronald. "The American Image of Southeast Asia, 1790-1865." *Journal of Southeast
Asia Studies* 3, 2 (September 1972): 299-305.

Spivak, Gayatri. "Can the Subaltern Speak?" In *Colonial Discourse and Post-Colonial Theory:
A Reader,* ed. Patrick Williams and Laura Chrisman, 66-111. New York: Columbia University Press, 1994.

Srisurang Poolthupya. "The Changing Role of Thai Women." Paper presented at the Seventh Conference of the International Association of Historians of Asia, Bangkok, August
1977.

Stienstra, Deborah. "Madonna/Whore, Pimp/Protector: Prostitution and International
Law and Organization." *Studies in Political Economy* 51 (Fall 1996): 183-217.

Stowe, Judith. *Siam becomes Thailand: A Story of Intrigue.* London: Hurst and Company,
1991.

Strobel, Margaret. *Gender, Sex and Empire: Essays on Global and Comparative History.* Washington, DC: American Historical Association, 1993.

Suchit Bunbongkarn. *Thailand: State of the Nation.* Singapore: Institute of Southeast Asian
Studies, 1996.

Sukanya Hantrakul. "Prostitutes and Human Rights in Thailand." N.p., 1982.

–. "Prostitution in Thailand." Paper proposed to the Women in Asia Workshop. Monash
University, Melbourne, 22-4 July 1983.

–. "The Spirit of a Fighter: Women and Prostitution in Thailand." *Manushi* 18 (October/
November 1983): 27-35.

–. "Prostitution in Thailand." In *Development and Displacement: Women in Southeast Asia,*
ed. Glen Chandler, Norma Sullivan, and Jan Branson, 115-36. Clayton, Australia: Centre of Southeast Asian Studies, Monash University, 1988.

Sukhumbhand Paribatra. "State and Society in Thailand: How Fragile the Democracy?"
Asian Survey 33, 9 (September 1993): 879-93.

Sulak Sivaraksa. *Siam in Crisis.* Bangkok: Kamol Keemthong Foundation, 1980.

–. *Siamese Resurgence.* Bangkok: Asian Cultural Forum on Development, 1985.

Surin Maisrikrod. "Emerging Patterns of Political Leadership in Thailand." *Contemporary
Southeast Asia* 15, 1 (June 1993): 80-97.

Suteera Thomson. "Gender Issues in Thailand Development." Paper prepared for the
United Nations Development Programme. Bangkok: Gender and Development Research
Institute, July 1990.

Suwadee T. Patana. "Thai Society's Expectations of Women 1904-1935: An Approach to
Women's History." Paper Presented to 12th International Association of Historians of
Asia. Conference, University of Hong Kong, 24-8 June 1991.

Szanton Blanc, Christina. "The Thoroughly Modern 'Asian': Capital, Culture, and Nation
in Thailand and the Philippines." In *Ungrounded Empires: The Cultural Politics of Modern
Chinese Nationalism,* ed. Aihwa Ong and Donald Nonini, 261-86. New York: Routledge,
1997.

Tannenbaum, Nicola. "Buddhism, Prostitution and Sex: Limits on the Academic Discourse on Gender in Thailand." In *Gender and Sexualities in Modern Thailand,* ed. Peter A.
Jackson and Nerida M. Cook, 243-60. Chiang Mai: Silkworm, 1999.

Thailand National Commission on Women's Affairs. *Aspects of Thai Women Today.* Presented by the Delegation of Thailand as a background document to the World Conference of The United Nations Decade for Women, Copenhagen, 14-30 July 1980.
Bangkok, Thailand National Commission on Women's Affairs, 1980.

Thak Chaloemtiarana. *Thailand and the Politics of Despotic Paternalism.* Bangkok: Thammasat University, 1979.

Thamsook Numnonda. "Pibulsongkram's Thai Nation-Building Programme during the Japanese Military Presence, 1941-1945." *Journal of Southeast Asian Studies* 9, 2 (September 1978): 234-47.

Thitsa, Khin. *Providence and Prostitution: Image and Reality for Women in Buddhist Thailand.* London: Change International, 1980.

Thongbai Thongpao. "The State of Human Rights in Thailand in 1985." *Thai Development Newsletter* 3, 4 (1986): 10-4.

Thongchai Winichakul. *Siam Mapped: A History of the Geo-body of a Nation.* Chiang Mai: Silkworm, 1994.

Trumbach, Randolph. "Sex, Gender, and Sexual Identity in Modern Culture: Male Sodomy and Female Prostitution in Enlightenment London." In *Forbidden History: The State, Society and the Regulation of Sexuality in Modern History,* ed. C. Fout, 89-106. Chicago: University of Chicago Press, 1992.

Truong, Thahn-dam. *Sex, Money and Morality: Prostitution and Tourism in Southeast Asia.* London: Zed, 1990.

UNESCO. "Thailand." In *Identification of Issues Concerning Women and Their Consideration in Development Planning.* Bangkok: UNESCO, 1987.

United Nations. *Convention for the Suppression of the Traffic in Persons and of the Exploitation of the Prostitution of Others.* 1950.

–. "Prostitution in Selected Countries of Asia and the Far East." *International Review of Criminal Policy* 13 (1958): 44-55.

–. Department of Economic and Social Affairs. *Study on Traffic in Persons and Prostitution (Suppression of the Traffic in Persons and of the Exploitation of the Prostitution of Others).* New York: United Nations, 1959. ST/SOA/SD/8.

United Nations Development Programme. *The UN in Thailand.* Bangkok: UNDP, 1986.

Vandergeest, Peter. "Constructing Thailand: Regulation, Everyday Resistance, and Citizenship." *Society for Comparative Study of Society and History* 35, 1 (1993): 133-58.

–. "Real Villages: National Narratives of Rural Development." In *Creating the Countryside: The Politics of Rural and Environmental Discourse,* ed. E. Melanie DuPuis and Peter Vandergeest, 279-302. Philadelphia: Temple University Press, 1996.

Van Esterik, Penny. *Women of Southeast Asia.* Monograph Series on Southeast Asia. Occasional Paper Number 9. DeKalb, IL: Northern Illinois University Center for Southeast Asian Studies, 1982.

–. "Thai Prostitution and the Medical Gaze." In *Gender and Development in Southeast Asia,* Vol. 2, ed. Penny and John Van Esterik, 133-50. CCSEAS (Canadian Council for Southeast Asian Studies) 20. Montreal: Canadian Asian Studies Association, 1991.

–. *Materializing Thailand.* New York: Berg, 2000.

Van Landingham, Mark, Chanpen Saengtienchai, John Knodel, and Anthony Pramualratana. *Friends, Wives and Extramarital Sex in Thailand: A Qualitative Study of Peer and Spousal Influence on Thai Male Extramarital Sexual Behavior and Attitudes.* Bangkok: Institute for Population Studies, Chulalongkorn University, 1995.

Van Praagh, David. *Thailand's Struggle for Democracy: The Life and Times of M.R. Seni Pramoj.* New York: Holmes and Meier, 1996.

Vella, Walter F. *Chaiyo! King Vijiravudh and the Development of Thai Nationalism.* Honolulu: University of Hawaii Press, 1978.

–. *The Impact of the West on Government in Thailand.* Berkeley: University of California Press, 1955.

Vibul Thamavit, and Robert D. Golden. "The Family in Thailand." In *Aspects and Facets of Thailand,* ed. Witt Siwasariyanon, 1-9. Bangkok: Public Relations Department, 1958.

Vipa Chulachart. "Introduction." In *Aspects of Thai Women Today.* Presented by the Delegation of Thailand as a background document to the World Conference of The United Nations Decade for Women, Copenhagen, 14-30 July 1980, 1-5. Bangkok: Thailand National Commission on Women's Affairs, 1980.

Vitit Muntarbhorn, Wimolsirir Jamnarnvej, and Tanawadee Boonlue. *Status of Women: Thailand.* Social and Human Sciences in Asia and the Pacific RUSHAP Series on

Monographs and Occasional Papers, 26. Bangkok: UNESCO Principal Regional Office for Asia and the Pacific, 1990.

Walker, Dave, and Richard S. Ehrlich. *"Hello My Big Big Honey": Love Letters to Bangkok Bar Girls and Their Revealing Interviews*. Bangkok: Dragon Dance Publications, 1992.

Walkowitz, Judith. *Prostitution and Victorian Society: Women, Class and the State*. New York: Cambridge University Press, 1980.

Wathinee Boonchalaksi, and Philip Guest. *Prostitution in Thailand*. IPSR Publication No. 171. Bangkok: Institute for Population and Social Research, Mahidol University, 1994.

Wawer, Maria J., Chai Podhisita, Uraiwan Kanungsukkasem, Anthony Pramulratana, and Regina McNamara. "Origins and Working Conditions of Female Sex Workers in Urban Thailand: Consequences of Social Context for HIV Transmission." *Social Science and Medicine* 42, 3 (1996): 453-63.

Weatherbee, Donald E. *The United Front in Thailand: A Documentary Analysis*. Studies in International Affairs No. 8. Columbia: Institute of International Studies, University of South Carolina, 1970.

Winkler, Mary Packard. "Construction of Knowledge and Discourse in Middle Class Marriage: Implications for Coping with Sexual Risk Among Urban Thai." Paper Presented at the Sixth International Conference on Thai Studies, Chiang Mai, Thailand, October 1996.

Women Lawyers Association of Thailand. *Status of Women in Thailand*. Bangkok: Women Lawyers Association, 1972.

Yuangrat Wedel. "Current Thai Radical Ideology: The Returnees from the Jungle." *Contemporary Southeast Asia* 4, 1 (June 1982): 1-18.

Yuangrat Wedel, with Paul Wedel. *Radical Thought, Thai Mind: The Development of Revolutionary Ideas in Thailand*. Bangkok: Assumption Business College Administration, 1987.

Yuval-Davis, Nira, and Floya Anthias, eds. *Woman-Nation-State*. New York: St. Martin's Press, 1989.

Yuval-Davis, Nira. *Gender and Nation*. London: Sage, 1997.

Newspapers

The *Bangkok Post*
The *Nation* (Thailand)
The *Globe and Mail*
Week in Review. On-line (*Bangkok Post*)

Newsletters

Thai Development Newsletter. 1983-97. Thai Development Support Committee, Bangkok.
Thailand Monitor. 1996-9. International Understanding Program, Institute of Asian Studies, Chulalongkorn University, Bangkok.

Index

DATE DUE

MAY 7 2003	
DEC — 4 2003	
DEC 2 7	
DEC 3 0 2008	
MAY 1 7 2010	
MAY 0 1 2012	

DEMCO, INC. 38-2931